The BIG BOOK of AMAZING LEGO® CREATIONS with Bricks You Already Have

SARAH DEES

author of the bestselling *LEGO® Creations* book series
and creator of Frugal Fun for Boys and Girls

PAGE STREET
PUBLISHING CO.

TO JORDAN AND OUR LEGO-LOVING KIDS—

AIDAN, GRESHAM, OWEN, JONATHAN AND JANIE. IT'S AMAZING TO INVENT NEW LEGO PROJECTS WITH YOU ALL!

First published in 2021 by
Page Street Publishing Co.
27 Congress Street, Suite 105
Salem, MA 01970
www.pagestreetpublishing.com

Distributed by Macmillan, sales in Canada by The Canadian Manda Group.

25 24 23 22 21 1 2 3 4 5

ISBN-13: 978-1-64567-350-7
ISBN-10: 1-64567-350-2

Library of Congress Control Number: 2021931385

Cover and book design by Meg Baskis for Page Street Publishing Co.
Photography by Sarah Dees

Printed and bound in China

Page Street Publishing protects our planet by donating to nonprofits like The Trustees, which focuses on local land conservation.

CHECK OUT THE OTHER BOOKS IN THE SERIES

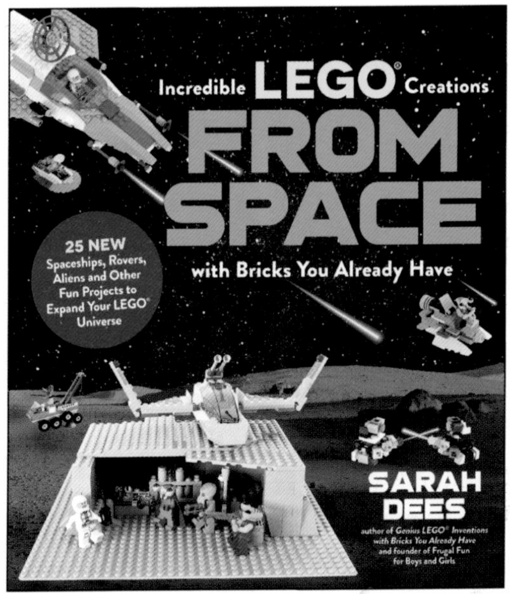

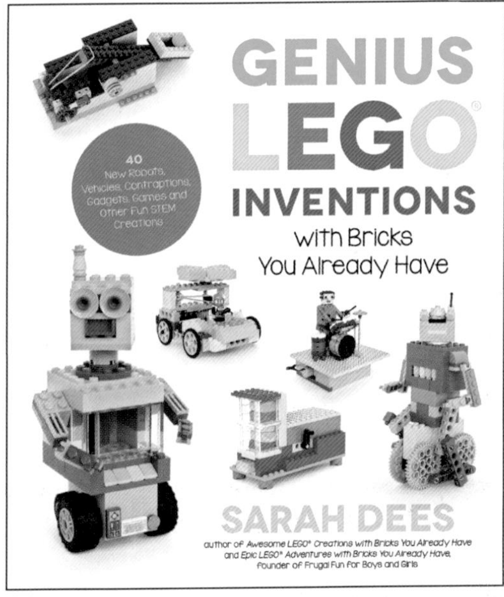

CONTENTS

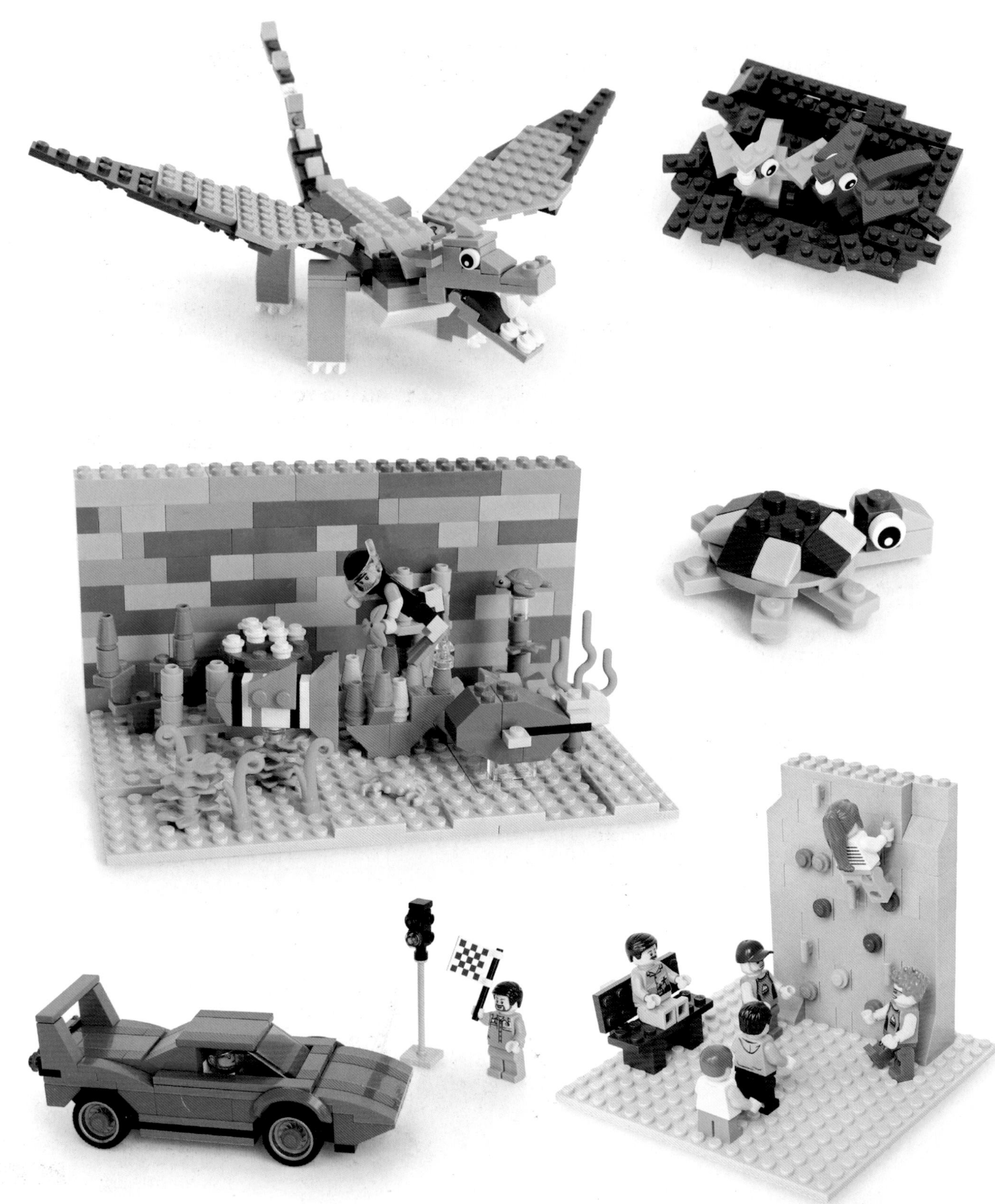

HOW TO USE THIS BOOK

Welcome, LEGO fans! If you love to build, construct, design, create and imagine, this book is for you. These next couple of pages will help you get the most out of this big book of amazing building ideas.

FIRST, ACTIVATE YOUR IMAGINATION!
Get ready to build awesome vehicles, city scenes, robots, fairytale creatures and even works of art made out of bricks. This book is all about IMAGINATION! The goal is not for you to build everything exactly like the pictures. Instead, the idea is to inspire you to take your big tub of random bricks and taken-apart sets and build new and amazing things with them.

The projects in this book will teach you some new building techniques and give you fresh ideas to inspire you to create some really cool things with your bricks. Think of the ideas here as a launching point for you to imagine and build creations of your own.

THE INSTRUCTIONS WILL HELP YOU BUILD.
Many of the projects in this book have step-by-step instructions. These instructions are not exactly the same as the LEGO manuals that come with a set. You can use the pictures to see which bricks to add next and where to put them. The captions with the pictures will also tell you which bricks to put where, and they'll help you figure out the names of the bricks being used in each step, in case you want to order individual bricks to supplement what you have.

If you don't have the exact pieces shown, that's totally okay. You can substitute different colors or even different types of bricks. In fact, you may discover a modification for a project that actually makes it better! And if you really DO want your project to look just like the one in the book, I'll explain how to order individual bricks in just a moment.

TRY ORGANIZING YOUR BRICKS.
Some kids like to organize their bricks and some don't. It's totally up to you! But it can definitely be faster and easier to build when your bricks are sorted.

If you've never organized your bricks before, just start making piles. Put all the wheels together, all the minifigure parts together, all the basic bricks together and so on. You might want to separate out plates with handles and clips that form joints and bricks that have modifications added to them like wheel holders, bars or clips. Another helpful idea is just to sort out tiny pieces from larger bricks. You can sort by color or you can sort by shape. The important thing is to develop a system that helps you know where to find the piece you're looking for.

THERE ARE TWO TYPES OF PROJECTS IN THIS BOOK.
This book contains both step-by-step projects and creative challenges. The projects that have full step-by-step instructions have a parts list included that lists every brick you'll need to complete the project as shown.

The creative challenges have a key elements list that names the most important pieces. The creative challenges are meant to be just that—creative! Use our ideas as a launching point, but build them the way you want. For example, when building the Cozy Bedroom project on page 91, you can customize it to look like your own bedroom, or you can design your dream room. It's up to you!

You can use both the parts lists and the key elements lists to organize your bricks before building or to figure out which bricks you need if there is something that you don't have on hand. Please note that a few of the simple creative challenges are exceptions—they have full parts lists, but they don't have full instructions.

ORDER INDIVIDUAL ELEMENTS ONLINE IF YOU WANT TO SUPPLEMENT THE BRICKS YOU HAVE.
If there is a project that you want to build just like the picture but you don't have all the pieces, it's easy to order the bricks you want. One option is to order through the Pick-A-Brick or Bricks & Pieces sections of Lego.com. You can select the bricks you want by using the brick name or the ID number. Each LEGO brick has a very tiny ID number, usually located on the bottom of the brick. These numbers can be hard to see, but once you find the number, you can enter it on Lego.com and find the exact element you need. Note that the ID number is specific to the brick shape only, not the color.

Another great option for ordering individual LEGO bricks is to visit BrickLink.com. Brick Link is a site that hosts many different sellers of LEGO bricks. You can buy individual bricks, both new and used, as well as minifigures and new or retired sets. The prices on Brick Link are related to supply and demand, so you'll pay a lower price for a basic brick in a common color than you will for a rare collectible minifigure.

Keep in mind that each seller on Brick Link charges separately for shipping, so you'll want to find one seller that has several different things you need. You don't want to order seven types of bricks from seven different vendors and pay a separate shipping fee each time! In addition, be aware that some Brick Link sellers have a minimum purchase amount that you must meet before ordering.

The Brick Link site has a helpful color guide, and the colors are also listed on the Pick-A-Brick section of Lego.com. One difference, however, is that Brick Link's color guide includes both current and discontinued colors. The Brick Link color system is used in this book, but please note that the current light gray and dark gray bricks are actually referred to as light bluish gray and dark bluish gray on Brick Link.

Be sure to get permission from your grown-ups before making any purchases, and get their help when using websites such as Brick Link and the official LEGO site!

BRICK GUIDE

Did you know that LEGO bricks have names? You may not know any brick names because you don't need to know the names of the bricks to put together a LEGO set. The names aren't even used in the instructions. However, if you want to order individual LEGO elements online, you'll need to know either the names of the bricks or their ID numbers.

There are thousands of different LEGO elements available. This brick guide does not describe every type of brick, but it will help you understand the names and categories of the bricks you'll need for the projects in this book.

Remember, if you want to search for a brick by its ID number, you can find the tiny ID number printed on each brick, usually on the underside. Once you have the number, you can enter it on the Pick-A-Brick or Bricks & Pieces sections of Lego.com or on BrickLink.com and easily find the LEGO element you are looking for.

Please note that the names for bricks vary depending on whether you are using Lego.com or Brick Link. This book primarily uses the Brick Link system of names, although the names of some bricks have been changed or simplified for clarity. For example, you'll see bricks labeled "windscreens" on BrickLink.com, but in this book I call them "windshields."

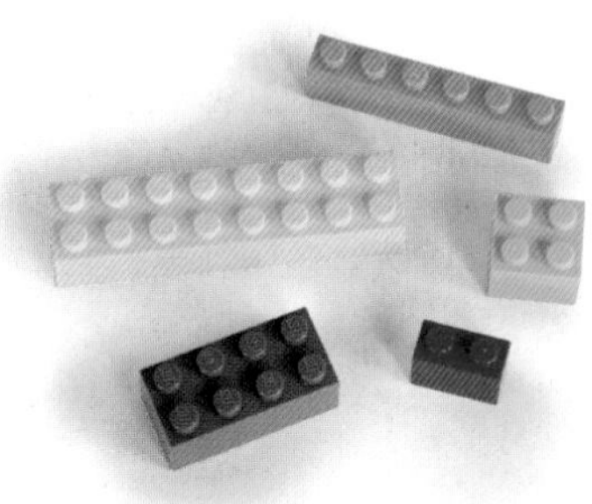

BRICKS
These are bricks. Count the number of studs to determine the size. For example, the yellow brick is a 2 x 8 and the red brick is a 1 x 2.

MODIFIED BRICKS
Bricks can be modified in many different ways. They may have extra studs on the side like the tan brick in the picture, a modified shape such as a curved top like the lime green brick in the picture or added clips and pins. The light gray brick has two added pins, and the dark gray brick has a clip. If a LEGO element you are looking for is brick-shaped with something extra added to it, you'll probably find it under modified bricks.

PLATES AND TILES

The flat bricks are called plates. A plate is one-third the height of a regular brick. Plates are also referred to by size. The dark gray plate in this photo is a 2 x 6. Tiles are plates that do not have any studs on the top, such as the 2 x 2 dark gray tile in the photo.

MODIFIED PLATES

As you might have guessed, modified plates are plates that have been modified in some way. They may have an added clip like the yellow plate, a handle like the dark gray plate or a wheel holder, for example. Some have a pin hole or even a ladder. The dark tan plate in the photo is a 1 x 2 plate with one stud on top and is also called a jumper plate.

SLOPES

Slope bricks are bricks that have an angled top. They are referred to as "slopes" on Brick Link and "roof tiles" on Pick-A-Brick. The blue brick in the picture is a 2 x 3 slope. The lime green brick is a 1 x 3 curved slope because it has a rounded top. The orange brick is a 2 x 2 inverted slope because it slopes the opposite way.

ROUND BRICKS

These are round bricks, and they are measured in size the same way as square and rectangular bricks. The dark gray brick is a 4 x 4 round brick. The lime green brick is a 2 x 2 dome. There are also round plates that are the same height as the other plates but round in shape.

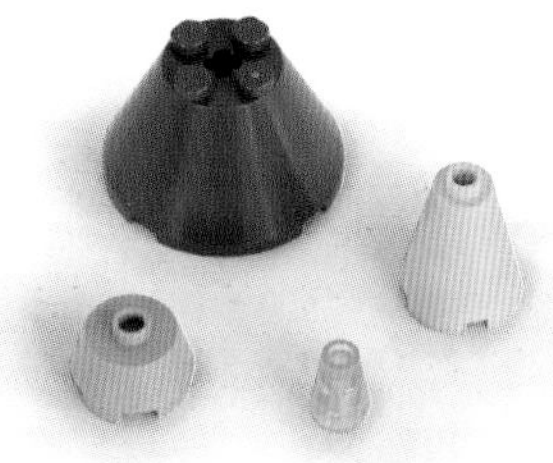

CONES

Cone bricks are quite useful, and they are used in this book. The translucent light blue brick is a 1 x 1 cone. The yellow brick is a 2 x 2 x 2 cone, meaning that it is 2 studs by 2 studs, and it is also 2 bricks high.

BRACKETS

Brackets are so useful for adding pieces on the side of a creation. They are called "brackets" on Brick Link, and Pick-A-Brick refers to them as "angle plates." The light gray bracket is a 1 x 2—1 x 4, and the larger dark gray bracket is a 1 x 2—2 x 2. The smaller dark gray bracket is an inverted bracket because the second side goes up instead of down. It's called a 1 x 2—1 x 2 bracket, inverted.

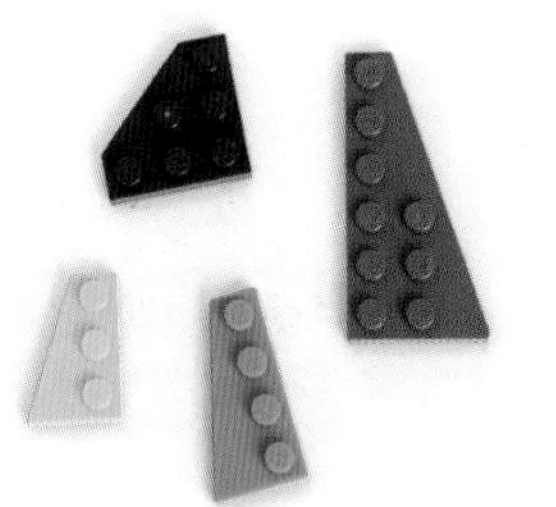

WEDGE PLATES

These plates are called wedge plates. The dark blue one is a 3 x 3 wedge plate with cut corners. Some wedge plates have a right or left orientation. The lime green plate is a 2 x 3 wedge plate, left. The dark gray plate is a 3 x 6 wedge plate, right.

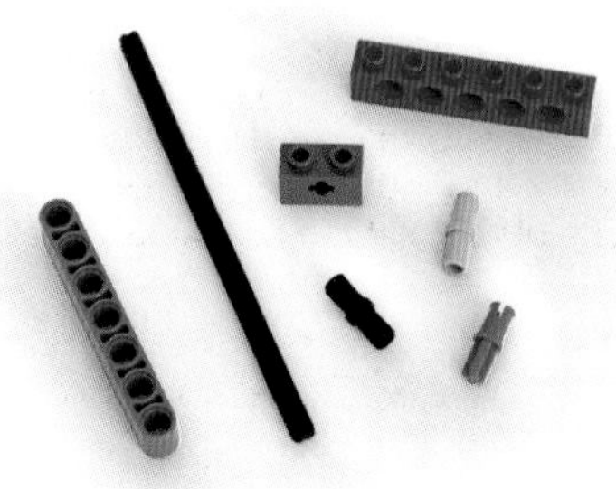

TECHNIC BRICKS AND ELEMENTS

This book uses a few Technic elements, but don't be concerned! Technic elements are used widely in lots of LEGO sets, not just Technic sets. There is a good chance that you own many of them already. Technic bricks, like the red brick in the photo, are bricks that have holes. Some of the 1 x 2 Technic bricks have axle-shaped holes, like the dark gray brick in the photo. On Brick Link, the blue element is a 1 x 7 Technic liftarm. The LEGO site refers to these as "beams."

AMAZING VEHICLES

Take your vehicle building skills to a whole new level with these inspiring designs! Construct some sweet race cars or build a rugged ATV that is ready for an outdoor adventure. Learn how to build a realistic military tank and Humvee, and then set up an epic battle scene. Each of these vehicles can be customized in the colors you want, and you can swap out different wheel types or make modifications to the design. Once you've built your vehicles, use your completed projects to create awesome scenes like a car show or a mountain expedition.

1960s RACE CAR

STEP-BY-STEP

This stylish race car combines high performance with sleek design. Build this 1960s-style car in any color scheme you choose. Make it a solid color or give it racing stripes. This car is patterned after the 1960s Plymouth Superbird, which was designed for NASCAR racing and was also available in limited numbers for consumers to purchase. It's a sweet-looking car!

PARTS LIST

DARK GRAY BRICKS

1—4 x 6 plate
4—2 x 6 plates
1—2 x 4 plate
2—1 x 6 plates
1—2 x 2 plate
1—1 x 4 plate
3—1 x 2 plates
1—2 x 4 brick
1—1 x 2 brick
2—2 x 2 bricks
4—1 x 4 curved slopes
1—2 x 4 curved slope
1—2 x 3 slope
2—1 x 2 x 2 slopes
2—2 x 4 tiles
1—1 x 6 tile
2—1 x 8 tiles
2—1 x 2 tiles
1—1 x 4 plate with two studs
2—2 x 4 Technic bricks with holes and a 2 x 2 cutout
2—2 x 2 round plates with a rounded bottom

LIGHT GRAY BRICKS

1—2 x 3 plate
2—2 x 2 plates
2—1 x 3 plates

RED BRICKS

1—4 x 4 plate
1—2 x 4 plate
3—1 x 6 plates
4—1 x 1 plates
1—2 x 2 brick
2—1 x 4 bricks
6—1 x 1 bricks
4—2 x 2 slopes, inverted
2—1 x 2 slopes, inverted
2—1 x 3 slopes, inverted
2—1 x 4 curved slopes
2—1 x 3 slopes
4—1 x 1 slopes, 30 degree
4—1 x 1 round plates
4—1 x 4 tiles
4—1 x 1 tiles
2—4 x 2½ x 1 vehicle mudguards with arch

BLACK BRICKS

1—4 x 10 vehicle base
1—2 x 4 plate
1—2 x 3 plate
1—2 x 2 plate
2—1 x 6 plates
1—1 x 4 plate
1—1 x 2 plate
2—2 x 2 corner plates
1—1 x 2 brick
1—2 x 2 slope, inverted
4—1 x 4 curved inverted slopes
3—1 x 2—1 x 2 brackets, inverted
2—1 x 1 round plates

ASSORTED BRICKS

1—2 x 2 x 2 white slope
2—1 x 2 white plates
1—steering wheel
4—tan Technic axle pins without friction ridges
1—4 x 3 x 2 windshield
2—1 x 1 translucent red round plates
4—wheels with axle holes

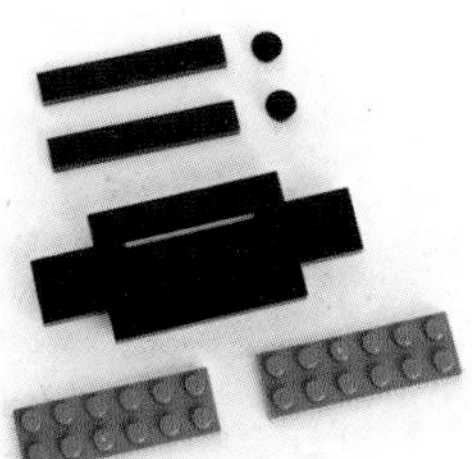

STEP 1: To build the base of the car, find two 2 x 6 dark gray plates, a 4 x 10 black vehicle base, two 1 x 6 black plates and two 1 x 1 black round plates.

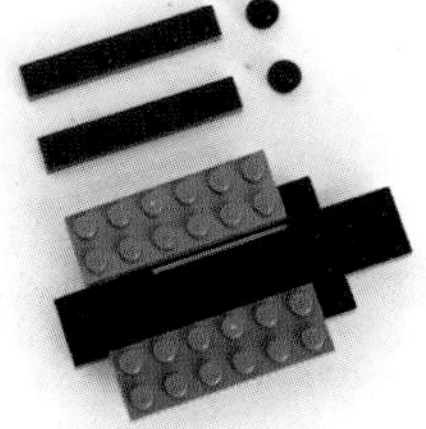

STEP 2: Attach the two 2 x 6 dark gray plates to the vehicle base as shown.

STEP 3: Flip over the vehicle base. Attach the 1 x 6 black plates and the 1 x 1 black round plates to the underside of the dark gray plates. Then find two more 2 x 6 dark gray plates and a 2 x 3 black plate.

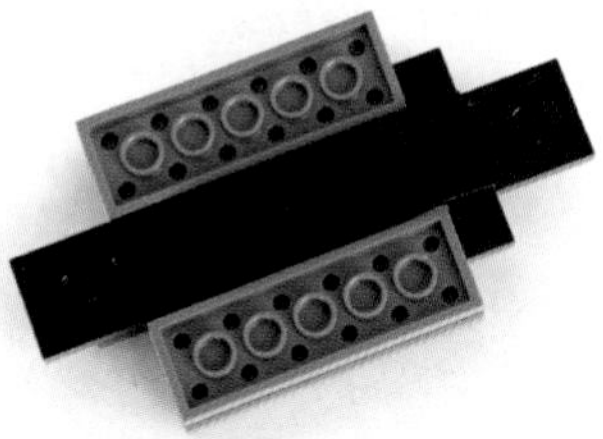

STEP 4: Add the two 2 x 6 dark gray plates and the 2 x 3 black plate to the underside of the vehicle.

STEP 5: Turn the vehicle right side up again. Then add a steering wheel, two 1 x 3 light gray plates and two 1 x 1 red slopes (30 degree).

STEP 6: Place a 1 x 1 red brick and a 1 x 1 red slope (30 degree) on each side of the steering wheel. Attach a 2 x 2 x 2 white slope to make the back of the driver's seat.

STEP 7: Find a 1 x 2 black plate, a 2 x 3 light gray plate and a 2 x 2 light gray plate.

STEP 8: Attach the 1 x 2 black plate to the very back of the vehicle base. Then add the 2 x 3 light gray plate in the back and the 2 x 2 light gray plate in the front.

STEP 9: Place a 2 x 4 red plate on top of a 4 x 4 red plate. Add this to the front of the car. Then find two red vehicle mudguards.

STEP 10: Attach the mudguards to the top of the 4 x 4 red plate.

STEP 11: Add a 2 x 2 red brick in between the mudguards. Then attach a 1 x 2 dark gray tile and two 1 x 1 red tiles.

STEP 12: Find the bricks shown for building the front hood.

STEP 13: Use a 1 x 6 red plate to connect the curved slopes. If you don't have the exact pieces shown, adapt the design with what you have. Make the hood a solid color by using three 2 x 4 curved slopes instead of the bricks shown.

STEP 14: Turn the hood section upside down. Add a 1 x 1 red plate on one side and place a 1 x 3 inverted slope on top of it, as shown. Repeat on the other side.

STEP 15: Attach the hood to the front of the car.

STEP 16: Use a 1 x 4 black plate to connect four 1 x 4 black inverted curved slopes.

STEP 17: Turn the vehicle over. Add the black curved slopes to the front of the car. Then gather the bricks shown.

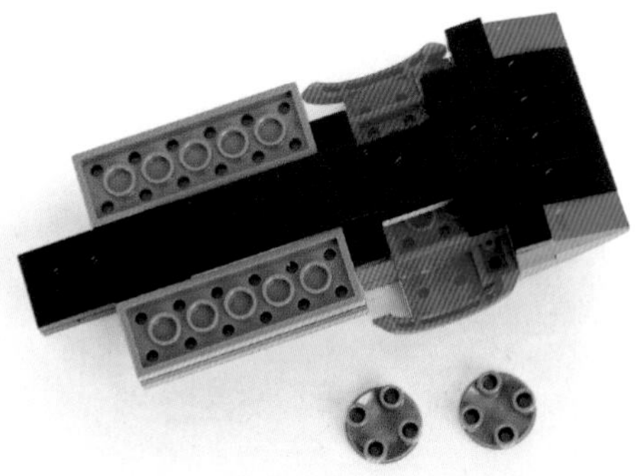

STEP 18: Add two 2 x 2 black corner plates to the front of the vehicle. This will help secure the bricks in that area.

STEP 19: Place two 2 x 2 dark gray round plates with a curved bottom on the underside of the car.

STEP 20: Turn the car over again. Add a 1 x 1 red brick on either side of the seat, and place two 2 x 2 red inverted slopes on the back of the car. Then find a 1 x 2 dark gray brick, a 1 x 2 dark gray plate and two 1 x 2 white plates.

STEP 21: Stack the white plates. Then, stack the dark gray brick and plate.

STEP 22: Attach the two white plates to the top of the seat and then add the dark gray brick and plate behind the seat.

STEP 23: Add a 2 x 2 dark gray brick in between the red inverted slopes. Then add two 1 x 1 red bricks.

STEP 24: Attach a 2 x 4 dark gray plate and a 1 x 4 dark gray plate to the back of the car. Then add a 2 x 2 light gray plate. Find two 1 x 4 red bricks and two 1 x 2 red inverted slopes.

STEP 25: Place one 1 x 4 red brick and one 1 x 2 red inverted slope on each side of the car.

STEP 26: Add a 1 x 6 dark gray plate to each side of the car. Then find two 1 x 8 dark gray tiles. Substitute with smaller tiles to fill in the same amount of space if you need to.

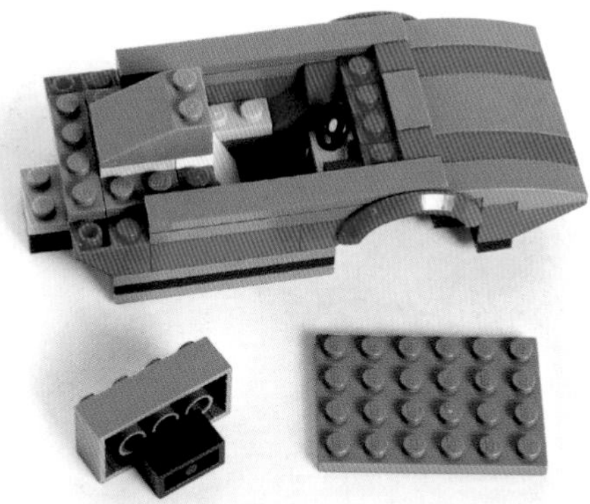

STEP 27: Attach a tile on each side of the car. Add a 2 x 3 dark gray slope on top of the white seat and the 2 x 2 light gray plate. Then attach a 1 x 2 black brick to the underside of a 2 x 4 dark gray brick. Find a 4 x 6 dark gray plate.

STEP 28: Add the dark gray brick with the black brick attached to the back of the car.

STEP 29: Attach the 4 x 6 plate on top of the dark gray brick you added in step 28.

STEP 30: Turn the car over and add two 2 x 2 red inverted slopes and a 2 x 2 dark gray brick. Then find a 2 x 2 black inverted slope.

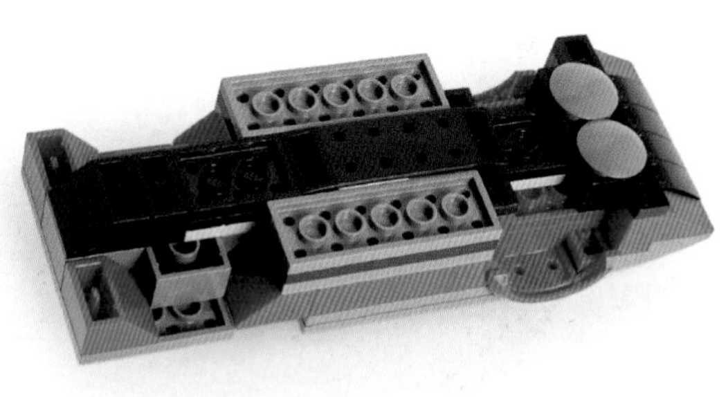

STEP 31: Attach the 2 x 2 black inverted slope to the underside of the car as shown.

STEP 32: Gather the bricks shown for building the taillights.

STEP 33: Use a 1 x 4 dark gray plate with two studs to connect three 1 x 2—1 x 2 inverted brackets. Then add a 1 x 2 dark gray tile and two 1 x 1 translucent red round plates.

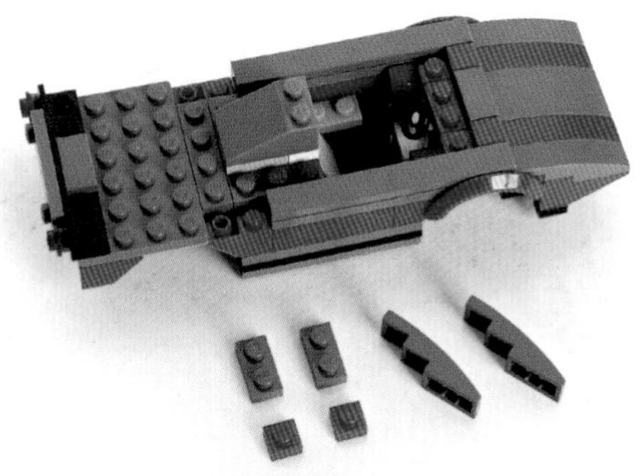

STEP 34: Attach the taillight assembly to the back of the car. Then find two 1 x 2 dark gray plates, two 1 x 1 red plates and two 1 x 4 dark gray curved slopes.

STEP 35: Place a 1 x 1 red plate and a 1 x 2 dark gray plate on each side just in front of the taillight assembly. Then add a 1 x 4 dark gray curved slope on each side.

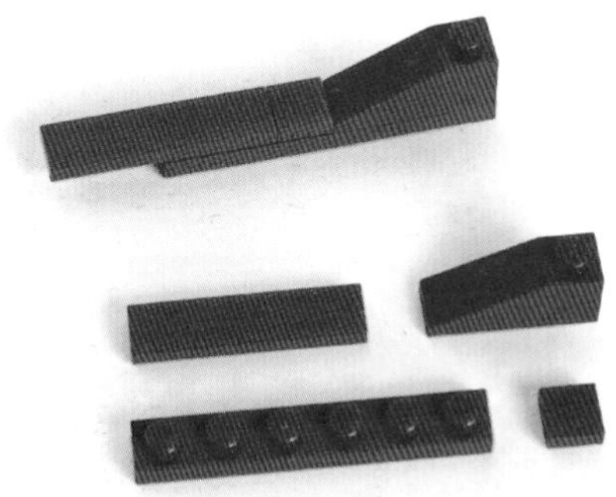

STEP 36: Find a 1 x 4 red tile, a 1 x 3 red slope, a 1 x 6 red plate and a 1 x 1 red tile. Attach them as shown with the 1 x 6 plate on the bottom. Then make a second one of these.

STEP 37: Attach these red slope sections to the car as shown. Then find a 2 x 4 black plate, a 2 x 4 dark gray tile, a 1 x 6 dark gray tile and two 1 x 2 x 2 dark gray slopes.

STEP 38: Build the wing on the back of the car using the two slope bricks and the 1 x 6 dark gray tile. Place the 2 x 4 black plate between the red bricks, and then add a 2 x 4 dark gray tile on top of it.

STEP 39: Add a 3 x 2 windshield to the car, and then find a 2 x 4 dark gray tile and two 1 x 4 red tiles for the roof.

STEP 40: Attach the tiles to the roof. Then find the bricks shown for building the wheels. The wheel holders are called 2 x 4 Technic bricks with holes and a 2 x 2 cutout.

STEP 41: Use tan axle pins to attach the wheels to the Technic bricks. Add red 1 x 1 round plates to the wheels for extra decoration. Add a 2 x 2 dark gray plate to the Technic brick that holds the front wheels. You can substitute different wheels and wheel holders based on what you have.

STEP 42: Attach the wheels, and your 1960s race car is complete!

Here's a way to modify the design a bit and create a car that looks more like a muscle car: Instead of building the wing on the back of the car, give it a square back end. This car looks really awesome with one large stripe down the center!

AWESOME HOT RODS

STEP-BY-STEP

Car fans love to modify and improve their cars, and hot rods are the perfect vehicles to tinker with and customize! Build some awesome hot rods with powerful engines and give them cool designs with great colors and flames on the sides. Then build a hot rod shop equipped with tools for making modifications.

PARTS LIST

BLACK BRICKS

2—2 x 6 plates
4—1 x 4 plates
2—1 x 3 plates
3—1 x 2 plates
2—2 x 2 plates
1—2 x 4 brick
3—1 x 4 bricks
2—1 x 1 bricks
2—1 x 1 bricks with a stud on the side (headlight)
2—1 x 4 x 1 panels
2—1 x 2 grills
1—2 x 4 brick, modified with wheel holders and a 2 x 2 cutout

RED BRICKS

1—4 x 4 plate
2—2 x 4 plates
2—2 x 3 plates
1—1 x 4 plate
1—1 x 2 plate
2—2 x 3 bricks
1—1 x 2 brick
1—2 x 4 x 1⅓ curved slope with four recessed studs
2—1 x 1 slopes, 30 degree
1—steering wheel

DARK GRAY BRICKS

1—4 x 12 vehicle base with a 4 x 2 recessed center and smooth underside
1—2 x 4 Technic brick with holes and a 2 x 2 cutout
2—2 x 2 plates
2—1 x 1 tiles with a clip on top
1—1 x 2 slope, 30 degree with printed dials

LIGHT GRAY BRICKS

1—2 x 4 plate
2—2 x 2 plates
1—1 x 2 plate
1—1 x 2—1 x 2 bracket
1—1 x 2—1 x 2 bracket, inverted
1—1 x 2—1 x 4 bracket
1—1 x 2 grill
1—1 x 4 curved slope, double
1—1 x 2 plate with bar handles
2—1 x 1 bricks with a stud on the side
4—1 x 1 round plates

ASSORTED BRICKS

1—1 x 4 yellow curved slope, double
1—2 x 3 yellow plate
1—1 x 2 yellow brick
2—1 x 2 white grills
2—tan Technic axle pins
2—1 x 2 x 1 clear panels
2—1 x 2 clear plates
2—1 x 1 clear round plates
2—1 x 2 translucent red round plates
2—Waves Rounded with Base Rim (Flame)
2—wheels with axle holes
2—wheels with a hole for a wheel holder

STEP 1: Gather the bricks shown for building the base of the hot rod.

STEP 2: Place a 2 x 4 light gray plate and a 2 x 2 light gray plate inside the vehicle base.

STEP 3: Attach the steering wheel to a 1 x 2 red plate. Attach a 1 x 2 slope with printed dials to a 1 x 2 red brick. Then place both of these inside the vehicle base.

STEP 4: Place a 2 x 4 red plate and a 2 x 2 light gray plate on the back of the car. Add a 2 x 2 black plate and a 1 x 2 black plate on the front of the car.

STEP 5: Find a 2 x 6 black plate, a 1 x 4 black brick, a 1 x 1 black brick, a 1 x 1 black brick with a stud on the side (headlight) and a 1 x 4 x 1 black panel for building the side of the car.

STEP 6: Attach the panel to the 2 x 6 plate.

STEP 7: Add the three black bricks next to the panel as shown.

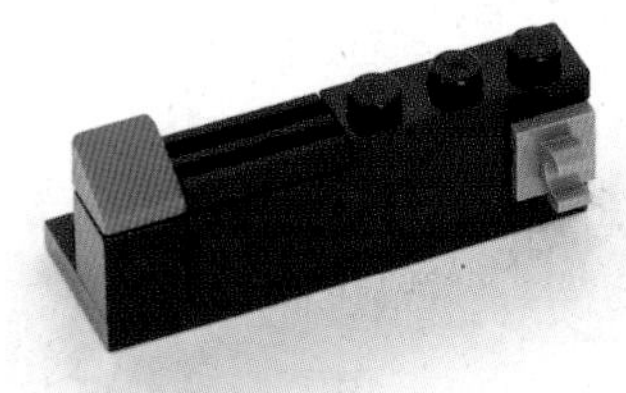

STEP 8: Place a 1 x 1 red slope (30 degree), a 1 x 2 black grill and a 1 x 3 black plate on top of the bricks. Then attach a 1 x 1 dark gray tile with a clip on top to the brick that has a stud on the side.

STEP 9: Make a second one of these. It should be a mirror image of the first.

STEP 10: Attach the sides to the vehicle base.

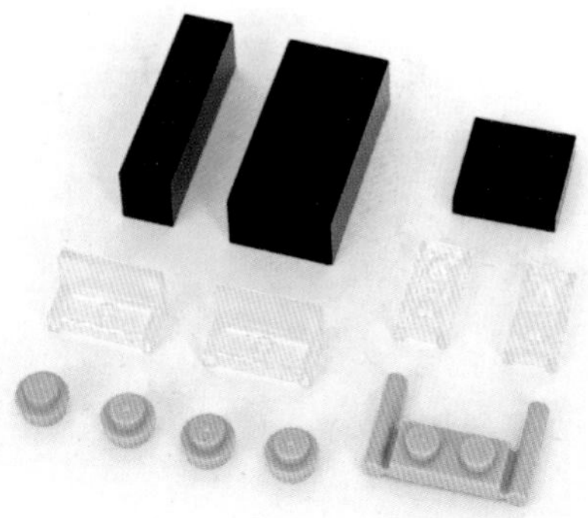

STEP 11: Find a 1 x 4 black brick, a 2 x 4 black brick, a 2 x 2 black plate, two 1 x 2 x 1 clear panels, two 1 x 2 clear plates, four 1 x 1 light gray round plates and a 1 x 2 light gray plate with bar handles.

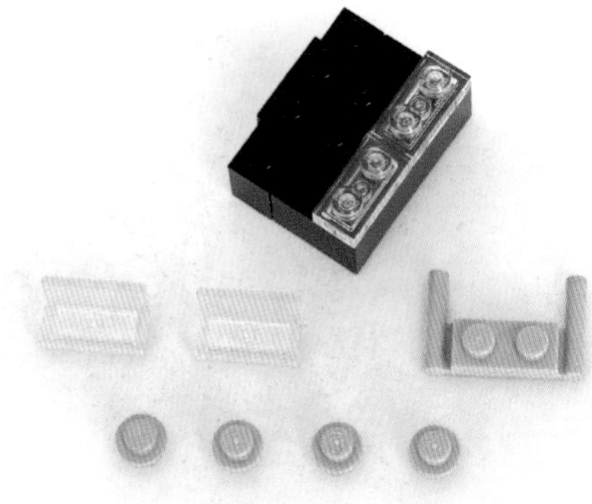

STEP 12: Use the 2 x 2 plate to connect the 1 x 4 brick and the 2 x 4 brick. Then add two 1 x 2 clear plates.

STEP 13: Make an exposed engine by adding a 1 x 2 plate with bar handles and four 1 x 1 light gray round plates.

STEP 14: Make the windshield by adding two 1 x 2 x 1 clear panels. Then attach the engine to the vehicle base.

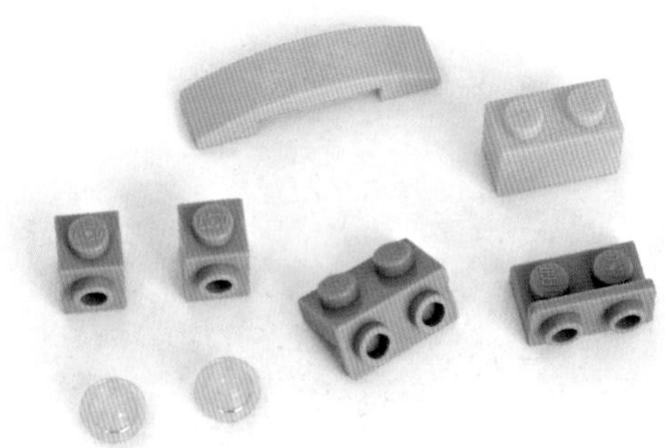

STEP 15: Gather the bricks shown for building the front grill and headlights for your hot rod.

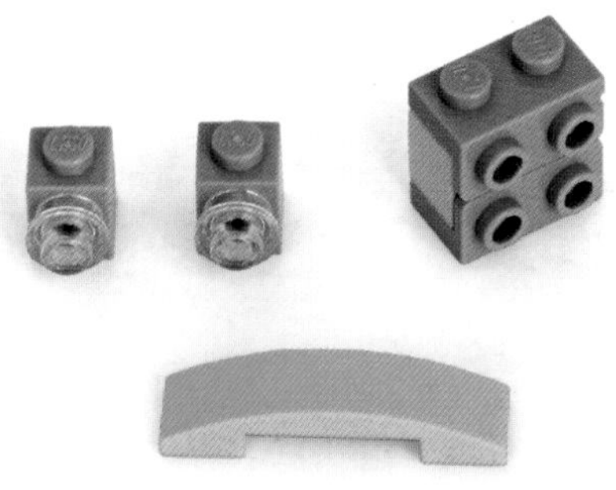

STEP 16: Grab a 1 x 2 yellow brick. Attach a 1 x 2—1 x 2 bracket to the top of it and attach a 1 x 2—1 x 2 inverted bracket to the bottom.

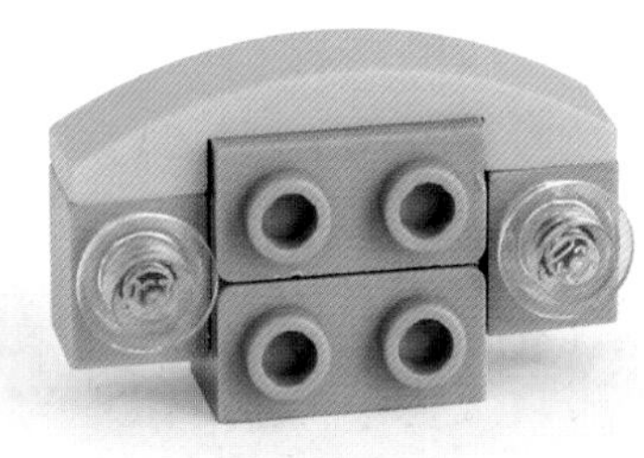

STEP 17: Place a 1 x 4 yellow double curved slope on top of the bracket. Then attach a 1 x 1 light gray brick with a stud on the side to each end. Add 1 x 1 clear round plates to make headlights.

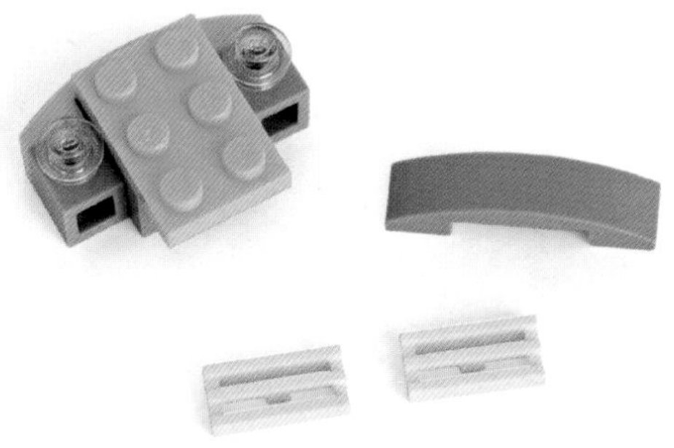

STEP 18: Attach a 2 x 3 yellow plate to the headlight assembly. Then find two 1 x 2 white grills and a 1 x 4 light gray double curved slope.

STEP 19: Place the white grills and light gray curved slope on the headlight assembly.

STEP 20: Attach the headlight assembly to the front of the hot rod.

STEP 21: Grab four 1 x 4 black plates. Make two stacks with two plates in each one.

STEP 22: Attach the sets of two 1 x 4 black plates to the underside of the hot rod, one on each side.

STEP 23: Gather the bricks shown for building the curved back end of the hot rod.

STEP 24: Attach two 2 x 3 red bricks to a 4 x 4 red plate. Then add a 1 x 4 red plate.

STEP 25: Add a 1 x 4 x 1⅓ curved slope with four recessed studs.

STEP 26: Fill in the remaining space with two 2 x 3 red plates.

STEP 27: Attach the red section to the back of the hot rod.

STEP 28: Gather the bricks shown for building the front wheels. The wheels will be attached to a 2 x 4 black brick modified with wheel holders and a 2 x 2 cutout.

STEP 29: Connect the wheels to the wheel holders. Then add a 2 x 2 dark gray plate in the center and a 1 x 2 black plate on each side.

STEP 30: To make the car look like an awesome hot rod, you'll want to make the back wheels larger than the front wheels. Grab the bricks shown for the back wheels.

STEP 31: Place a 2 x 2 dark gray plate in the center of a 2 x 4 dark gray Technic brick with holes and a 2 x 2 cutout. Then add a 1 x 2—1 x 4 light gray bracket and a 1 x 2 light gray plate.

STEP 32: Add two 1 x 1 translucent red round plates and a 1 x 2 light gray grill to the bracket. Then insert two tan axle pins.

STEP 33: Attach the wheels to the axles, and then attach the wheel assembly to the car.

STEP 34: Give the car a finishing touch by attaching flames to the dark gray clips on the sides of the car. Your hot rod is complete and ready to rev its engine!

Now use the picture to try making a different style of hot rod. This one is built on a base of plates rather than using a vehicle base. Unlike the first hot rod, this car also has a flat windshield and a roof. The exposed engine on this hot rod is built from hinge bricks with a 1 x 1 black round plate and 1 x 1 dark gray round tiles attached to them.

If you prefer an open design, this same car also looks great without a roof. Use clear panels for the windshield instead of a full-sized windshield.

Now set up a hot rod shop! Build a rolling tool cart to hold all the things your minifigures will need to fix up their cars.

Your minifigures can swap out the tires for different ones or add more power to the hot rod's engine. Or maybe they'll want to try making the car a different color or adding a different style of headlights. So many possibilities!

CLASSIC POLICE CAR

STEP-BY-STEP

Get ready to go after the bad guys with an awesome police car! This patrol car features a classic design, translucent bricks that mimic flashing lights and a trunk that really opens in case you need to store some extra handcuffs or radios. Your police officers will have no trouble chasing down the bank robber with this powerful car!

PARTS LIST

BLUE BRICKS

1—2 x 4 brick
2—1 x 4 bricks
1—1 x 4 brick with four studs on the side
2—1 x 1 bricks with a stud on the side (headlight)
5—1 x 6 plates
7—1 x 4 plates
7—1 x 2 plates
4—1 x 1 plates
3—2 x 4 plates
1—2 x 2 plate
6—1 x 2 slopes, inverted
4—1 x 4 tiles
1—1 x 2 tile
4—1 x 1 slopes, 30 degree
2—2 x 1 slopes, 45 degree with cutout without stud

DARK GRAY BRICKS

1—4 x 4 plate
2—2 x 6 plates
1—2 x 4 plate
3—1 x 6 plates
2—1 x 4 plates
2—1 x 1—1 x 1 brackets, inverted
2—1 x 2 slopes with four slots
1—1 x 2 plate with door rail

LIGHT GRAY BRICKS

2—1 x 2 plates with a handle on the side
2—1 x 1 plates
2—1 x 1 plates with a vertical clip
2—1 x 1—1 x 1 brackets
2—1 x 2 plates with a clip on the side
1—2 x 2 round plate
1—2 x 4 tile
1—steering wheel

WHITE BRICKS

1—4 x 4 plate
2—1 x 4 plates
1—1 x 2 plate
2—1 x 1 plates
2—1 x 2 plates with door rail
1—1 x 2—1 x 2 bracket
1—1 x 2—2 x 2 bracket, inverted
1—1 x 2—1 x 2 bracket, inverted
1—2 x 4 tile
2—1 x 2 x 1 panels
1—2 x 2 curved slope
1—1 x 2 slope, 30 degree
1—4 x 4 x ⅔ wedge, triple curved
1—2 x 4 x 1⅓ curved slope with four recessed studs

ASSORTED BRICKS

1—4 x 10 black vehicle base with a 4 x 2 recessed center
1—2 x 4 black plate
2—1 x 1 black plates with a light attachment
2—1 x 4 black plates with wheel holders
1—2 x 6 translucent black windshield
1—3 x 6 translucent black windshield
1—1 x 2 translucent blue plate
1—1 x 2 translucent blue tile
1—1 x 2 translucent red plate
1—1 x 2 translucent red tile
2—1 x 1 translucent red round plates
2—1 x 1 translucent yellow round tiles
2—1 x 1 clear round tiles
4—wheels

STEP 1: Grab a 4 x 10 black vehicle base with a 4 x 2 recessed center and the plates shown for building the base of the police car.

STEP 2: Attach a 2 x 6 dark gray plate to the underside of the vehicle base on both sides. Then add a 4 x 4 dark gray plate on the underside of the back end.

STEP 3: Turn the vehicle base upside down. Attach two 1 x 6 dark gray plates on the sides. Then attach a 1 x 4 dark gray plate and a 2 x 4 black plate on the front end.

STEP 4: Flip the vehicle base over again. Attach two 1 x 4 blue plates and a 2 x 2 blue plate on the front end.

STEP 5: Place a 2 x 4 blue brick and two 2 x 4 blue plates on the front of the car. Then find the bricks shown.

STEP 6: Attach a 2 x 4 blue plate and a 1 x 2 blue plate to the underside of a 4 x 4 x ⅔ white wedge (triple curved).

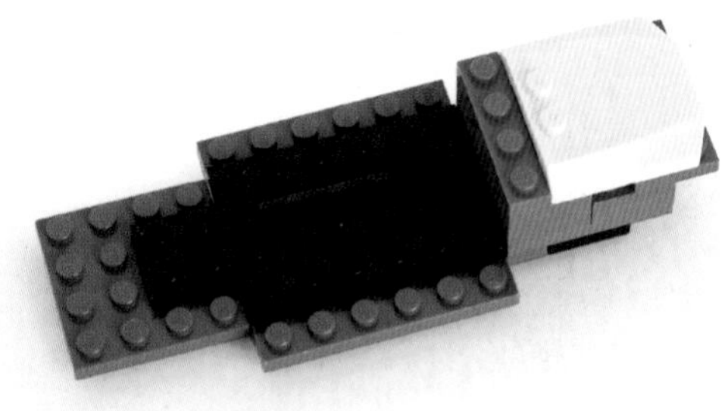

STEP 7: Add the white wedge to the front of the police car. Place a 1 x 4 blue plate right behind it.

STEP 8: Build the sides of the car by placing two 1 x 2 blue inverted slopes and a 1 x 4 blue brick on each side.

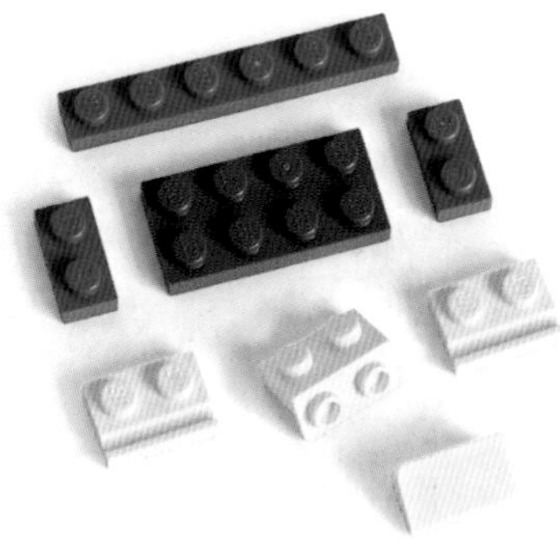

STEP 9: Gather the bricks shown for building the front bumper.

STEP 10: Use a 1 x 6 blue plate to connect a 1 x 2 blue plate, a 2 x 4 dark gray plate and another 1 x 2 blue plate.

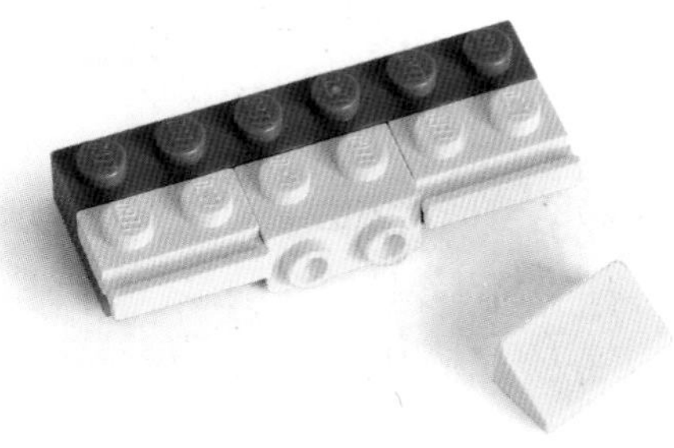

STEP 11: Attach a 1 x 2—1 x 2 white bracket and two 1 x 2 white plates with door rail.

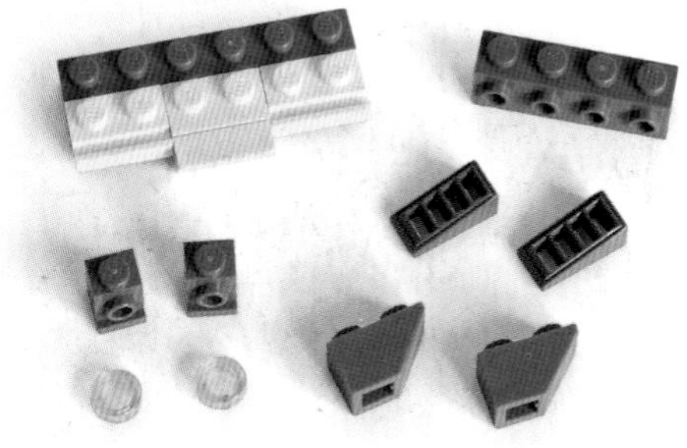

STEP 12: Place the 1 x 2 white slope (30 degree) on the white bracket. Then gather the bricks shown.

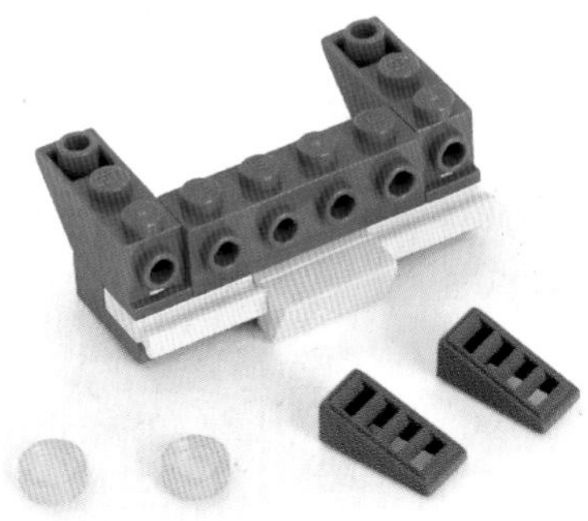

STEP 13: Add two 1 x 2 blue inverted slopes, two 1 x 1 blue bricks with a stud on the side (headlight) and a 1 x 4 blue brick with four studs on the side to the front bumper.

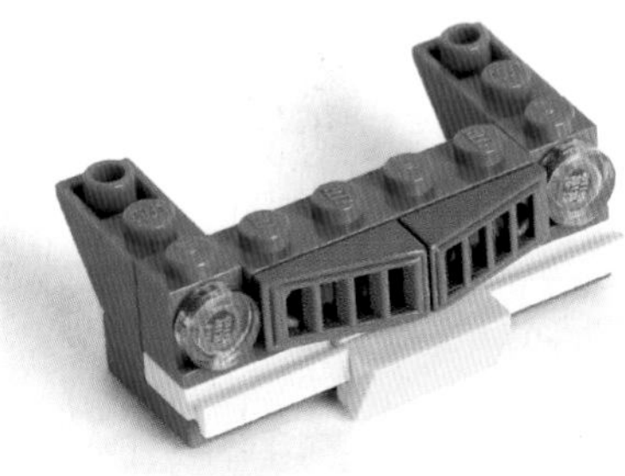

STEP 14: Use two 1 x 1 translucent yellow round tiles and two 1 x 2 dark gray slopes with four slots to build headlights and a grill on the front of the car.

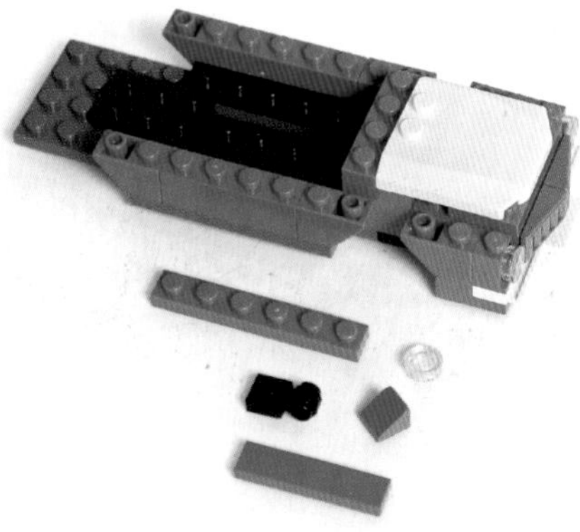

STEP 15: Attach the front bumper and grill to the police car. Then find the bricks shown.

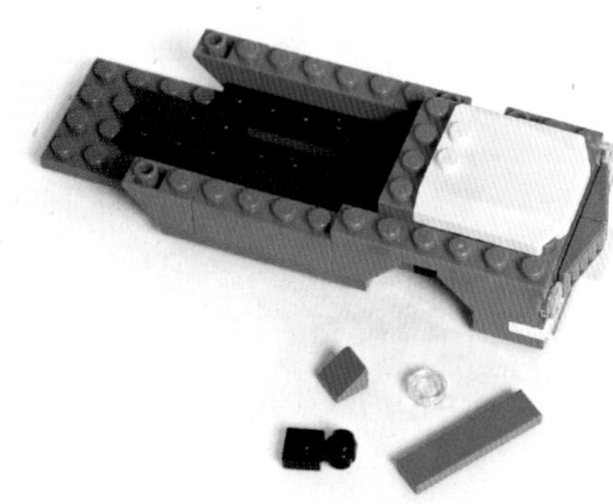

STEP 16: Place a 1 x 6 blue plate next to the hood so that it attaches to both 1 x 2 inverted slopes.

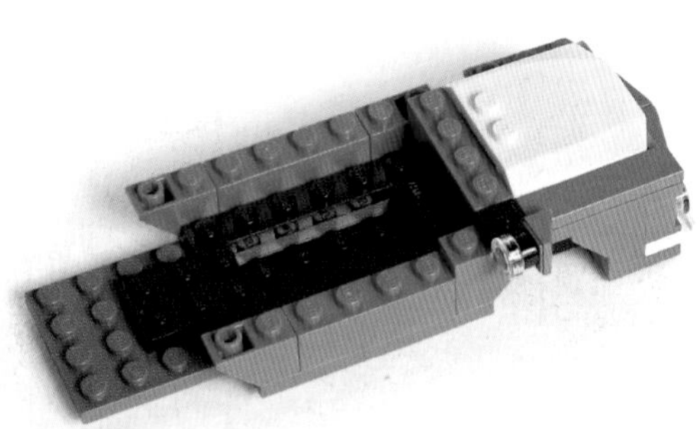

STEP 17: Add a 1 x 4 blue tile next to the hood. Just behind that, add a 1 x 1 black plate with a light attachment. Attach a 1 x 1 clear round tile for a rearview mirror.

STEP 18: Repeat steps 16 and 17 on the other side of the car. Then add a steering wheel and place a 1 x 2 blue tile at the back of the car as shown.

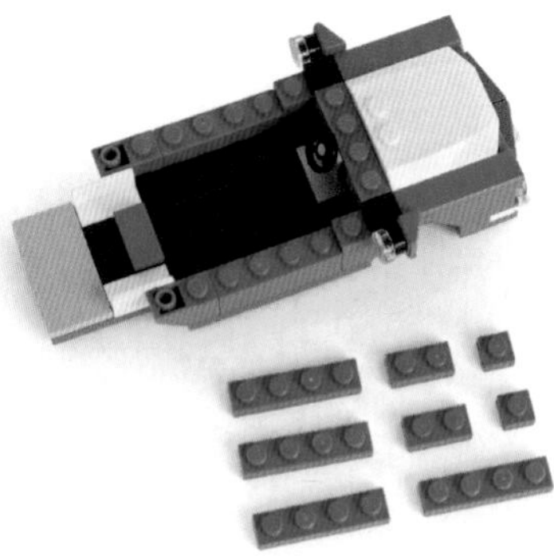

STEP 19: Place a 1 x 2 x 1 white panel on either side of the blue tile. Add a 2 x 4 light gray tile behind that. Then find the plates shown.

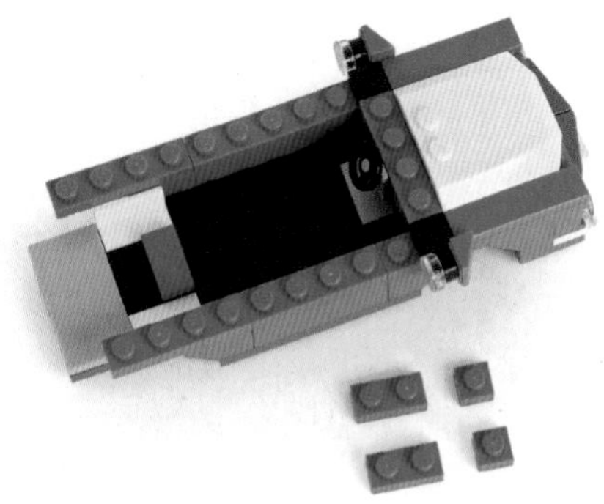

STEP 20: Attach two 1 x 4 blue plates on each side of the car.

STEP 21: Add a 1 x 2 blue plate and a 1 x 1 blue plate on each side of the car. Then find two 1 x 6 blue plates, two 1 x 2 blue plates and two 2 x 1 blue slopes (45 degree with cutout).

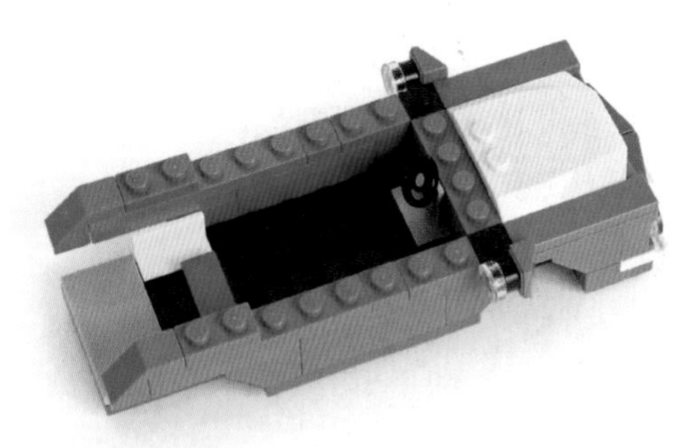

STEP 22: Attach a 1 x 6 blue plate to each side of the car. Then add the 2 x 1 slopes with cutout and put the 1 x 2 plates next to them.

STEP 23: Grab a 1 x 4 white plate, a 1 x 4 dark gray plate, two 1 x 1 blue plates, a 1 x 2—2 x 2 white inverted bracket and two 1 x 2 light gray plates with a clip on the side.

STEP 24: Place the white bracket and the two 1 x 1 blue plates on top of the 1 x 4 dark gray plate.

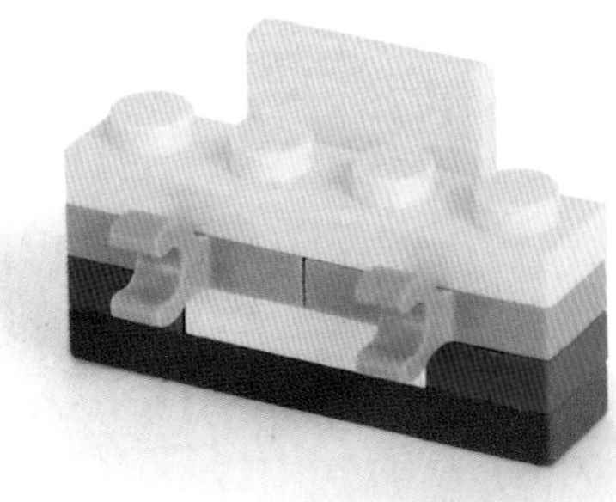

STEP 25: Add two 1 x 2 light gray plates with a clip on the side, and then add a 1 x 4 white plate.

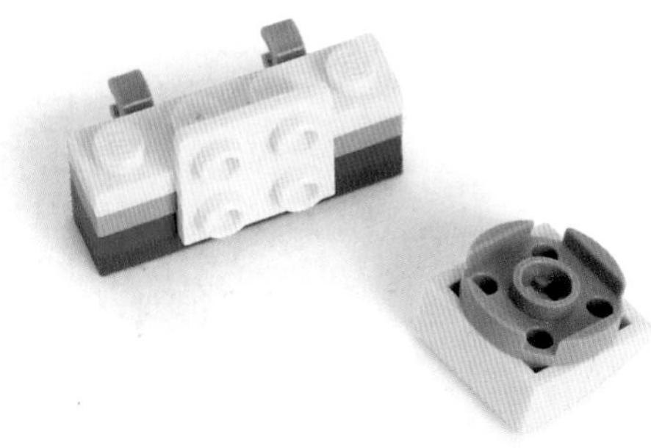

STEP 26: Build the back of the car's seat. Attach a 1 x 2 white plate to the underside of a 2 x 2 white curved slope. Then add a 2 x 2 light gray round plate.

STEP 27: Attach the seat back to the white bracket from step 24

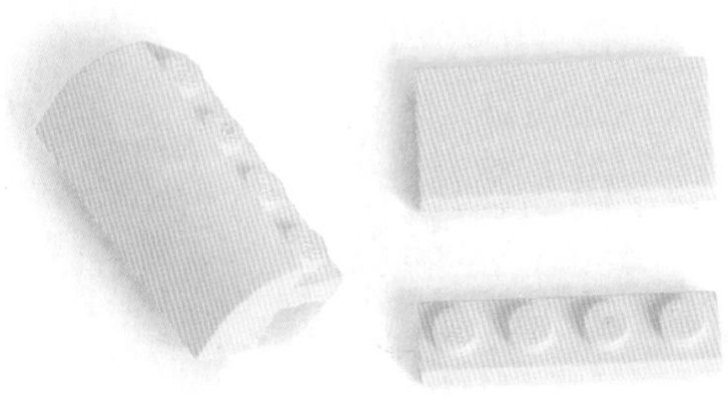

STEP 28: Find a 2 x 4 white curved slope with four recessed studs, a 2 x 4 white tile and a 1 x 4 white plate for building the trunk of the police car.

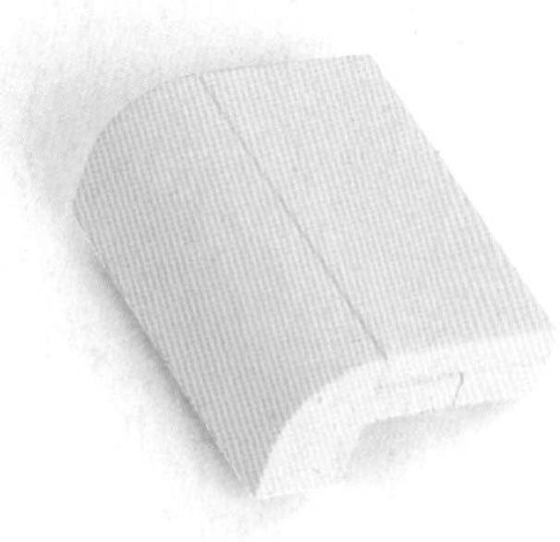

STEP 29: Attach the 2 x 4 tile to the 2 x 4 curved slope. Then attach the 1 x 4 plate under the tile.

STEP 30: Flip the trunk over and add two 1 x 2 light gray plates with a handle on the side.

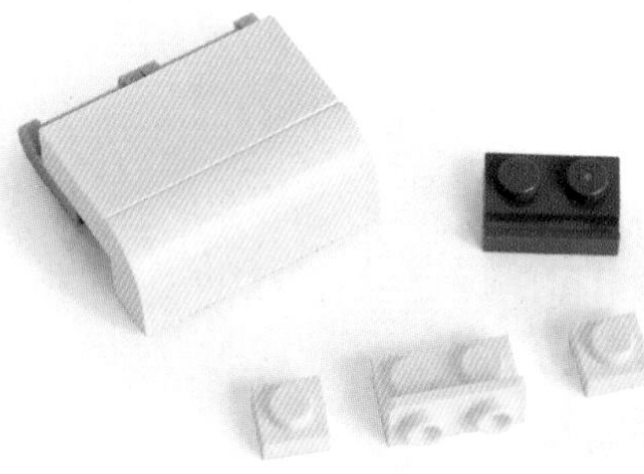

STEP 31: Turn the trunk back over and find two 1 x 1 white plates, a 1 x 2—1 x 2 white inverted bracket and a 1 x 2 dark gray plate with door rail.

STEP 32: Attach the bracket and the two 1 x 1 white plates to the bottom of the curved brick on the trunk.

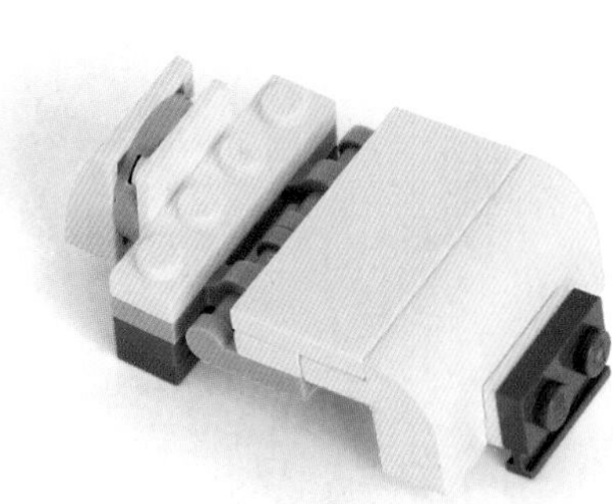

STEP 33: Place the 1 x 2 dark gray plate with door rail to the trunk. Then connect the trunk to the back of the seat using the clips and handle plates.

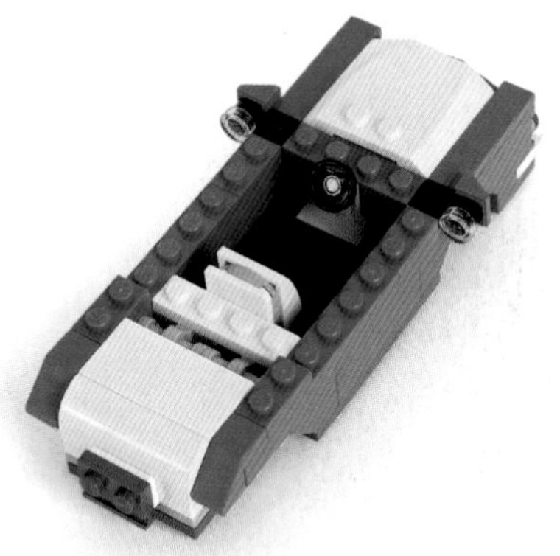

STEP 34: Attach the seat and trunk to the body of the police car.

STEP 35: Gather the pieces shown for building the taillights.

STEP 36: Place a 1 x 1 light gray plate on top of a 1 x 1 light gray plate with a vertical clip. Then add a 1 x 1—1 x 1 dark gray inverted bracket.

STEP 37: Attach a 1 x 1—1 x 1 light gray bracket. Then attach a 1 x 1 blue slope (30 degree) to that. Add a 1 x 1 translucent red round plate to the dark gray bracket.

STEP 38: Follow steps 35 to 37 again to build a second taillight. Then attach both taillights to the ends of a 1 x 6 dark gray plate.

STEP 39: Attach the plate and taillights to the back of the car as shown.

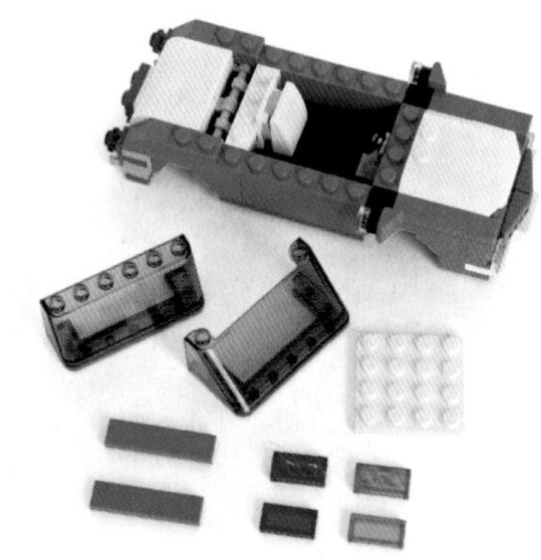

STEP 40: Gather the bricks shown for building the windshield and roof of the police car. One windshield is 2 x 6, while the other is 3 x 6. However, you can substitute with the windshields you have.

STEP 41: Attach the windshields to the car and place a 4 x 4 white plate on the roof. The white plate only attaches to the 2 x 6 windshield because the other one does not have studs on top.

STEP 42: Add a 1 x 4 blue tile on each side of the white plate. Then build the flashing lights. Both lights are built from a 1 x 2 plate with a 1 x 2 tile on top. Use only plates if you don't have the tiles.

STEP 43: Find two 1 x 4 black plates with wheel holders. Use these to attach the wheels to the bottom of the car. Your police car is complete!

The trunk easily opens and closes with the handle and clip joint. Your officers can use the trunk to carry extra handcuffs and other gear.

Officer Jackson was cruising down Seventh Street, just about to end his shift, when he saw a man run out of the bank with a crowbar and a fistful of cash. Ugh, not again! Pete the Swindler was already wanted on three counts of bank robbery! This time he was going behind bars.

Thankfully, Officer Jackson's recent endurance training at the gym was really paying off. He easily overtook Pete and loaded him into his squad car.

MILITARY HUMVEE

STEP-BY-STEP

The official term for what is commonly called a "humvee" is HMMWV, short for High Mobility Multipurpose Wheeled Vehicle. In the 1970s, the United States military began the process of replacing their fleet of jeeps with a more modern vehicle. A list of specifications was created for this vehicle. It needed to be lightweight, durable, have good performance both on the road and off and be able to carry a large amount of weight. The motor company AM General created a design that fit the standards, and they were awarded a contract to begin producing the vehicles in 1983. The Humvee is still the primary light vehicle used by the United States military, and they are also used around the world.

This LEGO Humvee can hold four soldiers, and it's equipped with a gun on the top. It is built in a desert tan color, but another option is to build your Humvee in a mix of tan, brown and green to make it camouflaged for forest areas. Once you're finished building, set up a combat scene!

PARTS LIST

TAN BRICKS

1—8 x 8 plate
1—4 x 8 plate
1—4 x 4 plate
6—2 x 4 plates
1—1 x 8 plate
3—1 x 6 plates
5—1 x 4 plates
1—2 x 2 plate
4—1 x 2 plates
6—1 x 6 bricks
2—1 x 4 bricks
1—2 x 4 brick
2—2 x 2 slopes, inverted
6—1 x 1 bricks with a stud on the side (headlight)
2—2 x 4 tiles
2—1 x 2 tiles
6—1 x 2 x 1 panels
2—1 x 1 round bricks
2—1 x 2 plates with one stud on top (jumper plate)
2—1 x 2 slopes, 30 degree
8—1 x 1 slopes, 30 degree
1—1 x 1 plate with a vertical clip

DARK GRAY BRICKS

1—1 x 6 plate
4—1 x 4 plates
8—2 x 2 plates with a pin hole
2—2 x 2 corner plates
5—1 x 1 tiles with a clip on top
1—1 x 2 plate with a ladder
2—1 x 2 grills
1—2 x 2 plate with one stud on top
2—1 x 2—2 x 2 brackets
2—1 x 1 Technic bricks
1—1 x 2 slope, 30 degree with printed gauges
1—2 x 2 barrel
2—1 x 14 Technic bricks

BLACK BRICKS

1—1 x 4 plate
2—1 x 2 plates
1—1 x 2 plate with two clips on the side
2—1 x 1 tiles
2—1 x 1 slopes, 30 degree
2—1 x 1 round plates
2—bars, 4 studs long
1—bar, 6 studs long with a stop ring
2—antennas (levers)
1—bar, 1 x 8 x 2
2—axles, 8 studs long
1—1 x 4 antenna
1—antenna whip
2—arms, mechanical (battle droid)
4—wheels with axle hole
1—wheel with pin hole

LIGHT GRAY BRICKS

2—antennas (levers)
1—1 x 2 plate with a handle on the side
1—steering wheel
4—1 x 1 plates with a vertical clip
1—1 x 1 tile
1—1 x 2 x ⅔ brick, modified with studs on the sides
1—pin, half length

ASSORTED BRICKS

8—blue Technic pins with friction ridges, 3 studs long
1—6 x 8 dark tan plate
1—1 x 6 dark tan plate
2—2 x 2 dark tan tiles
1—1 x 2 dark tan plate with one stud on top (jumper plate)
1—brown chair
1—1 x 2 brown grill
2—1 x 1 translucent red round plates
4—1 x 1 translucent yellow round tiles
1—1 x 1 translucent black slope, 30 degree
3—1 x 2 x 2 clear panels

STEP 1: Find a 1 x 14 Technic brick, four 2 x 2 plates with a pin hole and four blue pins with friction ridges (3 studs long).

STEP 2: Insert the pins into the Technic brick as shown.

STEP 3: Slide a 2 x 2 plate with a pin hole onto each pin. Then make a second one of these. They should be mirror images of each other as shown.

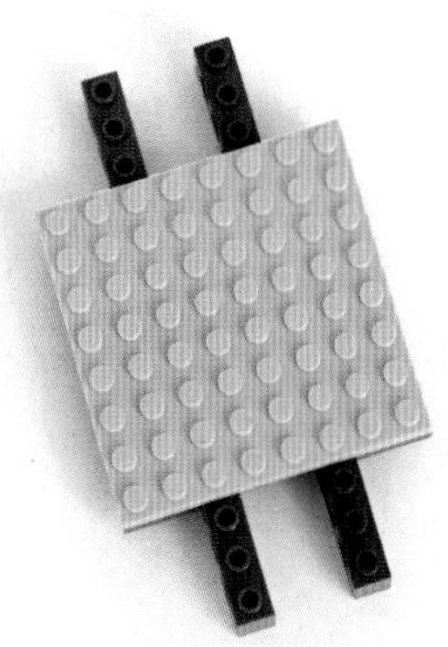

STEP 4: Turn the Technic bricks over and attach an 8 x 8 tan plate.

STEP 5: This is what the underside should look like.

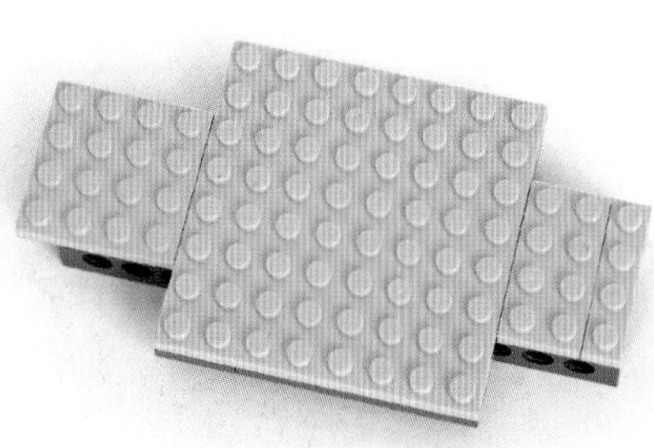

STEP 6: Turn the bricks back over and add a 4 x 4 tan plate, a 2 x 4 tan plate and a 1 x 4 tan plate.

STEP 7: Place a 1 x 4 tan brick and a 2 x 4 tan brick on the front of the vehicle. Then find the bricks shown.

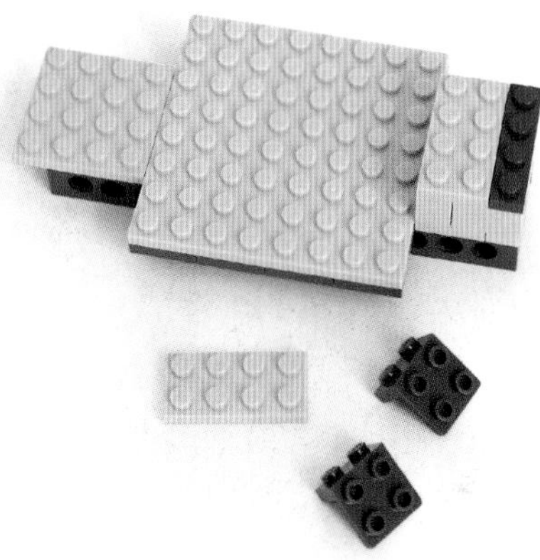

STEP 8: Place a 2 x 4 tan plate and a 1 x 4 dark gray plate on top of the bricks.

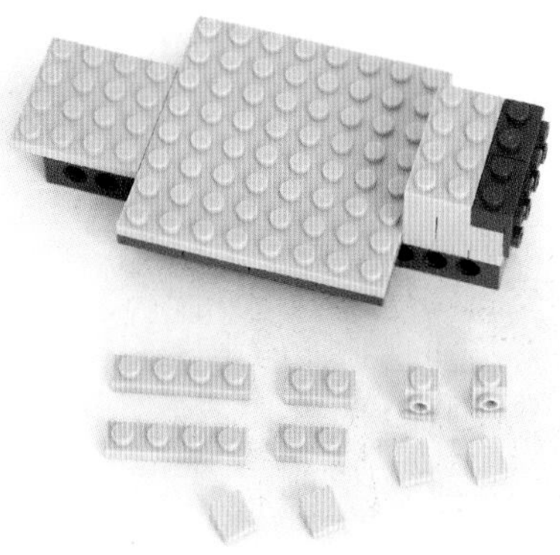

STEP 9: Then add a second 2 x 4 tan plate and place two 1 x 2—2 x 2 dark gray brackets on the front of the vehicle. Then gather the bricks shown.

STEP 10: Place a 1 x 1 brick with a stud on the side (headlight) and a 1 x 1 tan slope (30 degree) on both of the front corners of the 8 x 8 plate.

STEP 11: Grab two 1 x 4 tan plates. Attach a 1 x 2 tan plate to the underside of each one.

STEP 12: Attach the tan plates to the bricks from step 10. Add a 1 x 1 tan slope (30 degree) on top of each one.

STEP 13: Place a 4 x 8 tan plate on the front of the vehicle so that it attaches to the bricks and plates.

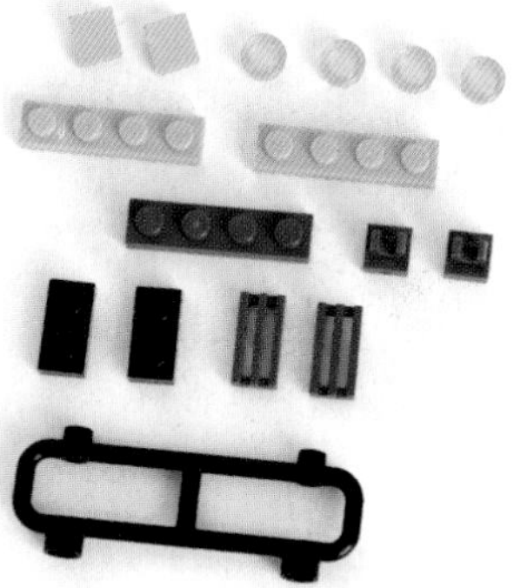

STEP 14: Gather the bricks shown for building the grill and headlights. The black piece is called a bar, 1 x 8 x 2.

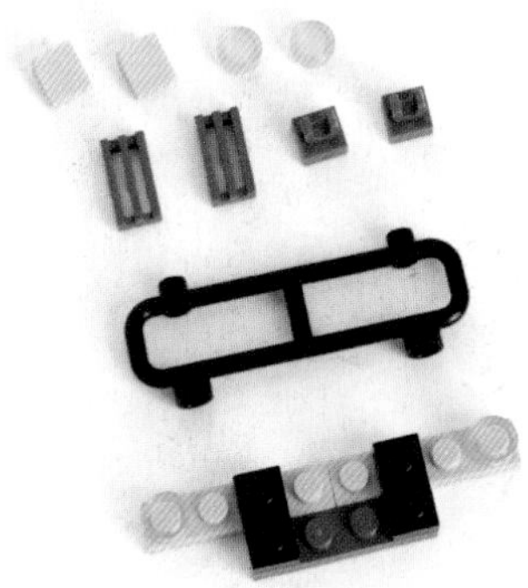

STEP 15: Use two 1 x 2 black plates to attach two 1 x 4 tan plates and a 1 x 4 dark gray plate. Then add two 1 x 1 translucent yellow round tiles.

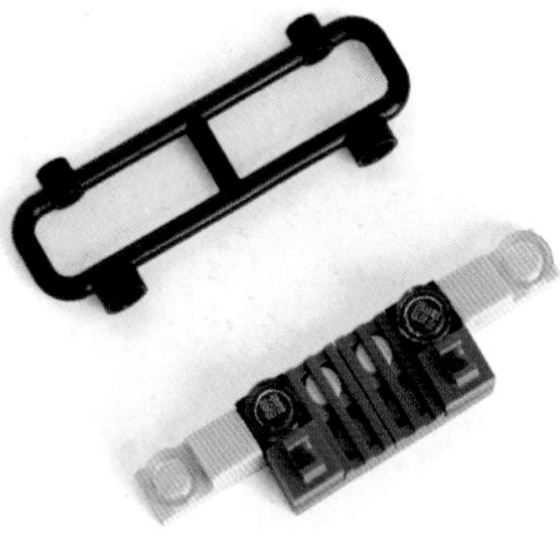

STEP 16: Add two 1 x 1 tan slopes (30 degree) and another pair of 1 x 1 yellow round tiles. Place two 1 x 2 dark gray grills in the center and add two 1 x 1 dark gray tiles with a clip, one on either side.

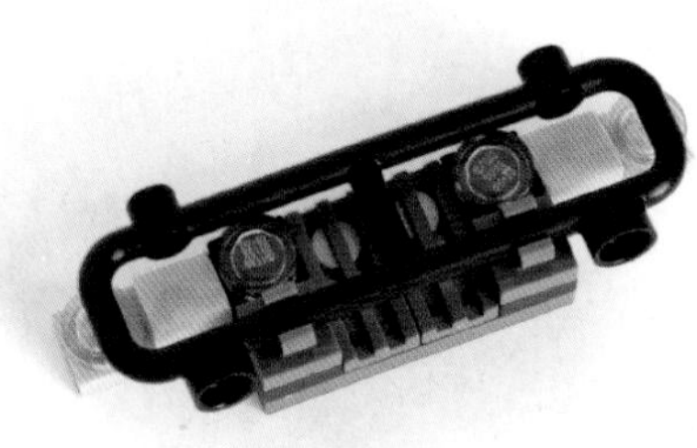

STEP 17: Insert the black bar into the clips on the headlight assembly.

STEP 18: Attach the headlights and grill to the brackets on the front of the vehicle.

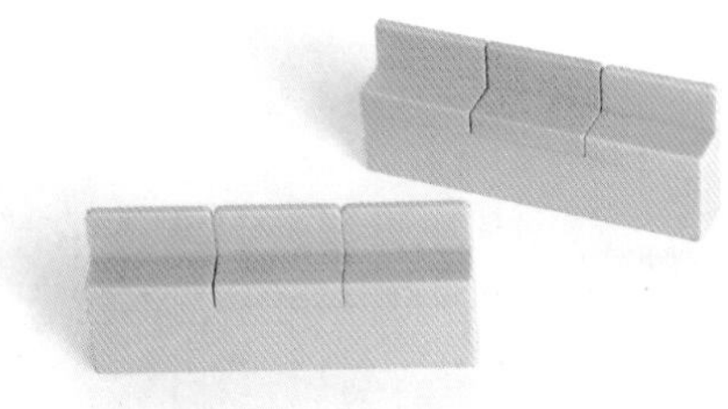

STEP 19: Find two 1 x 6 tan bricks. Place three 1 x 2 x 1 panels on top of each one.

STEP 20: Stack two 1 x 6 tan bricks. Then place three 1 x 2 x 2 clear panels on top of them to make the windshield.

STEP 21: Add the windshield and the side panels to the Humvee.

STEP 22: Place a 1 x 4 tan brick and two 2 x 2 tan inverted slopes on the back of the cab area. Then find a 1 x 6 dark gray plate and two 2 x 2 dark gray corner plates.

STEP 23: Add the 1 x 6 dark gray plate to the back of the cab. Then attach the two dark gray corner plates to the underside of the 4 x 4 tan plate.

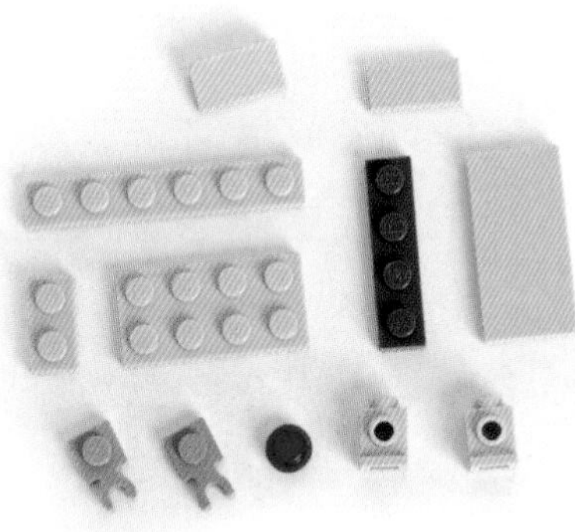

STEP 24: Gather the bricks shown for building the taillights.

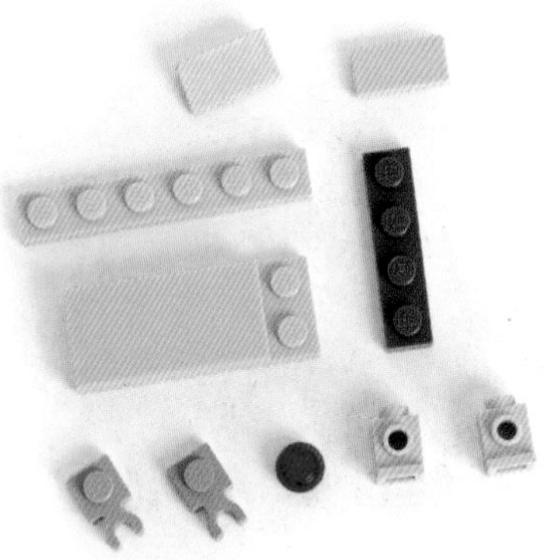

STEP 25: Use a 2 x 4 tan tile to attach a 1 x 2 tan plate and a 2 x 4 tan plate.

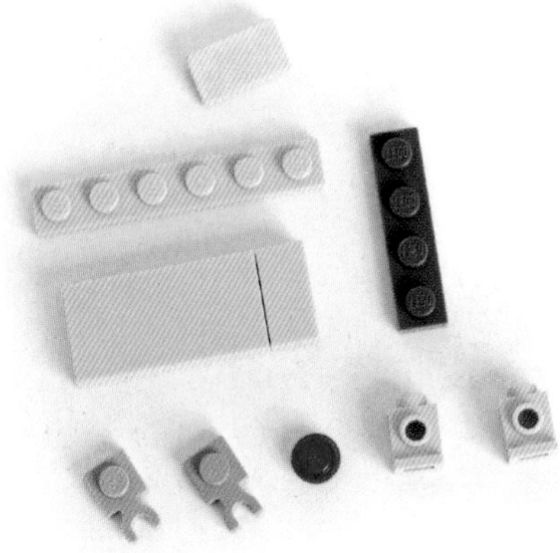

STEP 26: Add a 1 x 2 tan tile.

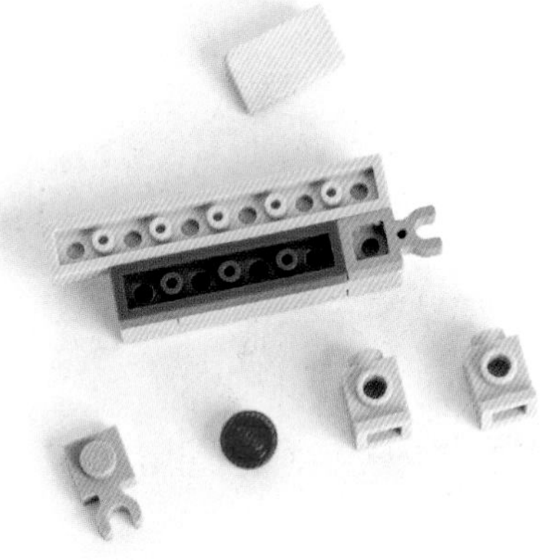

STEP 27: Turn the tiles over. Add a 1 x 6 tan plate, a 1 x 4 dark gray plate and a 1 x 1 light gray plate with a vertical clip.

STEP 28: Add two 1 x 1 bricks with a stud on the side (headlight), and then attach a 1 x 2 slope (30 degree) to them.

STEP 29: Insert a 1 x 1 translucent red round plate into the hole on the back of the headlight brick on the right side.

STEP 30: Then place a 1 x 1 light gray plate with a vertical clip on the headlight brick on the left.

STEP 31: Follow steps 24 to 30 again to build a second taillight assembly. Make this one a mirror image of the first one.

STEP 32: Attach the taillight assemblies to the Humvee. They will sit on the tan inverted slope bricks and the dark gray corner plates.

STEP 33: Build the dashboard. Find a 1 x 6 tan plate. Add a steering wheel, a 1 x 2 dark gray slope (30 degree) with printed gauges, and two 1 x 1 black tiles.

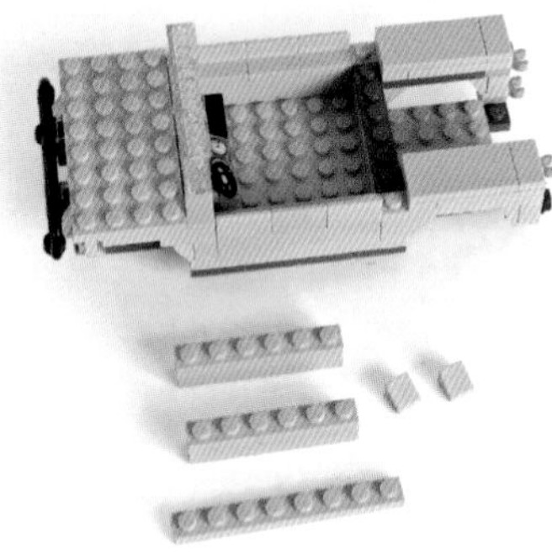

STEP 34: Place the dashboard inside the cab of the vehicle. Then find two 1 x 6 tan bricks, a 1 x 8 tan plate and two 1 x 1 tan slopes (30 degree).

STEP 35: Attach the 1 x 8 tan plate to the back of the cab. Then add two 1 x 6 tan bricks. Place a 1 x 1 slope (30 degree) on each side of the bricks.

STEP 36: Gather the bricks shown for building the spare tire.

STEP 37: Place a 2 x 2 dark gray plate with one stud on top on the center of a 2 x 4 tan plate. Place the black wheel inside the tire.

STEP 38: Attach the spare tire to the stud on the dark gray plate. Then place a 1 x 2 black plate with two clips on the side on top of a 1 x 4 black plate. Connect a 1 x 2 light gray plate with a handle on the side to the black clips. Place two 1 x 1 black round plates on the underside of the light gray plate.

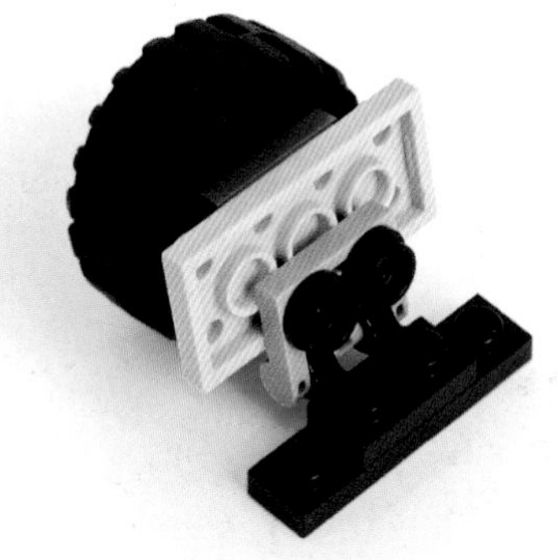

STEP 39: Attach the studs on the light gray plate to the tan plate.

STEP 40: Turn the Humvee over and attach the black plate to the dark gray corner plates on the underside of the vehicle.

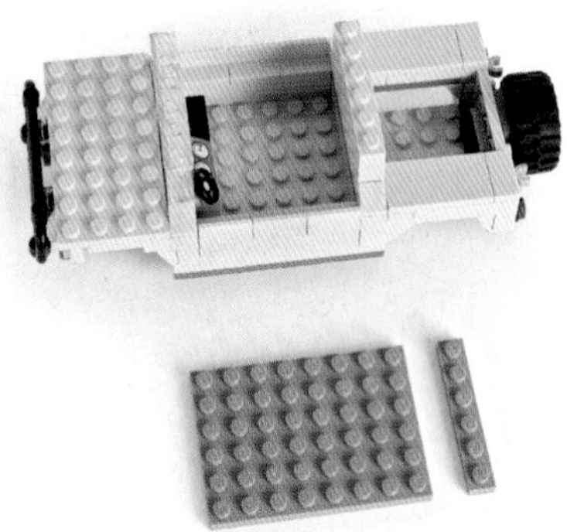

STEP 41: Flip the vehicle over again and find a 6 x 8 dark tan plate and a 1 x 6 dark tan plate.

STEP 42: Place the 1 x 6 dark tan plate on top of the bricks at the back of the cab. Then add the 6 x 8 plate for the roof.

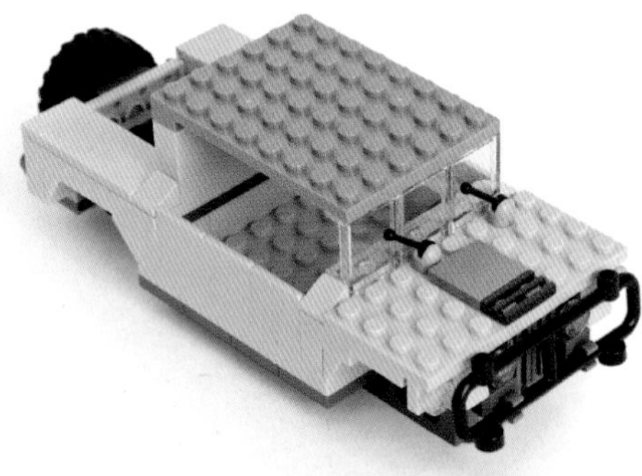

STEP 43: Add light gray antennas as windshield wipers. Decorate the hood with a 2 x 2 dark tan tile and a 1 x 2 brown grill.

STEP 44: Gather the pieces shown for building the push bar. The black bars are 4 studs long.

STEP 45: Attach the two 1 x 1 tiles with a clip on top to the tops of the two 1 x 1 Technic bricks. Insert a bar into the clips. Then use the two mechanical arms to attach another bar.

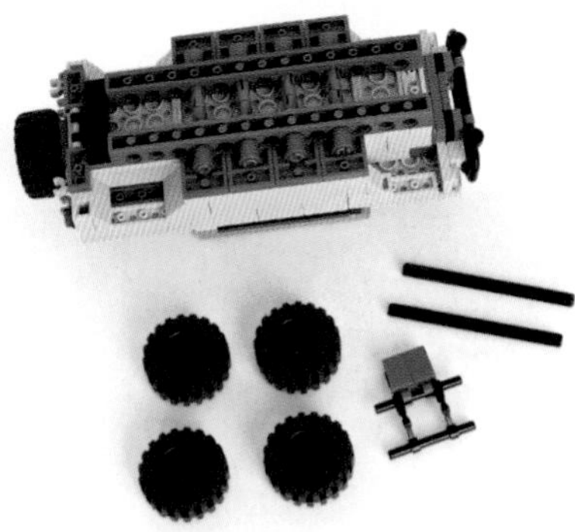

STEP 46: Turn the vehicle upside down. Find four wheels with X-shaped axle holes and two axles (8 studs long).

STEP 47: Slide the back axle through the holes in the Technic bricks and add the wheels. Slide the front axle through one Technic brick, then through the push bar, and then through the other Technic brick.

STEP 48: Slide the front wheels onto the axles and turn the Humvee over. Now it's time to add the final details. Attach accessories like a shovel into the clips on the back of the Humvee. Place a row of tiles and plates on the roof as shown.

STEP 49: Gather the bricks shown for building the gun on top of the Humvee. The light gray brick is a 1 x 2 x ⅔ brick modified with studs on the sides.

STEP 50: Attach the light gray brick to two 1 x 1 tan round bricks. Slide in a black bar (6 studs long with a stop ring).

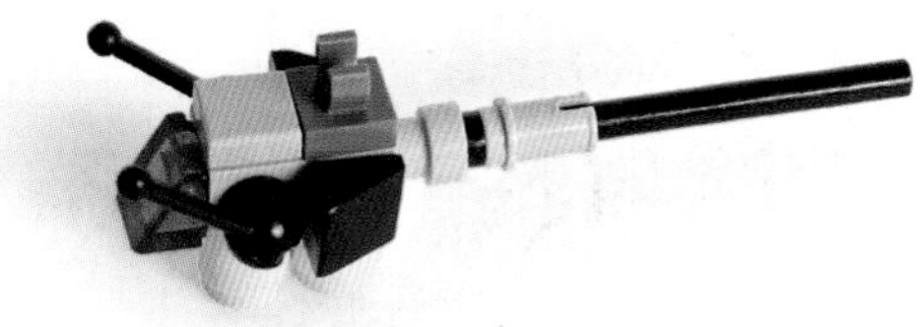

STEP 51: Slide a light gray pin (half length) onto the black bar. Then attach two 1 x 1 black slopes (30 degree), two black antennas, a 1 x 1 dark gray tile with a clip, a 1 x 1 light gray tile and a 1 x 1 translucent black slope (30 degree) to the studs on the light gray brick.

STEP 52: Place the gun on top of the Humvee and add a chair for the gunman to sit in. Attach an antenna to a 1 x 1 tan plate with a clip and add this to the roof of the vehicle. Place a dark gray barrel in the back of the Humvee or add other equipment. Your Humvee is complete!

Remove the roof to add troopers to the Humvee. The cab can hold four of them.

Set up a combat scene with rocks and land formations to hide behind. You might also want to build a military barracks with a place to park the Humvee.

BATTLE TANK

CREATIVE CHALLENGE

Create your own armored battle tank equipped with a large gun and space for soldiers. The gun turret really rotates, and the tank rolls on heavy-duty tracks. This open-ended project does not have a photo for every step; instead, use the photos as inspiration to create your own design based on the bricks you have. You can adjust the size of the tank and change the color if you want. Make the turret rotate with a 4 x 4 turntable base and a 4 x 4 round plate, and then design an awesome gun. Once your tank is finished, pair it with the Military Humvee on page 38 to create epic battle scenes!

KEY ELEMENTS

Various tank bricks and plates
1—8 x 16 light gray plate
1—4 x 4 black turntable base, locking
1—4 x 4 dark gray round plate
8—dark gray Technic gears, 24 tooth
2—Technic axles, 12 studs long
4—light gray Technic bush
2—1 x 5 black Technic liftarms
2—light gray Technic pins
4—tan Technic axle pins
2—1 x 14 dark gray Technic bricks
1—1 x 2 black hinge brick with a 2 x 2 hinge plate
1—1 x 1 x 6 brown solid pillar
About 86 link treads

This tank is built on an 8 x 16 light gray plate with two 1 x 14 dark gray Technic bricks under the plate to hold the gears and tracks. The bottom of the tank is made up of basic bricks and plates. Attach a 4 x 4 black turntable base with a 4 x 4 dark gray plate. This will allow the gun turret to turn. Place tiles on the base so that they are at an equal level with the turntable. The tiles will allow the gun turret to turn smoothly.

To add the gears, slide an axle (12 studs long) through the Technic bricks. Place a Technic bush on each axle before adding the gears. You can create a simple suspension system with the middle two gears on each side if you want. Attach a 1 x 5 liftarm to the Technic brick using a light gray pin. Then attach a 24-tooth gear to each end of the 1 x 5 liftarm using tan axle pins. The tank will be able to rumble over bumps really easily!

Once all your gears are attached, connect the link treads around the gears.

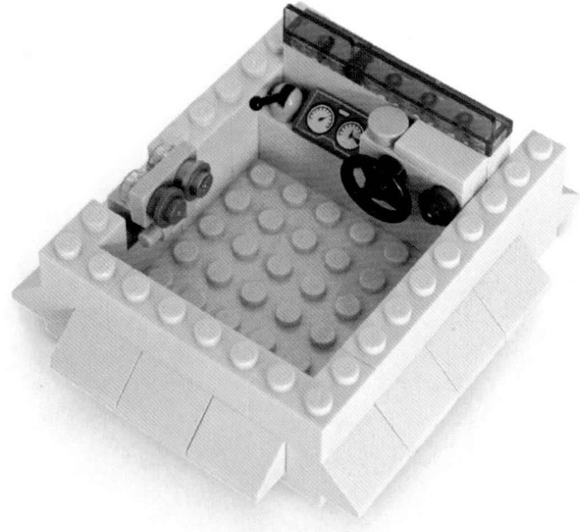

Build the gun turret. If you build it on an 8 x 8 plate, you can easily fit two minifigures inside. Customize your gun turret with controls and dials. Build a scope in the side of the gun turret so that the soldiers can easily watch enemy activity.

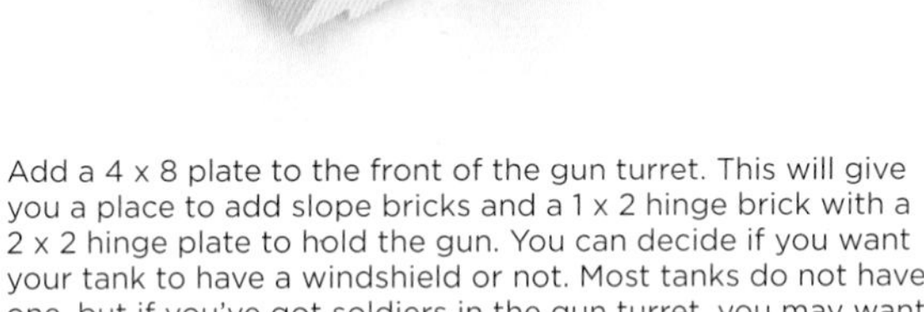

Add a 4 x 8 plate to the front of the gun turret. This will give you a place to add slope bricks and a 1 x 2 hinge brick with a 2 x 2 hinge plate to hold the gun. You can decide if you want your tank to have a windshield or not. Most tanks do not have one, but if you've got soldiers in the gun turret, you may want to build a way for them to see out.

Build a roof that opens on the top of the gun turret. Use 1 x 2 plates with a handle on the side and 1 x 2 plates with clips to make a hinge that allows the roof to open.

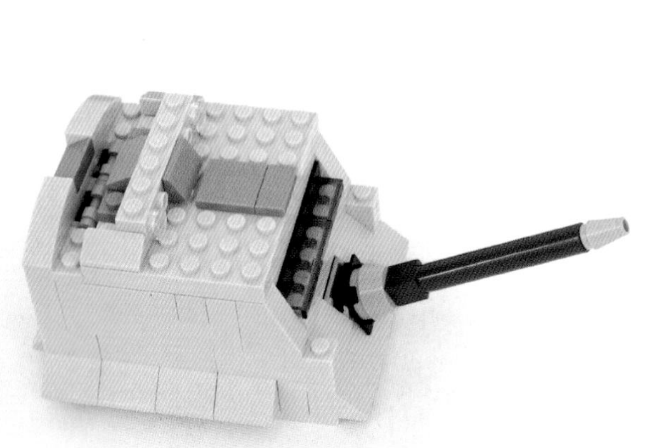

Attach the gun to the hinge brick and plate on the gun turret.

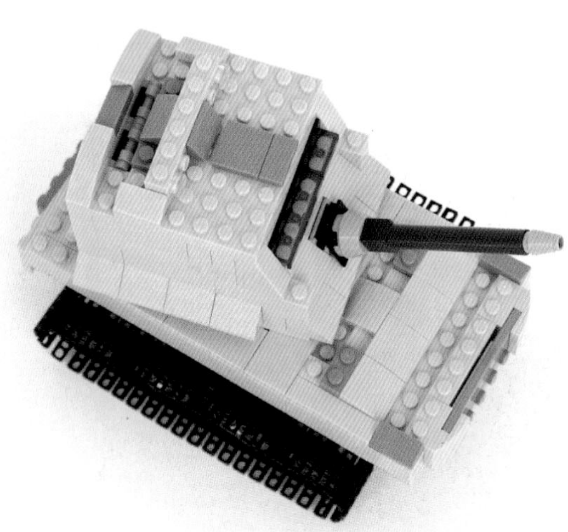

Connect the turret to the base of the tank, and you're ready for battle!

BUILDING TIP

Use 1 x 4 hinge plates to attach sections of rock together. This will allow you to pivot the sections and make a really awesome scene!

Now set up a battle scene! Grab your Military Humvee (page 38) and some minifigures. Use light gray bricks to build rocks to hide behind and add some desert plants and little trees.

Here's another awesome tank design to build. This tank's proportions are more realistic, but because of that, it does not have room for minifigures inside. The gun turret rotates with a 4 x 4 turntable.

This tank is built on top of a base made from plates that connect to make 8 studs by 16 studs. Once you have built the base, get creative with the bricks you have to design the body of the tank and the gun turret. The gun is a 1 x 4 light gray antenna. Slide two light gray pins (half length) onto the antenna and add a 1 x 1 dark gray round brick.

ADVENTURE ATV

STEP-BY-STEP

Sometimes, the most fun driving is done off the road rather than on it! Build an awesome all-terrain vehicle that is perfect for driving across fields, splashing through creeks and exploring rugged mountain roads. This ATV is big enough to hold four minifigures as well as gear and supplies for the journey.

PARTS LIST

DARK GRAY BRICKS

1—8 x 8 plate
1—4 x 12 plate
1—4 x 8 plate
1—2 x 8 plate
2—2 x 6 plates
6—2 x 4 plates
2—2 x 3 plates
2—1 x 8 plates
3—1 x 4 plates
3—2 x 6 bricks
4—2 x 4 bricks
2—1 x 6 bricks
1—1 x 4 brick
1—1 x 2 brick
3—2 x 2 slopes
2—1 x 1 plates
6—1 x 2 slopes, inverted
2—1 x 6 tiles
2—2 x 4 plates with two pins
1—1 x 2 grill
1—6 x 4 slope, double inverted with a 4 x 4 cutout and three holes
2—6 x 2 slopes, double inverted with a 2 x 4 cutout
1—1 x 2 slope, 30 degree with printed gauges
2—1 x 1 bricks with a stud on the side

LIGHT GRAY BRICKS

2—1 x 6 plates
1—1 x 4 brick with four studs on the side
1—1 x 2 tile
1—1 x 1 round plate
1—antenna (lever)

ASSORTED BRICKS

2—1 x 10 black plates
6—1 x 6 black plates
6—1 x 1 black round bricks
2—1 x 1 translucent orange round plates
2—1 x 1 translucent yellow round plates
4—chairs
1—steering wheel
1—2 x 6 windshield
4—wheels

STEP 1: Find two 2 x 6 dark gray bricks, four 2 x 4 dark gray bricks and a 4 x 12 dark gray plate.

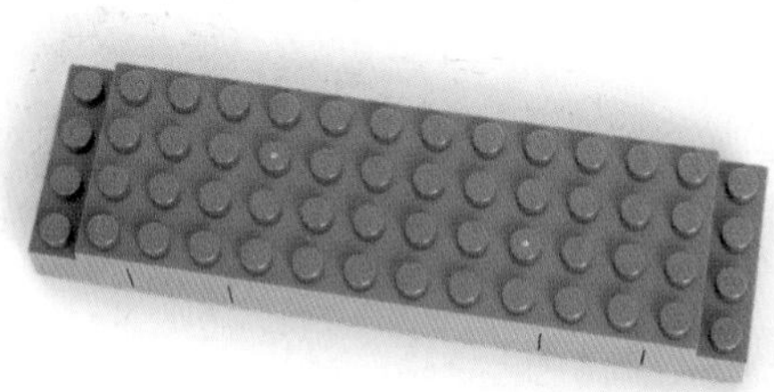

STEP 2: Use the 4 x 12 plate to connect the bricks as shown. There will be a 2 x 4 brick sticking out by one row of studs on each end.

STEP 3: Add a 1 x 4 dark gray plate to the back end of the vehicle (left side). Then find a 6 x 4 double inverted slope (with a 4 x 4 cutout), an 8 x 8 dark gray plate and a 2 x 4 dark gray plate.

STEP 4: Attach the 6 x 4 inverted slope to the vehicle so that it hangs off by one row of studs. Then add the two plates.

STEP 5: Grab a 1 x 6 dark gray brick and a 2 x 6 dark gray brick. Then find a 1 x 8 dark gray plate, a 2 x 6 dark gray plate, a 2 x 8 dark gray plate and two 1 x 2 dark gray inverted slopes.

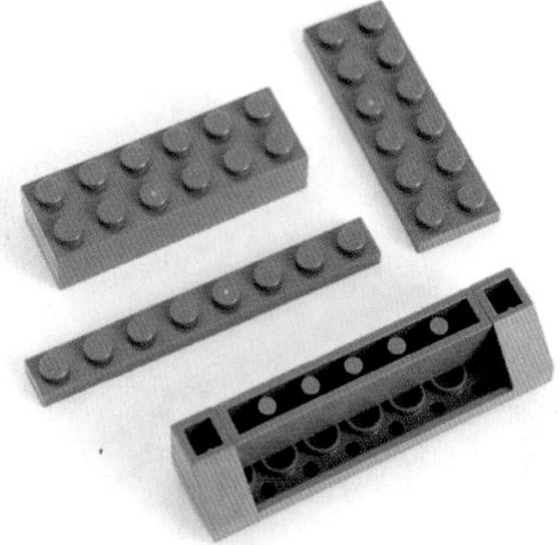

STEP 6: Attach a 1 x 6 brick and two 1 x 2 inverted slopes to the underside of a 2 x 8 plate.

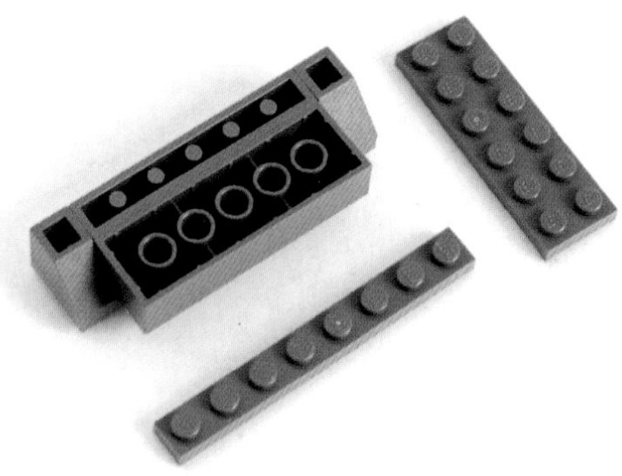

STEP 7: Then add a 2 x 6 brick.

STEP 8: Turn the bricks over and add a 1 x 8 plate and 2 x 6 plate as shown.

STEP 9: Attach this section to the body of the ATV. The inverted slope bricks will connect to the end of the 8 x 8 plate.

STEP 10: Gather the bricks shown for building the front hood and headlight area.

STEP 11: Use three 2 x 2 dark gray slopes to connect a 1 x 6 dark gray brick and a 1 x 4 light gray brick with four studs on the side.

STEP 12: Place a 1 x 1 brick with a stud on the side on each end of the light gray brick. Then attach a 1 x 2 dark gray brick and two 1 x 2 dark gray inverted slopes.

STEP 13: Attach this to the front end of the ATV. Then find a 2 x 4 dark gray plate, a 1 x 2 dark gray grill, two 1 x 1 translucent orange round plates and two 1 x 1 translucent yellow round plates.

STEP 14: Place the grill and the translucent round plates on the front of the vehicle.

STEP 15: Find two dark gray 6 x 2 double inverted slopes with a 2 x 4 cutout. Place two 2 x 4 dark gray plates inside each cutout area.

STEP 16: Turn the ATV upside down. Attach one of the 6 x 2 double inverted slopes on each side. Then find the bricks shown.

STEP 17: Place a 4 x 8 dark gray plate on the bottom of the ATV. Then add a 2 x 4 plate with two pins on each end of the 4 x 8 plate. These will hold the wheels.

STEP 18: Turn the vehicle back over. Add two 1 x 2 dark gray inverted slopes and a 1 x 4 dark gray plate on the back end of the vehicle.

STEP 19: Add a 1 x 1 dark gray plate and a 2 x 3 dark gray plate on each side of the back of the vehicle.

STEP 20: Place a 1 x 4 dark gray plate on each side and a 1 x 8 dark gray plate across the back.

STEP 21: Place a 1 x 6 dark gray tile on each side of the passenger area. Then build the dashboard. Stack two 1 x 6 light gray plates at the front of the cab. Add a steering wheel, a 1 x 2 dark gray slope with gauges printed on it and a 1 x 2 light gray tile.

STEP 22: Add a 2 x 6 windshield and four chairs for the passengers to ride in. Then build a gear shift by attaching a light gray antenna to a 1 x 1 light gray round plate.

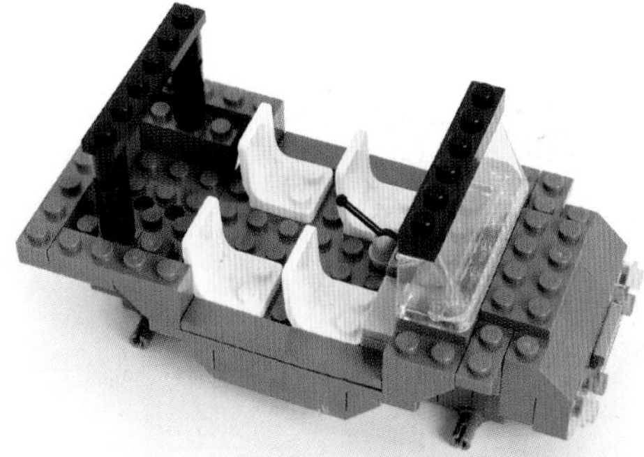

STEP 23: Place two 1 x 6 black plates on top of the windshield. On the back end, stack three 1 x 1 black round bricks and place one of these stacks on each side of the vehicle. Place a 1 x 6 black plate across them.

STEP 24: Add a 1 x 10 black plate on each side so that they connect the windshield to the bar at the back. Then place three 1 x 6 black plates across them.

STEP 25: Attach four wheels, and your adventure ATV is complete!

Now it's time to head out on a trip! Build soda cans by placing 1 x 1 light gray round tiles on top of 1 x 1 round bricks in different colors. Load up the ATV with drinks, snacks, cameras and other gear!

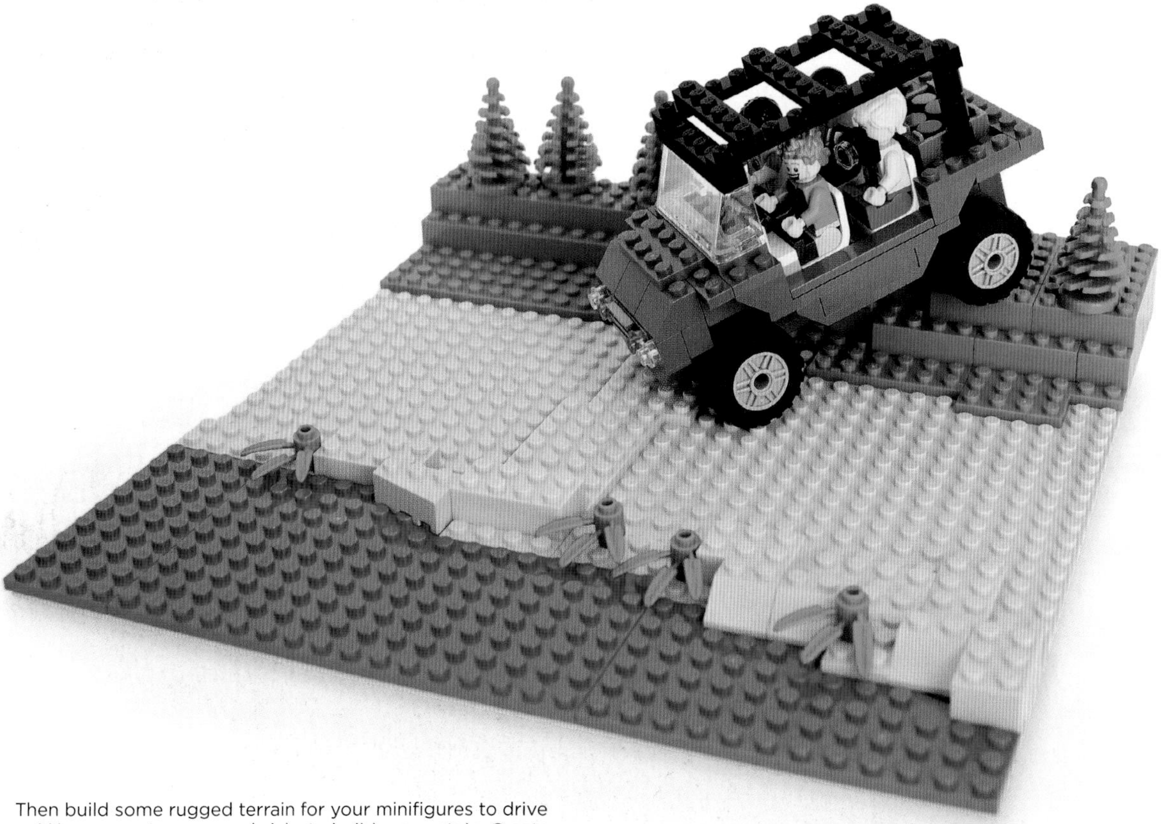

Then build some rugged terrain for your minifigures to drive on! Use green, tan or gray bricks to build a mountain. Create water areas out of blue plates and add plants along the edge of the water.

TINY CAR

STEP-BY-STEP

This petite sedan just might be the cutest car made out of bricks! Choose your favorite color of bricks for building this tiny car or make it a combination of colors. Because this car is small and easy to build, it's fun to assemble more than one of them and set up a car dealership. Your minifigures will have a great time shopping for a new car!

PARTS LIST

MAIN COLOR BRICKS (blue is pictured, but use whatever color you like)

3—2 x 4 plates
4—1 x 4 plates
1—2 x 3 plate
1—2 x 2 plate
5—1 x 2 plates
2—1 x 1 plates
2—2 x 2 corner plates
1—1 x 4 brick
2—1 x 3 bricks
2—1 x 2 bricks
2—1 x 1 bricks with a stud on the side
4—1 x 1 slopes, 30 degree
1—2 x 2 tile
2—1 x 2 tiles
2—1 x 2—2 x 2 brackets
2—car doors, one right and one left
2—2 x 4 vehicle mudguards with arch, studded with hole
2—1 x 1 plates with a light attachment
1—4 x 4 x ⅔ wedge, triple curved

ASSORTED BRICKS

1—2 x 6 white plate
2—2 x 2 black plates with a wheel holder
1—1 x 2 black grill
1—1 x 2—2 x 2 light gray bracket, inverted
1—1 x 2 white tile
1—steering wheel
2—2 x 4 x 2 windshields
1—1 x 2 translucent red plate
2—1 x 1 translucent red round plates
2—1 x 1 translucent orange round plates
2—1 x 1 clear round plates
4—small wheels

STEP 1: Find a 2 x 4 vehicle mudguard with arch, two 2 x 2 corner plates and two 1 x 1 plates.

STEP 2: Attach the corner plates to the mudguard. Then add a 1 x 1 plate to each corner plate.

STEP 3: Add a 1 x 2—2 x 2 light gray inverted bracket, and then place a 1 x 2 brick on top of the bracket.

STEP 4: Place a 1 x 1 brick with a stud on the side on each side of the bracket. Then add two 1 x 1 translucent orange round plates for headlights and add a 1 x 2 black grill.

STEP 5: Turn the car around and add one 1 x 2 plate on each side. Place two 1 x 2 plates in the center.

STEP 6: Attach a 1 x 4 plate just behind the headlights. Then add a 1 x 2 brick. Find two 1 x 1 clear round plates, two 1 x 1 slopes (30 degree) and two 1 x 1 plates with a light attachment.

STEP 7: Build rearview mirrors by adding a 1 x 1 plate with a light attachment to each side of the car. Place a 1 x 1 slope and a 1 x 1 clear round plate on each light attachment. Then find the plate and tiles shown.

STEP 8: Complete the front end of the car by adding a 1 x 4 plate in between the headlights and two 1 x 2 tiles and one 2 x 2 tile on the hood.

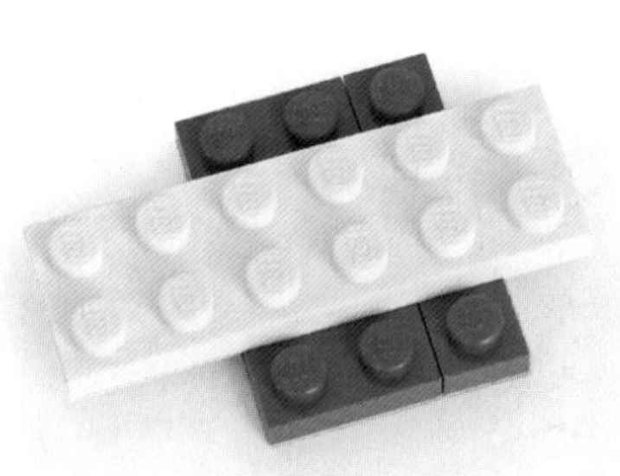

STEP 9: Start building the body of the car. Use a 2 x 6 white plate to connect a 2 x 4 plate and a 1 x 4 plate as shown.

STEP 10: Attach the front of the car to the end of the white plate.

STEP 11: Place a 1 x 3 brick on each side of the car. Then add a 2 x 3 plate in the middle. Place a 1 x 2 plate on top of the 2 x 3 plate.

STEP 12: Add a steering wheel to the car. Then attach a 2 x 4 mudguard to the back end of the white plate.

STEP 13: Fill in the recessed area in the mudguard with a 2 x 2 plate. Then add a 1 x 4 brick over the mudguard and place doors on both sides of the car.

STEP 14: Find a 1 x 4 plate, two 2 x 4 plates and two 1 x 2—2 x 2 brackets.

STEP 15: Place the 1 x 4 plate across the back of the car. Then add the brackets.

STEP 16: Attach one 2 x 4 plate to the face of the brackets and the other 2 x 4 plate on the top of them. Then find the bricks shown.

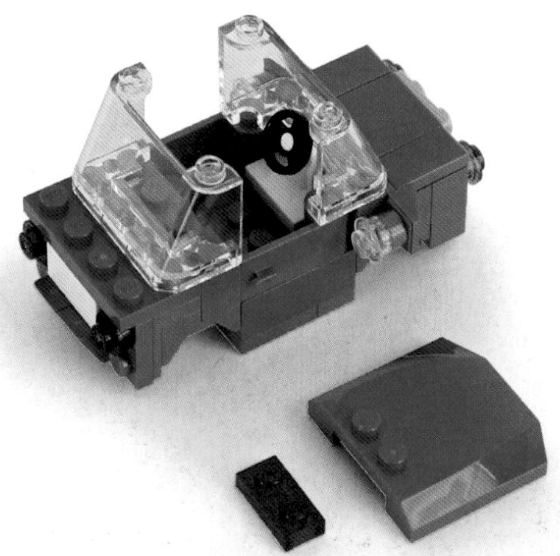

STEP 17: Add the taillights and license plate to the back of the car. Place two 1 x 1 slopes (30 degree) just below the license plate. Then add the windshields. Find a 1 x 2 translucent red plate and a 4 x 4 x ⅔ wedge (triple curved).

STEP 18: Attach the 1 x 2 translucent red plate to the underside of the wedge, and then attach it to the windshields. Find four small wheels. Attach them to two 2 x 2 plates with a wheel holder.

STEP 19: Add the wheels, and your cute little car is complete!

Hi, folks! What kind of car are we looking for today?

If you have enough bricks, try making another tiny car or two in other colors. It's fun to set up a car dealership and pretend your minifigures are shopping for a car! Mr. and Mrs. Thompson are looking for a vehicle to replace the old car that Mr. Thompson drives to work. He's ready for something new!

Now, once you sit down in these luxury leather seats, you'll never want to get back up!

The salesman will of course want to show off all the features of the car before letting the customers go on a test drive.

Looks like Mr. Thompson is loving the sporty look of the red car!

Mr. and Mrs. Thompson head inside the dealership to complete all the paperwork. Soon they're driving away with their brand-new car!

AMAZING IDEA

Try constructing a larger building for your car dealership! Add an office for the manager and a coffee station for customers. It would also be fun to create a service department for repairs and changing tires and oil. Add platforms for elevating the cars, workbenches with tools and a stash of extra tires.

SPORTS COUPE

STEP-BY-STEP

This open-top sports coupe is perfect for zooming around town on a sunny day! The car is shown in dark gray, but it would look great in any color. Build your sports car with a sleek, aerodynamic design. Once your car is complete, you'll want to build places around town to drive to. Try building a store, an ice cream shop or a coffee shop with a drive-through.

PARTS LIST

DARK GRAY BRICKS

7—2 x 6 plates
1—4 x 4 plate
3—2 x 4 plates
3—1 x 6 plates
8—1 x 4 plates
2—2 x 3 plates
3—1 x 2 plates
1—1 x 6 brick
1—2 x 4 brick
1—1 x 4 brick
2—1 x 4 curved slopes, double
2—1 x 4 x 1 panels
2—1 x 1 x 1 corner panels
2—1 x 1 tiles
2—1 x 1 slopes, 30 degree
2—2 x 1 slopes, 45 degree with cutout without stud
4—2 x 2 plates with a pin hole
1—1 x 2 slope, 30 degree with printed gauges
4—4 x 2½ x 2⅓ vehicle mudguards with arch, solid studs and rounded legs

BLACK BRICKS

1—4 x 10 vehicle base with a 2 x 4 cutout
1—2 x 4 plate
1—1 x 4 brick with four studs on the side
2—1 x 2 black plates with door rail
1—1 x 2—2 x 2 black bracket, inverted
1—1 x 2 plate
1—1 x 2 slope, 30 degree
2—1 x 2 slopes with four slots

ASSORTED BRICKS

1—1 x 4 light gray plate
1—1 x 2 light gray brick
2—1 x 4 tan plates
1—1 x 2 tan plate
1—1 x 4 tan curved slope, double
4—tan Technic axle pins
1—1 x 2 white tile
1—steering wheel
2—1 x 1 translucent red tiles
2—1 x 1 translucent red round tiles
2—1 x 1 translucent yellow round tiles
1—3 x 4 translucent black windshield
4—wheels with axle hole

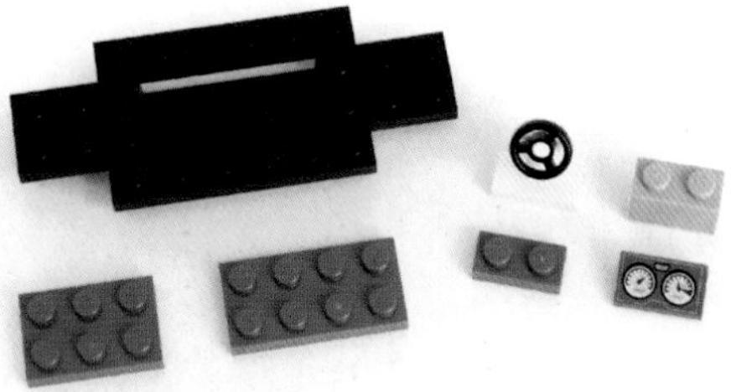

STEP 1: Gather the bricks shown for building the base of your sports coupe.

STEP 2: Attach a 2 x 4 dark gray plate under the vehicle base in the front and a 2 x 3 dark gray plate under the vehicle base in the back. Connect a steering wheel to a 1 x 2 dark gray plate. Build the dashboard by attaching a 1 x 2 dark gray slope with printed gauges to a 1 x 2 light gray brick.

STEP 3: Place the steering wheel and dashboard inside the vehicle base.

STEP 4: Find two dark gray vehicle mudguards, a 1 x 6 dark gray plate, a 1 x 4 black brick with four studs on the side and a 1 x 4 light gray plate.

STEP 5: Attach a 1 x 4 light gray plate to the underside of a 1 x 6 dark gray plate. Use the black brick to connect the mudguards on the front and the gray plates to connect the mudguards on the back.

STEP 6: Add a 2 x 4 black plate in the center of the front-end assembly. Then find a 2 x 6 dark gray plate and a 2 x 4 dark gray plate.

STEP 7: Turn the front-end assembly around. Add a 2 x 4 dark gray plate in the front and a 2 x 6 dark gray plate just behind that. Then find two 1 x 1 dark gray tiles and two 1 x 1 dark gray slopes (30 degree).

STEP 8: Place one 1 x 1 tile and one 1 x 1 slope (30 degree) on the mudguards on each side.

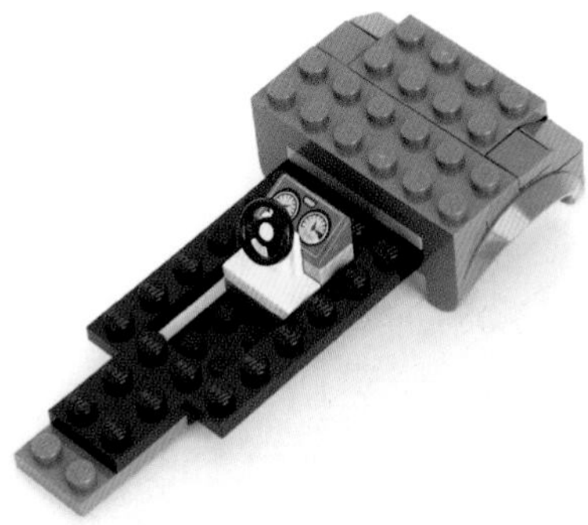

STEP 9: Attach the front-end assembly to the vehicle base.

STEP 10: Find two 2 x 6 dark gray plates, a 1 x 6 dark gray plate, a 1 x 4 x 1 dark gray panel and a 1 x 1 x 1 dark gray corner panel.

STEP 11: Stack the two 2 x 6 dark gray plates. Then add a 1 x 6 dark gray plate.

STEP 12: Add a 1 x 4 x 1 dark gray panel and a 1 x 1 x 1 corner panel on top of the 1 x 6 plate.

STEP 13: Build a second one of these panel sections, making sure that it is a mirror image of the first one as shown.

STEP 14: Attach the panel sections to the underside of the vehicle base on each side.

STEP 15: Add a 1 x 6 dark gray brick in front of the dashboard.

STEP 16: Find two more dark gray mudguards, a 4 x 4 dark gray plate, a 2 x 3 dark gray plate and two 1 x 4 dark gray plates.

STEP 17: Use two 1 x 4 dark gray plates to connect the mudguards. Then attach a 2 x 3 plate to the underside of a 4 x 4 plate.

STEP 18: Once you have the 4 x 4 plate with the 2 x 3 plate under it, place this piece on top of the car's back end. Then find a 2 x 4 dark gray brick, a 2 x 4 dark gray plate and two 1 x 4 dark gray double curved slopes.

STEP 19: Add the 2 x 4 brick, 2 x 4 plate and 1 x 4 double curved slopes to the vehicle as shown. Then find a 1 x 4 dark gray brick, a 1 x 4 dark gray plate and two 2 x 1 dark gray slopes (45 degree with a cutout).

STEP 20: Place the 1 x 4 brick on the vehicle and add the 1 x 4 plate in front of it.

STEP 21: Add the two 2 x 1 slopes (45 degree with a cutout) to the back of the vehicle.

STEP 22: Add a 1 x 2—2 x 2 black inverted bracket to the back of the vehicle. It attaches to the underside of this section.

STEP 23: Attach the rear section of the vehicle to the vehicle base. Add a 3 x 4 windshield, which adds stability as well as style to the front of the car.

STEP 24: Turn the vehicle over to expose the underside and find five 1 x 4 dark gray plates. Substitute with other colors if you need to.

STEP 25: Add the 1 x 4 plates to the underside of the car. These provide extra stability to hold the car together. There are two 1 x 4 plates at the very front of the car in this photo.

STEP 26: Add the wheels. Each wheel attaches to an axle pin and a 2 x 2 plate with a pin hole. Substitute with different wheels if you need to.

STEP 27: Build the front grill and headlight area. Grab a 2 x 6 dark gray plate and add a 1 x 2 white tile, two 1 x 1 translucent yellow round tiles and two 1 x 2 black slopes with four slots.

STEP 28: Attach the headlights and grill to the brick with four studs on the side at the front of the car.

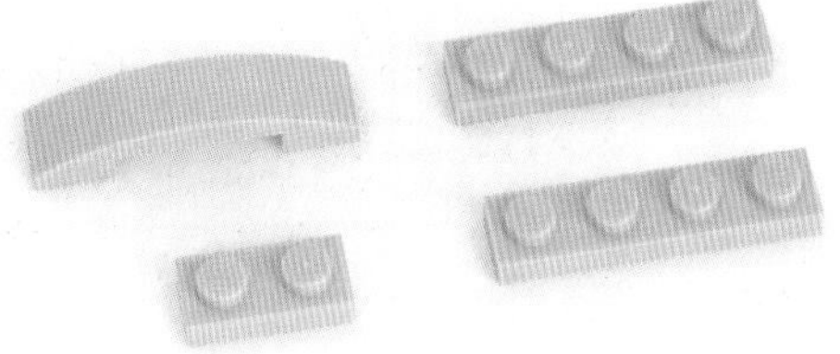

STEP 29: Find a 1 x 4 tan double curved slope, two 1 x 4 tan plates and a 1 x 2 tan plate for building the back of the driver's seat.

STEP 30: Stack the two 1 x 4 plates. Then add the 1 x 2 plate and put the 1 x 4 double curved slope on top.

STEP 31: Attach the tan bricks to the car just behind the driver's seat.

STEP 32: Build the back taillights and bumper. Find a 2 x 6 dark gray plate and add two 1 x 2 dark gray plates, two 1 x 1 translucent red round tiles and two 1 x 2 black plates with door rail.

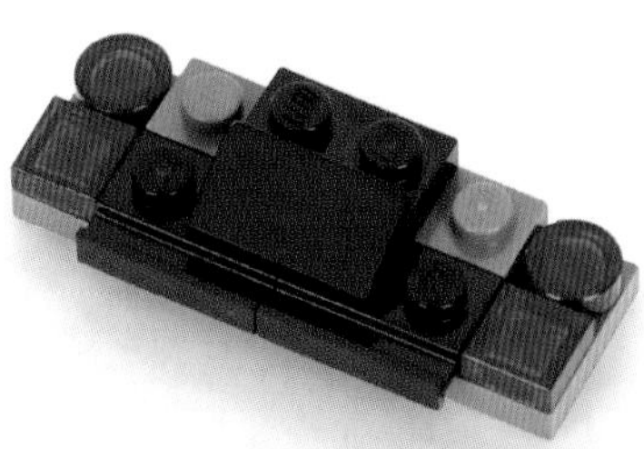

STEP 33: Finish up the back taillights by adding two 1 x 1 translucent red tiles, a 1 x 2 black slope (30 degree) and a 1 x 2 black plate. You can easily substitute pieces to create a different design for this area if you want.

STEP 34: Attach the rear bumper and taillights, and your sports coupe is complete!

Now it's time to go for a drive! Build some places to go, like the Trampoline Park on page 74 or the Workout Gym on page 87. You might also want to try building your favorite store or restaurant.

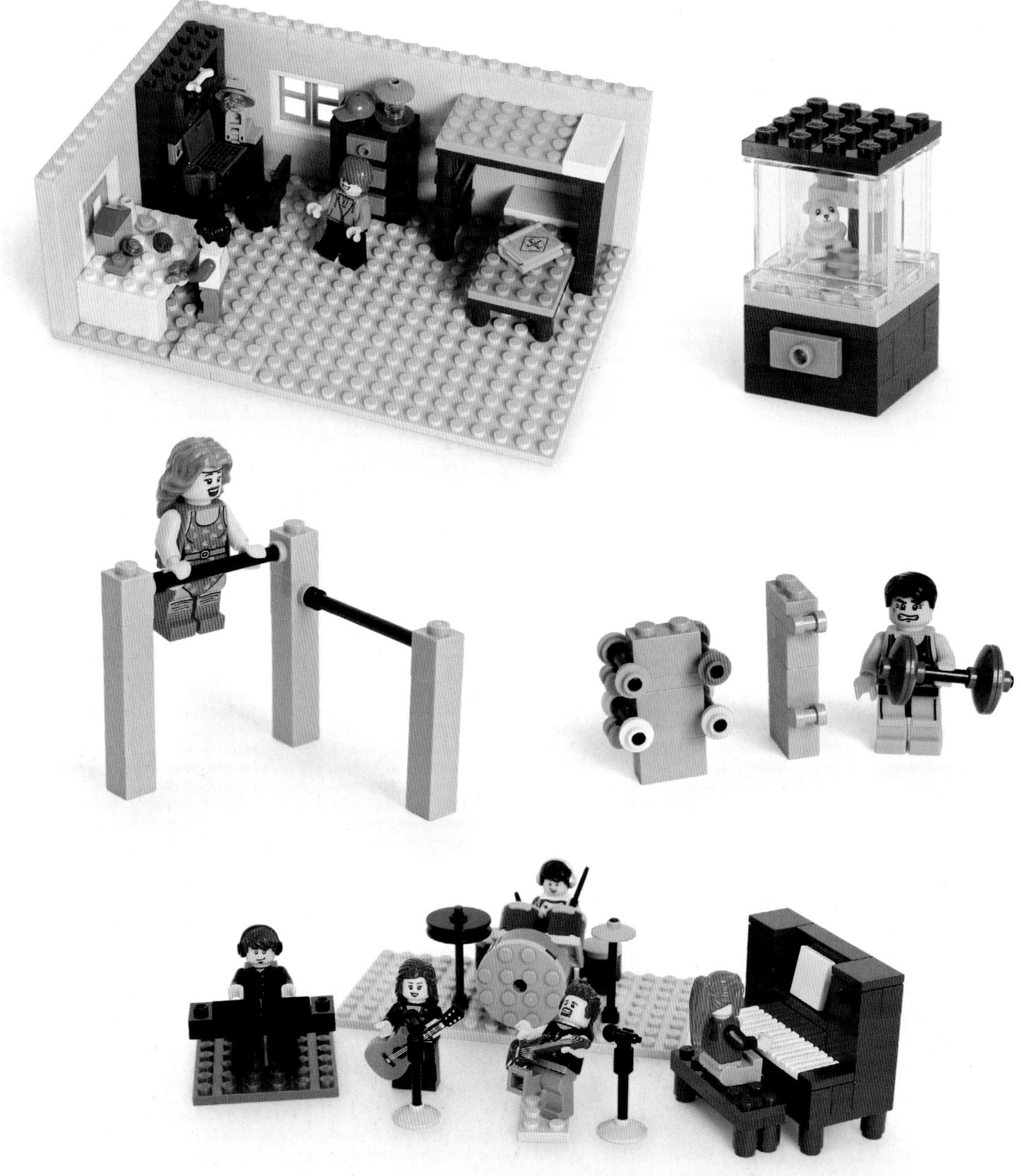

LIVING IN LEGO TOWN

Create your own LEGO town! It's fun to build environments from everyday life and then set up imaginative scenes, and these creative LEGO town ideas will get you started. Learn how to make an awesome trampoline park with jumping areas, a rock-climbing wall and arcade-style video games. Build a school classroom with desks and a chalkboard, and then design a bedroom that looks like yours. You can even build instruments for a garage band! Then see what else you can think of to build. Maybe you'll create an amazing playground modeled after your favorite park, build the karate studio you go to or design a zoo or museum that your minifigures can enjoy. LEGO town projects are the perfect way to spend a day!

TRAMPOLINE PARK

CREATIVE CHALLENGE

There's something for everyone to enjoy at the trampoline park! While some are jumping, others are testing their climbing skills on the rock-climbing wall. Build some cool arcade games and even an area for parents and grandparents to sit and visit while they're watching the kids have fun. Add fun accessories like drinks, pretzels and pizza.

KEY ELEMENTS

1—32 x 32 tan baseplate OR four 16 x 16 tan plates

TRAMPOLINES

3—6 x 8 black plates

3—6 x 8 white plates (or any color)

2—2 x 4 light gray plates

Various light gray bricks

5—1 x 2 light gray bricks (optional for basketball hoop)

1—1 x 2 light gray Technic brick with an axle hole (optional for basketball hoop)

1—basketball hoop (optional)

1—ball (optional)

2—1 x 2 x 2 clear panels (optional)

CLIMBING WALL

Various light gray bricks

About 8—1 x 1 light gray bricks with a stud on the side

About 5—1 x 1 light gray bricks with a bar handle

About 8—1 x 1 round plates in any colors

PICNIC TABLE

2—2 x 8 brown plates

2—1 x 2 brown plates

1—4 x 8 brown plate

2—1 x 2 brown bricks

2—1 x 8 brown bricks

Food items—pizza, pretzels, cups, etc.

BENCH

2—2 x 6 brown plates

2—1 x 2 brown bricks

2—1 x 2 brown plates with a handle on the end

2—1 x 2 light gray plates with a clip on the end

BLUE/GRAY GAME

1—2 x 4 blue brick

1—1 x 4 blue brick

2—2 x 2 blue slopes, inverted

2—1 x 2 x 2 light gray slopes

1—1 x 4 light gray plate with two studs

1—1 x 1 light gray tile

1—1 x 1 light gray tile, printed with a dial

1—2 x 2 black tile

1—1 x 1 orange round plate

1—1 x 1 lime green round plate

1—1 x 2 hinge brick with a 2 x 2 hinge plate

1—1 x 2 dark gray grill

YELLOW GAME

2—2 x 6 yellow bricks

2—1 x 6 yellow bricks

1—2 x 4 yellow brick

5—1 x 4 yellow bricks

4—1 x 3 yellow bricks

1—4 x 6 yellow plate

2—2 x 4 yellow plates

2—1 x 2 light gray hinge bricks with a 2 x 2 hinge plate

2—2 x 3 black plates

1—1 x 4 black tile

1—2 x 4 black tile

1—2 x 2 steering wheel

1—light gray antenna

1—1 x 1 red round plate

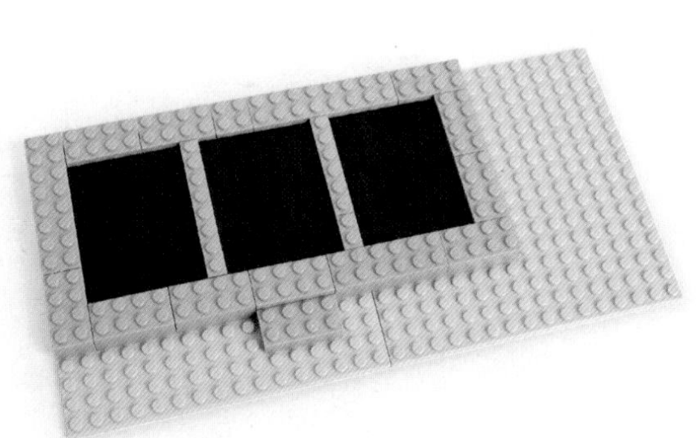

Build some trampolines! A 6 x 8 black plate is the perfect size for a trampoline. Build one or build a row with two or three. Each trampoline has a 6 x 8 plate (can be any color) under the black plate and light gray bricks around it. Use two 2 x 4 light gray plates to build a step up to the trampoline area.

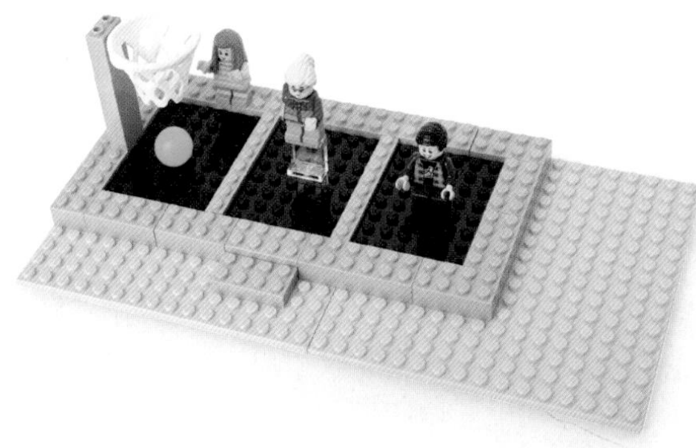

Add a basketball hoop to one of the trampolines if you have one! Build a post to mount the hoop by stacking five 1 x 2 light gray bricks. Then place a 1 x 2 light gray Technic brick with an axle hole on top. Insert the basketball hoop into the Technic brick. You can make your minifigures look like they are jumping by placing them on top of 1 x 2 x 2 clear panels!

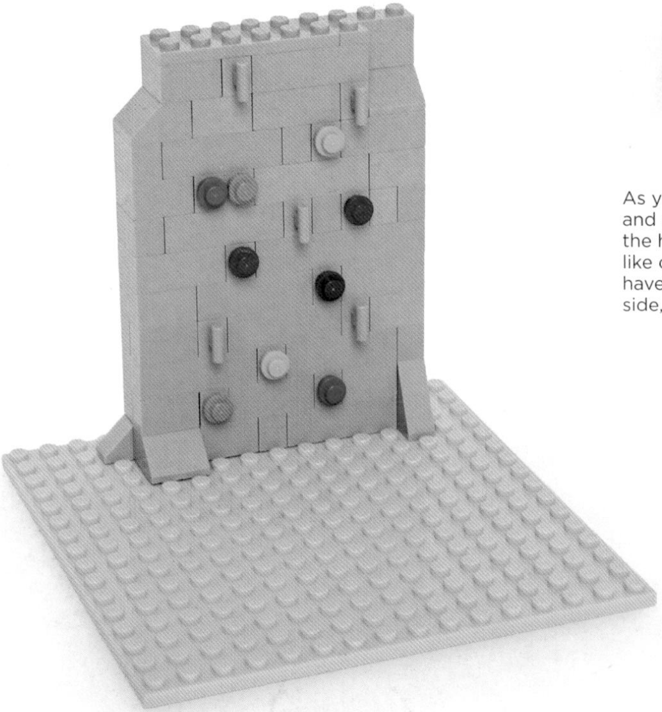

As you build, add in some 1 x 1 bricks with studs on the side and some 1 x 1 bricks with handles. Minifigures can hold on to the handles. You can add 1 x 1 round plates in any color to look like climbing grips. Or modify the design with the bricks you have! Use brackets in place of the bricks with a stud on the side, if needed.

Construct a rock-climbing wall! Use light gray bricks to build the wall. You may want to add a few slope bricks to make uneven rock edges.

Add a minifigure to help the climbers get started, and then build a bench for people who want to watch the climbers.

It's easy to build a bench with two 2 x 6 brown plates. Use two 1 x 2 light gray plates with a clip on the end and two 1 x 2 brown plates with a handle on the end to connect the two 2 x 6 plates. Then add two 1 x 2 brown bricks for legs.

Create some classic video games and set up a mini arcade at your trampoline park.

Let's start with the blue and gray arcade game. Grab a 1 x 4 blue brick, a 2 x 4 blue brick and two 2 x 2 blue inverted slopes.

Place the two inverted slope bricks and the 1 x 4 brick on top of the 2 x 4 brick. Then find a 2 x 2 black tile, a 1 x 2 dark gray grill and a 1 x 2 hinge brick with a 2 x 2 hinge plate.

Add the hinge brick and attach the 2 x 2 black tile to make the screen. Then add the 1 x 2 dark gray grill as shown.

Place two 1 x 2 x 2 light gray slopes on the video game, one on each side. Add a 1 x 4 light gray plate with two studs.

Finish up the game by adding 1 x 1 tiles and plates to look like buttons on the game.

Repeat the instructions again to build a second game in another color. This black one has a 1 x 4 black double curved slope and a 1 x 2 black plate on the top.

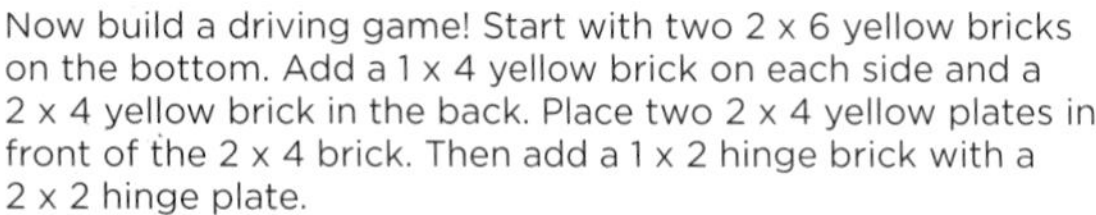

Now build a driving game! Start with two 2 x 6 yellow bricks on the bottom. Add a 1 x 4 yellow brick on each side and a 2 x 4 yellow brick in the back. Place two 2 x 4 yellow plates in front of the 2 x 4 brick. Then add a 1 x 2 hinge brick with a 2 x 2 hinge plate.

Build a screen by attaching a 2 x 4 black tile and a 1 x 4 black tile to two 2 x 3 black plates. Add another 1 x 2 hinge brick and attach the 2 x 2 hinge plate so that it tilts downward.

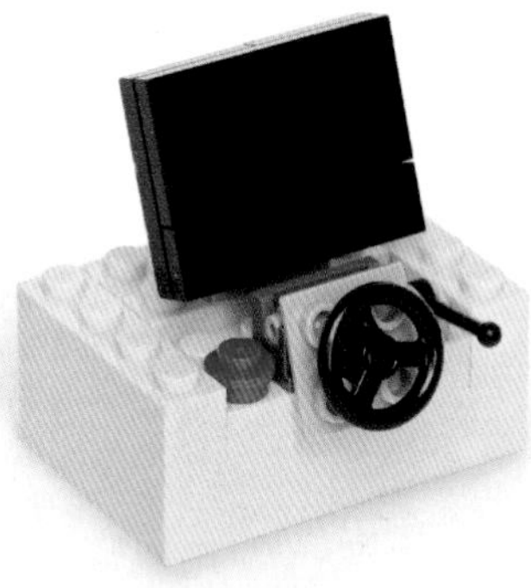

Add a steering wheel, a light gray antenna and a 1 x 1 red round plate.

Finish up the driving game by adding three more rows of yellow bricks and placing a 4 x 6 yellow plate on top.

Set up the arcade area in your trampoline park with a table for people to eat snacks.

To build the table, start with two 1 x 8 brown bricks. Place a 1 x 2 brown brick on top of the center of each one. Then find two 2 x 8 brown plates and two 1 x 2 brown plates.

Place a 1 x 2 brown plate on top of each 1 x 2 brick. Then add the two 2 x 8 plates to make the benches.

Finish up the table by adding a 4 x 8 brown plate. Then find food items like pizza, a pretzel and drinks. If you don't have these food items, substitute with what you have. You could even try designing a concession stand at the trampoline park for minifigures to buy snacks and drinks.

AMAZING IDEA

Try building an obstacle course to go with your trampoline area. You can create climbing features, ramps, monkey bars and more.

Now it's time for some fun! Create a scene with your minifigures having a blast playing at the trampoline park. You might also want to try setting up a birthday party. Build a little cake and gifts for the kids to bring to the party.

SCHOOL CLASSROOM

CREATIVE CHALLENGE

Build a classroom complete with a chalkboard, bookshelf, teacher's desk and even a cute hamster cage! Create desks for each kid in the class. You can customize this project to look like your own classroom at school. Does your classroom have a reading nook or a fish tank? Then design and build those things! The parts list for this project includes the colors shown in the pictures, but you can truly use whatever colors you have for the desks, chairs and other parts of this classroom. Be creative!

KEY ELEMENTS

2—16 x 16 tan plates
Various light gray bricks, 1 stud wide
3—1 x 4 x 3 windows
1—1 x 4 x 6 door

CHALKBOARD

1—6 x 10 light gray plate
1—4 x 10 black plate
1—1 x 10 black plate
1—1 x 2 x 1 white panel
2—1 x 4 x 1 white panels

DESKS (EACH DESK HAS)

1—2 x 4 tan tile
1—2 x 4 light gray plate
2—1 x 2 light gray bricks
2—1 x 2 light gray plates
1—yellow chair
1—2 x 2 yellow plate

BOOKSHELF

2—2 x 6 brown plates
4—1 x 2 brown bricks
2—1 x 4 brown tiles
5—1 x 1 brown round plates
2 x 2 plates in various colors for books
2 x 2 tiles in various colors for books
1—2 x 2 blue round brick
3—1 x 1 green round plates with three leaves
1—1 x 1 pink flower

TEACHER'S DESK

1—4 x 6 brown plate
2—1 x 4 brown plates
2—1 x 3 brown bricks
1—1 x 6 brown brick
1—brown chair
1—2 x 2 white turntable
1—1 x 2 tile, printed with a keyboard
1—2 x 2 black tile
1—1 x 2 hinge brick with a 2 x 2 hinge plate

HAMSTER CAGE

8—2 x 4 brown plates
1—2 x 4 brown brick
1—1 x 4 brown brick
2—1 x 1 brown bricks
2—1 x 1 brown bricks with a stud on the side
1—1 x 2 dark tan plate with one stud on top (jumper plate)
2—1 x 4 x 3 clear panels
2—1 x 2 x 3 clear panels
1—4 x 4 light gray plate
1—2 x 2 tan plate
1—1 x 1 tan round plate
1—1 x 1 magenta round brick
1—1 x 2 yellow plate
1—1 x 2 lime green round brick
1—1 x 1 green flower
1—hamster

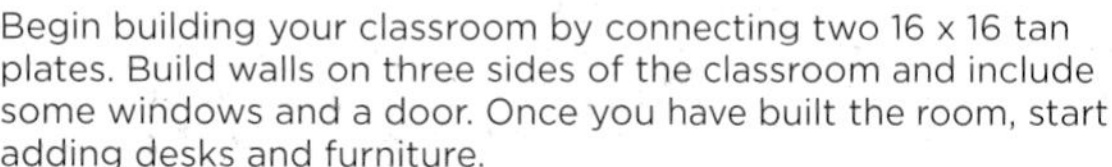

Begin building your classroom by connecting two 16 x 16 tan plates. Build walls on three sides of the classroom and include some windows and a door. Once you have built the room, start adding desks and furniture.

Each desk is built with a 2 x 4 tan tile and a 2 x 4 light gray plate. Make each leg with a 1 x 2 light gray brick and a 1 x 2 light gray plate. Make the chair the perfect height for the desk by attaching a 2 x 2 plate under it.

BUILDING TIP

It's easy to modify the desk to accommodate a wheelchair by swapping the 1 x 2 plate for a 1 x 2 brick!

Build a desk for the teacher. The top of this desk is a 4 x 6 brown plate. Build a computer by attaching a 2 x 2 black tile to a hinge brick. Then add a keyboard and an apple for the teacher! Grab a chair and place a 2 x 2 plate under it to make it the right height.

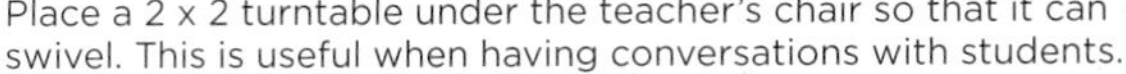

Place a 2 x 2 turntable under the teacher's chair so that it can swivel. This is useful when having conversations with students.

Build a bookshelf for the classroom. Start with a 2 x 6 brown plate for the bottom, and place a 1 x 1 brown round plate under each corner. Add two 1 x 2 brown bricks on each side and another 2 x 6 plate on top. Two 1 x 4 brown tiles on the bottom of the shelf will make the books slide more easily. Each book is made from a 2 x 2 plate and a 2 x 2 tile of the same color.

Give the class a special pet! Build a hamster cage. Make a base out of brown bricks and plates. Use two 1 x 1 brown bricks with a stud on the side to hold a 1 x 2 dark tan plate with one stud on top. Place a 4 x 4 light gray plate on top of the base. Then build a play structure for the hamster.

Use clear panels to build the sides of the hamster cage. Pictured are two 1 x 4 x 3 clear panels and two 1 x 2 x 3 clear panels.

Complete the cage by placing two 2 x 4 brown plates (or a 4 x 4 plate) on the top. If you don't have a hamster, make the cage for a little LEGO bunny or turtle! Another option is to build an aquarium plant instead of the climbing structure and add a fish.

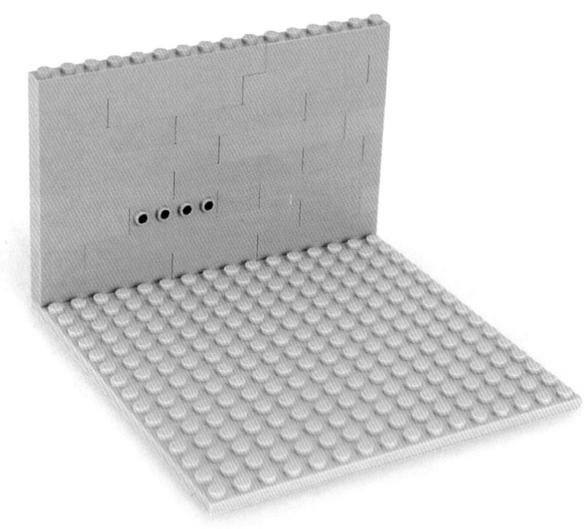

The chalkboard is attached to a 1 x 4 brick with four studs on the side that is built into the classroom wall.

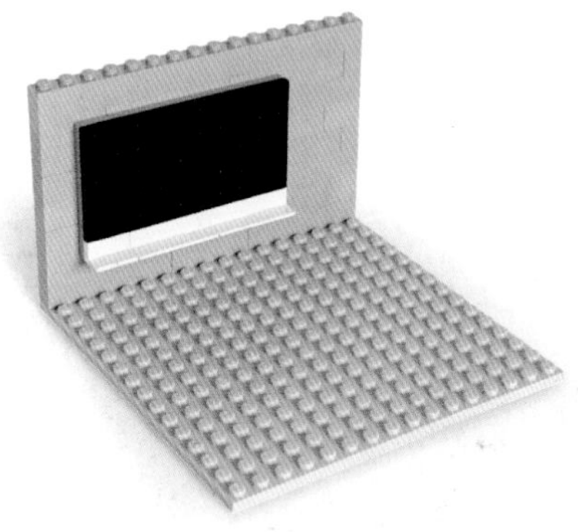

Build the chalkboard out of a 6 x 10 light gray plate. Cover the plate with a 4 x 10 black plate and a 1 x 10 black plate. Then add a chalk rail by adding two 1 x 4 x 1 white panels and a 1 x 2 x 1 white panel across the bottom. Attach the chalkboard to the wall.

AMAZING IDEA

Add on to your school! It would be fun to create a gym with basketball hoops. Or, use a green 16 x 16 plate to create an outdoor playground area to go with your classroom. Build a climbing structure with a slide, and then add a picnic table or bench.

ROCKIN' GARAGE BAND

STEP-BY-STEP

It's Saturday night, and the best garage band in town is taking the stage for a concert at the city park! Build an awesome band setup with a piano, keyboard, drum set and singers. Grab some minifigure guitars if you have them and set up your band for an evening of rockin' good music!

PARTS LIST

DRUMS

1—8 x 16 tan plate
1—2 x 4 tan plate
4—2 x 2 light gray round tiles
1—1 x 2—1 x 2 light gray bracket
1—4 x 4 light gray round plate
1—1 x 1 light gray tile with a clip
1—2 x 2 light gray dish
1—1 x 2 dark gray brick
1—1 x 2 dark gray hinge brick with a 2 x 2 hinge plate
1—4 x 4 dark gray round brick
1—1 x 2 dark gray plate with a handle on the end
1—1 x 2 dark gray plate with one stud on top (jumper plate)
1—1 x 2 brown plate
4—2 x 2 brown round bricks
4—1 x 1 brown round plates
1—1 x 4 brown antenna
1—2 x 2 black round brick
1—1 x 4 black antenna
2—3 x 3 black Technic disks

KEYBOARD

1—6 x 6 dark gray plate
2—1 x 1 black plates
2—1 x 1 black round plates
2—1 x 1 black cones
1—2 x 6 black plate
1—1 x 4 black plate
2—1 x 2 black plates with one stud on top (jumper plate)
2—1 x 2 black slopes, 30 degree
1—1 x 4 white tile

PIANO

Various brown bricks and plates (can also use black)
6—1 x 2 white grills for the keys
1—2 x 2 white tile for sheet music

MICROPHONE

1—2 x 2 tan dish
1—black bar, 3 studs long
1—black bar holder with clip
1—minifigure microphone OR light gray lightsaber hilt
1—1 x 1 black round plate

DRUMS

STEP 1: Build a drum set! Grab an 8 x 16 tan plate as a base for the drum set. Place a 1 x 2 brown plate on the base as shown. Then find a 1 x 2 dark gray brick, a 1 x 2—1 x 2 light gray bracket, a 1 x 2 dark gray hinge brick with a 2 x 2 hinge plate, two 2 x 2 light gray round tiles, two 2 x 2 brown round bricks and a 2 x 4 tan plate.

STEP 2: Attach both brown round bricks and light gray round tiles to the 2 x 4 tan plate to make the small drums, called toms. Then place the 1 x 2 dark gray brick and the 1 x 2—1 x 2 light gray bracket on top of the brown plate.

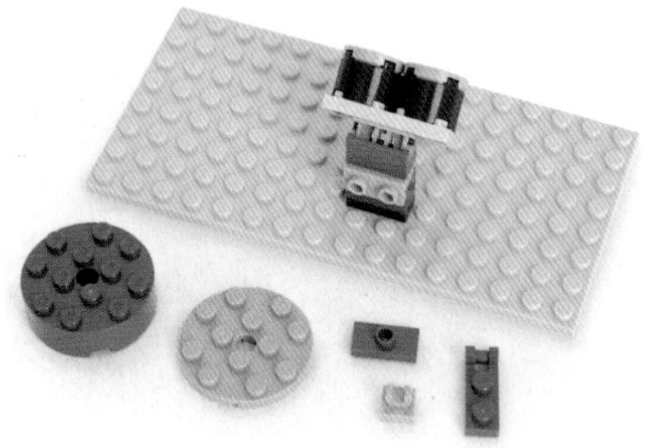

STEP 3: Place a 1 x 2 hinge brick on top of the bracket. Use the plate on the hinge brick to hold the toms. Then find the bricks shown for building the base drum.

STEP 4: Attach a 1 x 2 dark gray plate with a handle on the end to a 1 x 1 light gray tile with a clip. This will be the pedal for the bass drum. Attach it to the base as shown. Then attach a 1 x 2 dark gray plate with one stud on top (jumper plate) to the light gray bracket. Build the base drum by putting a 4 x 4 light gray round plate on top of a 4 x 4 dark gray round brick.

STEP 5: Connect the bass drum to the jumper plate.

STEP 6: Turn the drum set around. Add a 2 x 2 black round brick for the drummer's throne. Then place two 1 x 1 brown round plates on each side as shown. Build two more drums with 2 x 2 brown round bricks and 2 x 2 light gray round tiles.

STEP 7: Place the final two drums on top of the brown round plates. Then build cymbals with 1 x 4 antennas, a 2 x 2 light gray dish and two 3 x 3 black disks. Your drum set is complete!

Now you just need a drummer and some drumsticks! Magic wands work very well for drumsticks. Another good option is to use light gray flick missiles.

KEYBOARD

STEP 1: Now build a keyboard! Start by placing two 1 x 1 black round plates in between the studs on a 6 x 6 dark gray plate as shown.

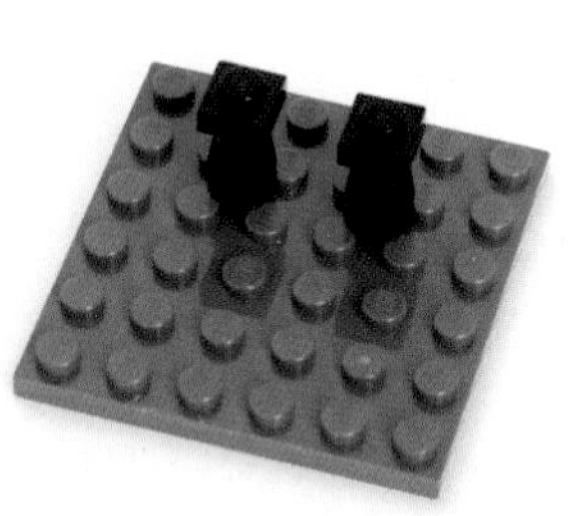

STEP 2: Add a 1 x 1 black cone and a 1 x 1 black plate on top of each black round plate.

STEP 3: Find a 2 x 6 black plate, a 1 x 4 black plate, two 1 x 2 black plates with one stud on top (jumper plate), two 1 x 2 black slopes (30 degree) and a 1 x 4 white tile.

STEP 4: Attach the white tile, black jumper plates and 1 x 4 black plate to the 2 x 6 plate.

STEP 5: Add two 1 x 2 black slopes (30 degree) on top of the 1 x 4 black plate.

STEP 6: Attach the keyboard to the legs, and your instrument is complete! Now find a minifigure to play the keyboard.

PIANO

See if you can use the pictures to build your own piano! You can make it black or brown or any color you like. Try using 1 x 2 white grills for the piano keys.

The piano is built on a 4 x 8 brown plate. The back of the piano has 2 x 2 bricks on the ends and 1 x 4 bricks in the center. This leaves a 1 x 4 cutout for a music stand. A 2 x 2 white tile or plate is perfect for sheet music!

MIC STAND

You'll also want to have some singers! Give your singers guitars if you have them, or just let them sing.

You can easily build a microphone stand with the pieces shown.

Attach a black bar holder with clip to a black bar (3 studs long). Insert the bar into a 2 x 2 dish. Then use the clip to hold the microphone.

If you don't have a minifigure microphone, you can use a lightsaber hilt and a 1 x 1 black round plate as a microphone! It will work with the same microphone stand.

WORKOUT GYM

CREATIVE CHALLENGE

Whether they're working on strength training or preparing for their next 5K, your minifigures will love working out in this top-of-the-line gym! Build treadmills and a bench press set. Then create some pull-up bars, exercise mats and a rack of free weights. Turn up the music on the boom box and let's get exercising!

KEY ELEMENTS

2—16 x 16 tan plates

6—2 x 4 medium azure plates for exercise mats

TREADMILL

1—4 x 6 dark gray plate

2—1 x 4 dark gray plates

2—1 x 2 dark gray plates with one stud on top (jumper plates)

1—1 x 2 dark gray slope, 30 degree

4—1 x 1 dark gray round plates

2—1 x 1 dark gray round bricks

2—1 x 1 dark gray cones

1—1 x 2 light gray plate with two clips on the side

2—1 x 1 light gray tiles with a clip

1—2 x 4 black plate

1—1 x 2 black plate

1—black bar, 4 studs long

1—1 x 2 black slope, 30 degree

BENCH PRESS

1—4 x 6 tan plate

2—1 x 2 dark gray plates with one stud on top (jumper plate)

2—1 x 1 dark gray round bricks

1—2 x 6 dark gray plate

2—2 x 2 dark gray dishes

3—2 x 2 black tiles

1—black bar, 6 studs long with a stop ring

2—1 x 1 x 3 light gray bricks

2—1 x 1 light gray bricks with a stud on the side

2—1 x 1 light gray bricks

2—1 x 1 light gray slopes, 30 degree

PULL-UP BARS

2—black bars, 6 studs long with a stop ring

4—1 x 1 light gray bricks with a stud on the side

3—1 x 1 x 3 light gray bricks

1—1 x 1 light gray brick

WEIGHTS RACK

6—1 x 2 light gray bricks

1—1 x 2 light gray plate

2—1 x 2 light gray plates with a handle on each end

2—1 x 2 light gray plates with a handle on the end

Black bars, 3 studs long

8—1 x 1 round plates with an open stud in various colors (must have the open stud)

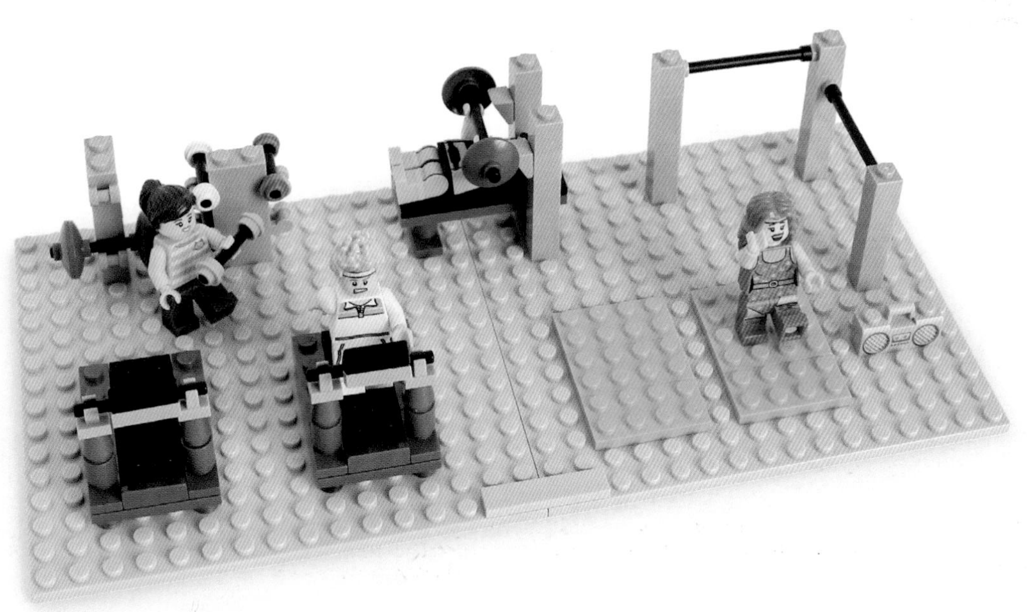

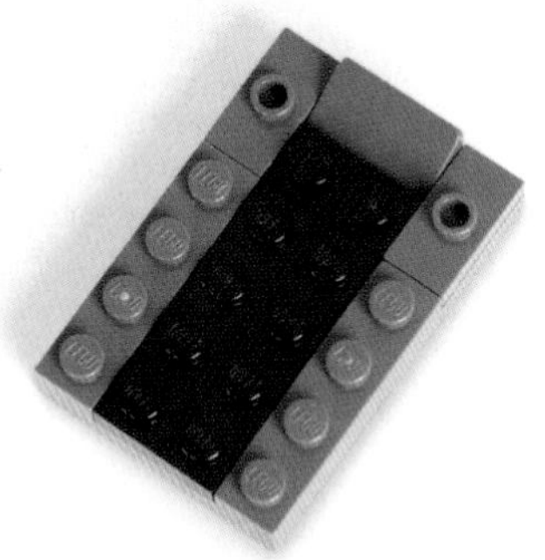

TREADMILL

STEP 1: Find a 4 x 6 dark gray plate, two 1 x 4 dark gray plates, two 1 x 2 dark gray plates with one stud on top (jumper plates), a 1 x 2 dark gray slope (30 degree), a 2 x 4 black plate and a 1 x 2 black plate.

STEP 2: Attach the plates and the 1 x 2 slope to the 4 x 6 plate as shown.

STEP 3: Turn the plate over and add a 1 x 1 dark gray round plate in each corner; this will raise the treadmill off the ground.

STEP 4: Then turn the treadmill back over and add two 1 x 1 dark gray round bricks and two 1 x 1 dark gray round cones. Find the bricks shown.

STEP 5: Place a 1 x 1 light gray tile with a clip on top of each dark gray cone. Then attach a black bar (4 studs long) to the clips. Build a screen by attaching a 1 x 2 black slope to a 1 x 2 light gray plate with two clips on the side. Clip that onto the treadmill.

Then get one of your minifigures ready to run on the treadmill!

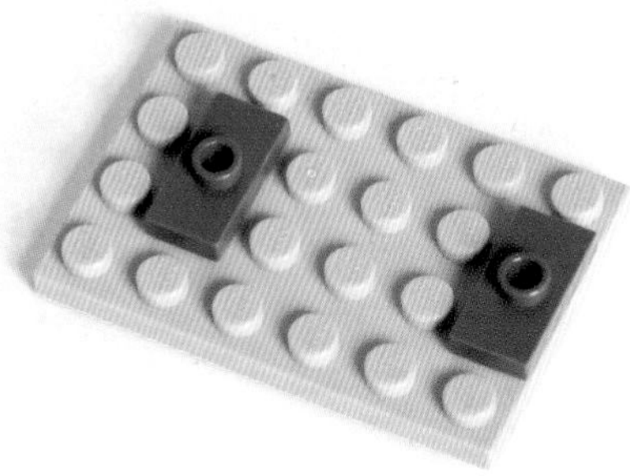

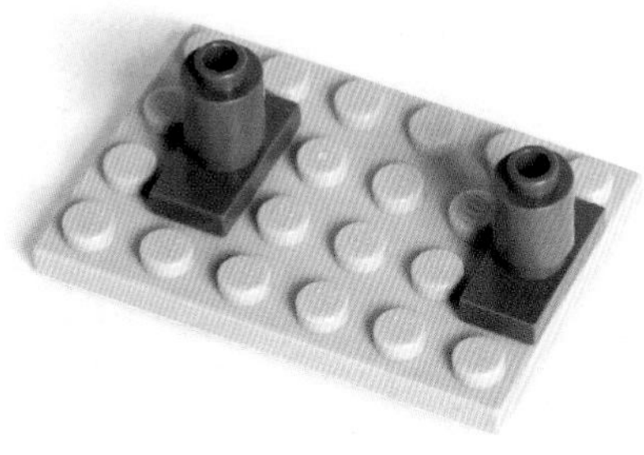

BENCH PRESS

STEP 1: Attach two 1 x 2 dark gray plates with one stud on top (jumper plates) to a 4 x 6 dark gray plate so that there are three studs in between.

STEP 2: Add a 1 x 1 dark gray round brick on each jumper plate.

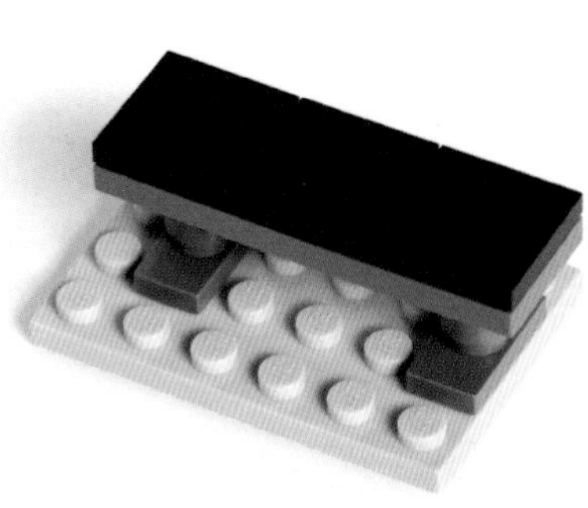

STEP 3: Place a 2 x 6 dark gray plate on top of the round bricks. Cover the 2 x 6 plate with three 2 x 2 black tiles.

STEP 4: Build a stand for the weights. Place a 1 x 1 x 3 light gray brick (that means it's three bricks high) on either side of the bench. Then add a 1 x 1 light gray brick with a stud on the side and a 1 x 1 light gray brick on each side. Attach 1 x 1 slopes (30 degree) to the studs. The slopes can hold up a weight made from a black bar (6 studs long with a stop ring) and two 2 x 2 dark gray dishes.

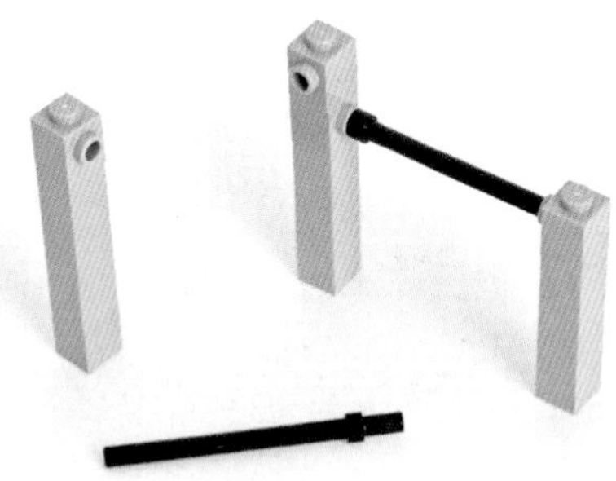

PULL-UP BARS

Build some pull-up bars for your minifigures! Their hands can hold on to the bars.

Use black bars that are 6 studs long with a stop ring. You can insert the ends of the bars into 1 x 1 bricks with a stud on the side.

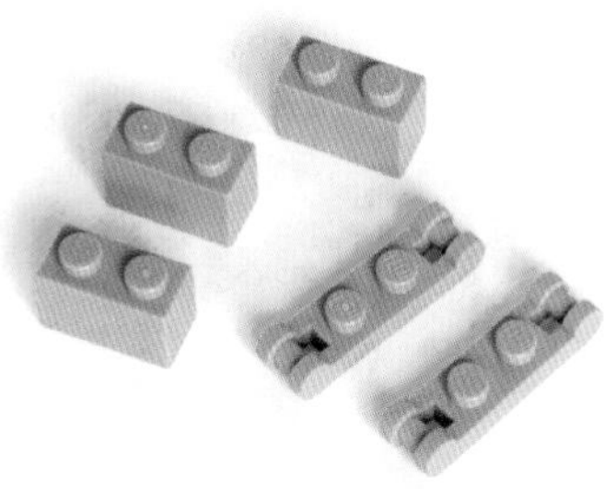

FREE WEIGHTS RACK

Build some free weights and a rack to store them. Make a rack that holds weights on both sides by using 1 x 2 light gray bricks and 1 x 2 plates with a handle on both ends.

Build weights with black bars that are 3 studs long. Slide on 1 x 1 round plates with an open stud in any color you choose.

Make a larger weight with a bar that is 4 studs long. Slide two 2 x 2 dishes onto each end.

Now it's workout time! Turn up the music!

AMAZING IDEA

Expand your gym if you want by building a running track around the perimeter or by adding a swimming pool. It would also be fun to build a racquetball court or a basketball goal!

COZY BEDROOM

CREATIVE CHALLENGE

Build a bedroom out of bricks! You can make this project look like your own bedroom, or you can design a room for your favorite minifigures. Make bunk beds or single beds—it's up to you! Create a desk with a lamp for a cozy place to do homework. You can tell that this bedroom belongs to a LEGO fan . . . it has a table for building a miniature LEGO city!

KEY ELEMENTS

1—16 x 16 tan plate
1—8 x 16 tan plate
Various yellow bricks, 1 stud wide, or use any color you'd like
2—1 x 4 x 3 windows

BUNK BEDS

12—1 x 1 brown round bricks
2—4 x 8 brown plates
3—1 x 4 brown plates
5—1 x 4 brown bricks
2—2 x 6 lime green plates
1—4 x 4 bright light blue plate
1—2 x 4 bright light blue plate
2—2 x 4 white plates
2—2 x 4 white tiles

DRESSER

4—2 x 4 brown plates
9—1 x 2 brown bricks
6—1 x 1 brown bricks with a stud on the side
3—1 x 2 dark tan plates with one stud on top (jumper plates)
1—2 x 2 dark gray round tile with one stud
1—1 x 1 clear round brick
1—2 x 2 dark tan dish

DESK

1—4 x 6 brown plate
4—1 x 4 brown bricks
1—1 x 3 brown brick
4—1 x 2 brown bricks
4—1 x 2 brown slopes, inverted
1—1 x 1 brown brick with a stud on the side
1—2 x 2 brown round brick
2—2 x 6 brown plates
3—1 x 2 brown plates
2—2 x 2 brown corner plates
1—1 x 4 brown plate
1—1 x 4 brown tile
1—1 x 2 light gray plate with one stud on top (jumper plate)
2—1 x 1 light gray plates with a horizontal clip
2—1 x 1 light gray plates with a bar handle
1—2 x 2 dark tan dish
1—1 x 1 clear round plate
1—brown chair
Accessories like a laptop, mug, hat and a 2 x 2 tile with a picture on it

LEGO TABLE

2—2 x 6 white plates
3—2 x 4 white plates
2—1 x 4 white bricks
2—1 x 4 white plates
Assorted tiny bricks—use what you have

BUNK BEDS

Build some bunk beds! The top bunk has a ladder on one side so that it's easy to climb up to bed. The other side is simply a stack of five 1 x 4 brown bricks. The bed is made from a 4 x 8 brown plate. Cover it with two 2 x 6 plates in any color (lime green is pictured), and then add a 2 x 4 white plate and a 2 x 4 white tile to make a pillow.

The bottom bunk is not connected to the top but simply sits underneath it. Build the bed in the same way that you built the top bunk, and then add four 1 x 1 brown round bricks as legs.

DESK

Make a desk with a hutch. A 4 x 6 plate is the perfect size for the top of the desk. Build legs on each side with a 1 x 4 brick and two 1 x 2 inverted slopes.

Start building the hutch by adding a 1 x 4 brick, two 1 x 2 bricks, a 1 x 3 brick and a 1 x 1 brick with a stud on the side. The stud will be used to hold a tile with a picture printed on it.

Create a shelf by adding a 2 x 6 plate. Then find a 1 x 4 tile, a 1 x 4 brick and two 1 x 2 bricks.

Place the 1 x 4 tile on the front of the shelf. Then add the bricks around the edges.

Finish the shelf by adding two rows of plates around the edges. Then place a 2 x 6 plate on the top. Grab a chair and attach it to the top of a 2 x 2 round brick.

BUILDING TIP

Use two 1 x 1 light gray plates with a clip and two 1 x 1 light gray plates with a handle to create a tiny posable desk lamp!

Then it's time to add some details! Attach a 2 x 2 tile with a map or other picture to the hutch. Then find things to display, like a tiny car, a fossil bone or a shell.

DRESSER

Build a dresser and a lamp. Attach 1 x 2 plates with one stud on top to the dresser to look like drawers. Make a tiny lamp from a 2 x 2 round tile with one stud on top, a 1 x 1 clear round brick and a 2 x 2 dish.

Place the lamp on top of the dresser, and then add a hat. Or think about the things you keep on your dresser and build those. Maybe you can top the dresser with a fish tank or a sports trophy.

LEGO TABLE

You can even build a LEGO table for your bedroom! Create a simple table design, and then add tiny bricks on top to look like a miniature LEGO town.

Now set up a bedroom scene! It would be fun to put together a minifigure that looks like you. If you share a room, build your sister or brother too. Do you have a bookshelf in your room? A pet cage? Or maybe a video game system? Build those things too! Then set up a scene with what you would be doing with a free afternoon to hang out.

FAIRYTALE CHRONICLES

Build your own fairytale world with knights, dragons, trolls, beanstalks and little pigs that run their own bakery in a gingerbread house in the forest. Construct a wise old wizard with a raven for a companion, plus some magical unicorns with colorful manes. Send your knights on a mission to rescue a baby dragon from the clutches of an evil witch, and then celebrate with the heroes as they outsmart some terrible trolls. It's always an adventure in Fairytale Forest!

EDMUND THE SPIKE-TAIL DRAGON

STEP-BY-STEP

Edmund is a majestic dragon with impressive wings and a row of spikes down his back and tail. He's a powerful dragon, but he enjoys helping Little Red deliver treats through her ForestDash business as much as he enjoys breathing fire at his enemies. Build Edmund the dragon with posable wings, posable legs, a posable head and a mouth that can open and close.

PARTS LIST

DARK GRAY BRICKS

2—2 x 6 bricks
2—2 x 4 bricks
1—3 x 12 wedge plate, right
1—3 x 12 wedge plate, left
1—3 x 8 wedge plate, right
1—3 x 8 wedge plate, left
4—2 x 4 plates
4—2 x 3 plates
2—1 x 2 plates
1—2 x 4 wedge plate
2—1 x 2 slopes
6—1 x 2 slopes, 30 degree
4—1 x 2 plates with one stud on top (jumper plates)
1—1 x 2 plate with a handle on the end
1—1 x 2 plate with a horizontal clip on the end
1—1 x 2 plate with two fingers on the end
8—1 x 2 plates with a ball on the side
2—1 x 1 plates with a horizontal tooth

LIGHT GRAY BRICKS

2—6 x 6 wedge plates
1—4 x 10 plate
1—4 x 6 plate
1—4 x 4 plate
1—2 x 6 plate
6—2 x 4 plates
2—2 x 3 plates
5—2 x 2 plates
2—1 x 4 plates
5—1 x 2 plates
4—2 x 2 bricks
1—1 x 2 brick
4—2 x 2 x 2 slopes
2—1 x 1 plates
1—2 x 2 plate with one stud on top
1—2 x 2 curved slope
1—2 x 2 x ⅔ modified brick with a curved slope end
2—1 x 1 bricks with a stud on the side (headlight)
5—1 x 2 slopes, 30 degree
1—1 x 2 plate with a handle on the side
1—1 x 2 plate with two clips on the side
1—1 x 2 plate with one finger on the side
4—1 x 2 plates with a socket on the side
4—1 x 2 plates with a socket on the end

MEDIUM AZURE BRICKS

2—1 x 6 plates
1—2 x 4 plate
2—1 x 3 curved slopes
10—1 x 1 slopes, 30 degree

WHITE BRICKS

1—6 x 4 wedge, triple inverted curved
2—2 x 2 slopes, inverted
3—4 x 2 slopes, double inverted
1—2 x 4 plate
1—1 x 2 plate with a handle on the end
1—1 x 2 plate with a horizontal clip on the end
1—1 x 2 plate
4—1 x 2 plates with three teeth
2—1 x 1 plates with a vertical tooth
6—1 x 1 round plates

ASSORTED BRICKS

2—1 x 2 red curved slopes
2—eyes

STEP 1: Find a 2 x 6 light gray plate, a 2 x 4 light gray plate and a 2 x 2 x ⅔ light gray modified brick with a curved slope end.

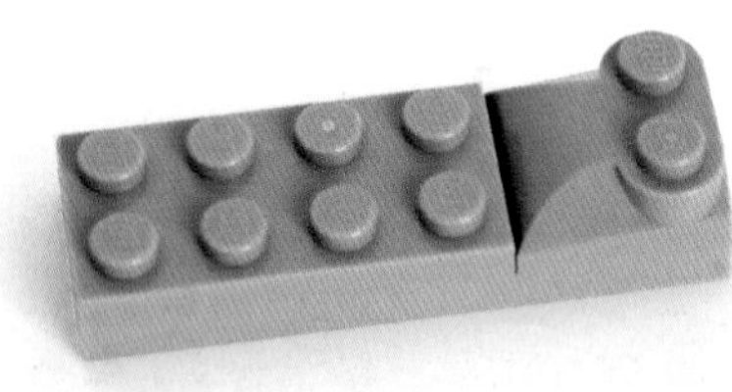

STEP 2: Attach the 2 x 4 plate and the curved slope brick to the 2 x 6 plate.

STEP 3: Add a 1 x 2 light gray brick, two 1 x 1 light gray bricks with a stud on the side (headlight) and a 1 x 2 light gray slope (30 degree). Find two eyes and a 1 x 2 light gray plate.

STEP 4: Attach the eyes and place the 1 x 2 plate on the back of the head.

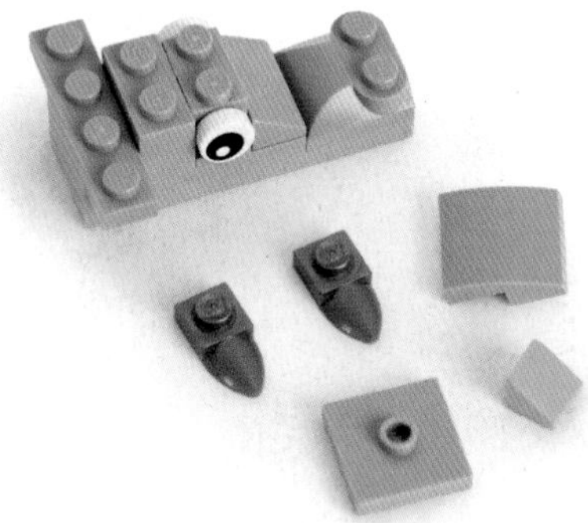

STEP 5: Add a 1 x 4 light gray plate to the back of the head. Then find the bricks shown.

STEP 6: Attach a 2 x 2 light gray plate with one stud on top of the head. Give the dragon a spike by placing a 1 x 1 medium azure slope (30 degree) on top of the head. Add a 2 x 2 light gray curved slope and two 1 x 1 dark gray plates with a horizontal tooth to the back of the head.

STEP 7: Give the dragon teeth! Add two 1 x 1 white round plates and two 1 x 1 white plates with a vertical tooth to the underside of the dragon's head.

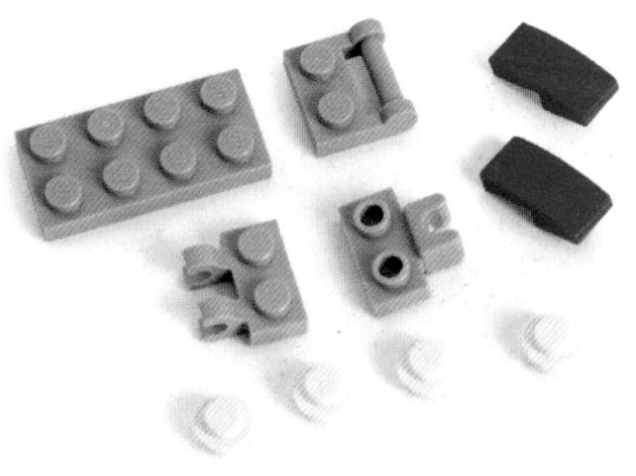

STEP 8: Gather the bricks shown for building the dragon's bottom jaw.

STEP 9: Attach a 1 x 2 light gray plate with a handle on the side and four 1 x 1 white round bricks to a 2 x 4 light gray plate.

STEP 10: Add two 1 x 2 red curved slopes to make the dragon's tongue. Place a 1 x 2 light gray plate with a socket on the side on top of a 1 x 2 light gray plate with clips. Connect this to the handle.

STEP 11: Attach the bottom jaw to the dragon's head as shown. He can now open and close his mouth.

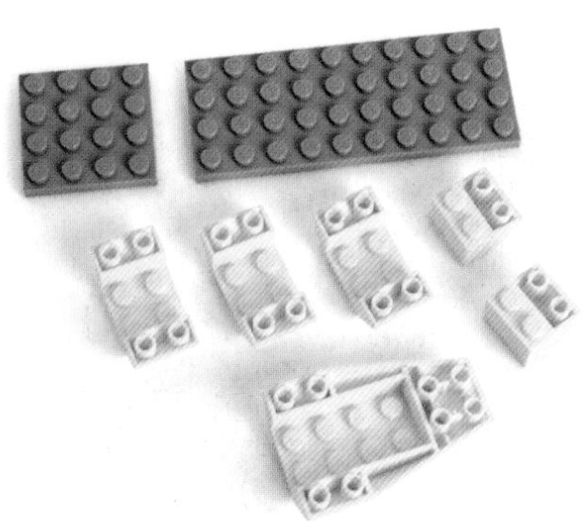

STEP 12: Gather the bricks shown for building the dragon's body.

STEP 13: Use the white inverted slope bricks and double inverted slopes to connect the two light gray plates.

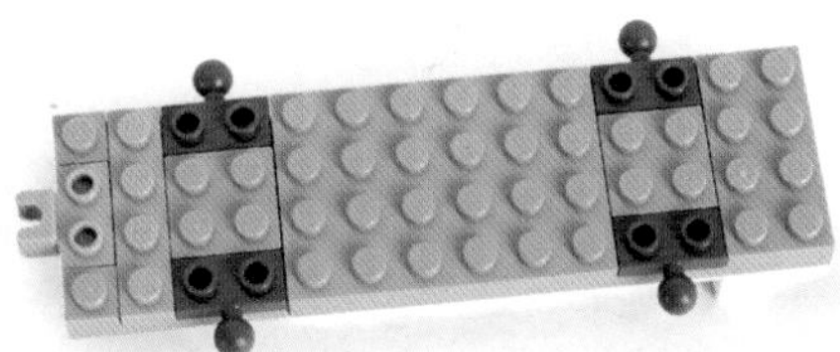

STEP 14: Turn the dragon body over. Make sure that the 2 x 2 inverted slope bricks are on the right. Then add the plates shown. The plates with a ball on the side will hold the legs.

STEP 15: Add (from left to right) a 2 x 4 dark gray plate, two 2 x 4 dark gray bricks, two 2 x 6 dark gray bricks and a 2 x 4 light gray plate.

STEP 16: Add a 1 x 2 dark gray plate and a 1 x 2 dark gray plate with a ball on the side to the front of the body. Then gather the bricks shown.

STEP 17: Place a 1 x 2 dark gray slope on each side of the front of the body and add two 1 x 3 medium azure curved slopes in between those. Then add two 1 x 1 medium azure slopes (30 degree).

STEP 18: Place two 2 x 4 dark gray plates and two 1 x 2 dark gray plates with a ball on the side on the top of the body. The plates with a ball will hold the wings.

STEP 19: Add a 2 x 4 medium azure plate and two 1 x 6 medium azure plates.

STEP 20: Place three 1 x 2 dark gray slopes (30 degree) on each side of the dragon's body. Then find the bricks shown.

STEP 21: Attach a 2 x 4 dark gray wedge plate at the back of the body.

STEP 22: Add two 1 x 2 dark gray plates with one stud on top (jumper plates) and a 1 x 2 dark gray plate.

STEP 23: Place a 1 x 1 medium azure slope (30 degree) on each jumper plate.

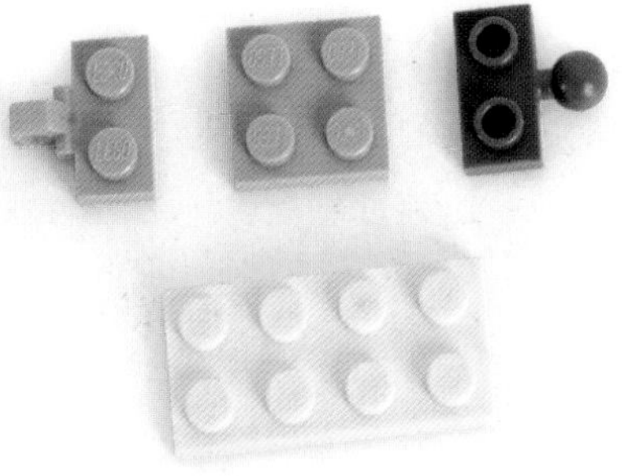

STEP 24: Find a 2 x 2 light gray plate, a 1 x 2 dark gray plate with a ball on the side, a 1 x 2 light gray plate with one finger and a 2 x 4 white plate.

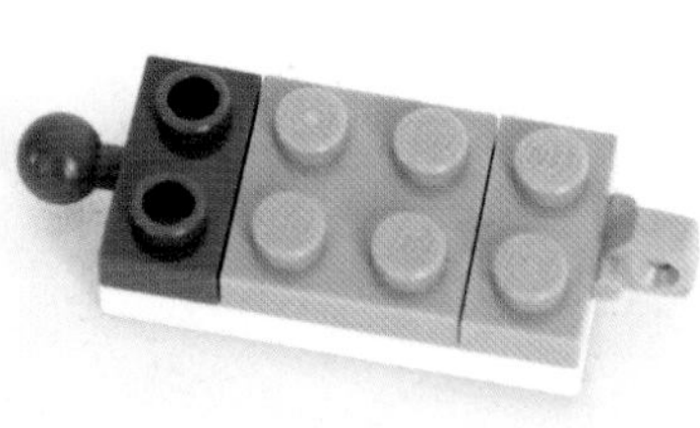

STEP 25: Attach the three gray plates to the 2 x 4 white plate as shown.

STEP 26: Add a 2 x 4 dark gray plate and two 1 x 2 dark gray plates with one stud on top (jumper plates). Then find the pieces shown.

STEP 27: Build the dragon's tail by attaching plates with handles and clips. If you don't have the exact pieces shown, get creative with other types of joints.

STEP 28: Add spikes to the tail by adding five 1 x 1 medium azure slopes (30 degree). Or use whatever colors you like!

STEP 29: Attach the head and tail to the body.

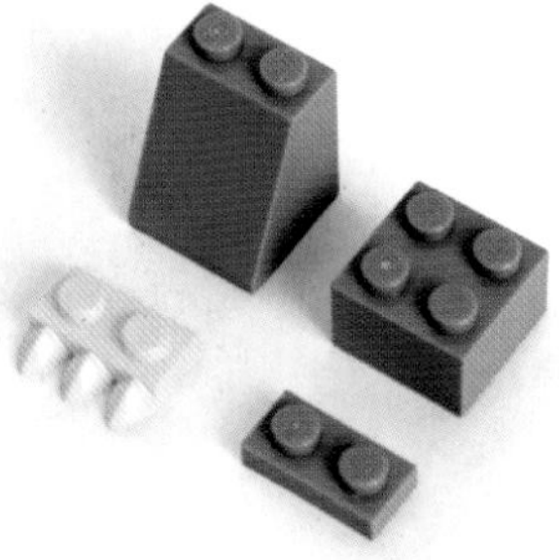

STEP 30: Build the legs. You'll need four sets of the bricks shown.

STEP 31: Attach a 1 x 2 white plate with three claws and a 1 x 2 light gray plate to the underside of a 2 x 2 light gray brick. Add a 2 x 2 x 2 light gray slope. Then find a 1 x 2 slope (30 degree) and a 1 x 2 light gray plate with a socket on the end.

STEP 32: Build four legs as shown. Substitute pieces if you need to or change the design of the legs.

STEP 33: Attach the legs to the dragon. He's starting to look really awesome!

STEP 34: Gather the pieces shown for building one dragon wing. You'll need two sets of these, but you can substitute them with other wedge plates if needed.

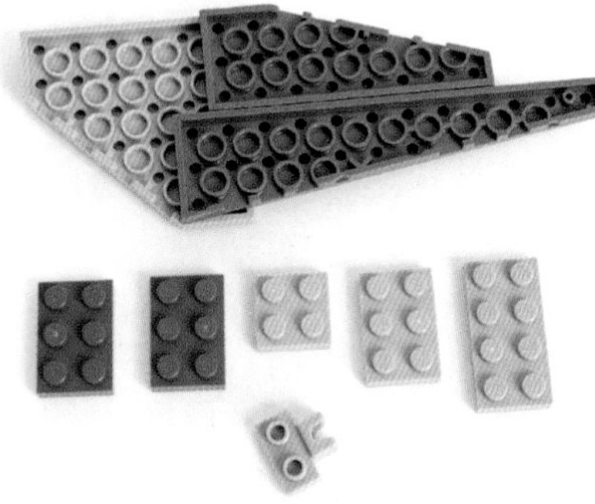

STEP 35: Attach a 3 x 12 dark gray wedge plate and a 3 x 8 dark gray wedge plate to the underside of a 6 x 6 light gray wedge plate.

STEP 36: Then add a 2 x 3 dark gray plate, a 2 x 2 light gray plate and a 1 x 2 light gray plate with a socket on the end.

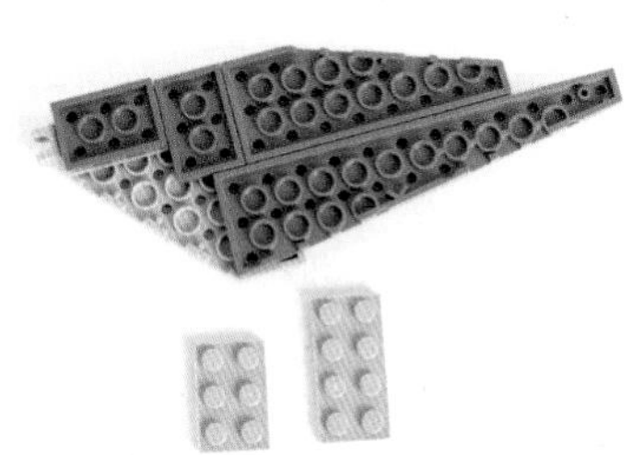

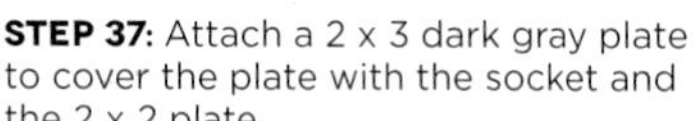

STEP 37: Attach a 2 x 3 dark gray plate to cover the plate with the socket and the 2 x 2 plate.

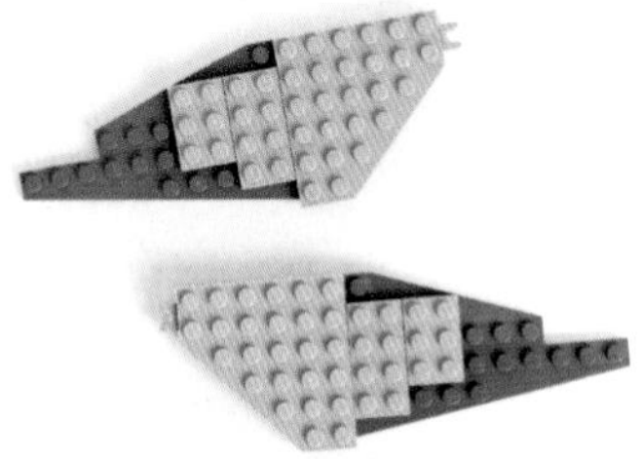

STEP 38: Flip the wing over and add a 2 x 3 light gray plate and a 2 x 4 light gray plate. Then build a second wing that is a mirror image of the first.

STEP 39: Attach the wings and your dragon is complete!

Now Edmund the dragon is ready to transport Little Red all over the forest, delivering treats to one and all! A 3 x 4 crate will easily attach to the dragon's back so that you can fill it with cookies, fruit and other goodies.

THE THREE LITTLE PIGS BAKE SHOP

CREATIVE CHALLENGE

After the unfortunate incident with the house of bricks and the Big Bad Wolf coming down the chimney, the Three Little Pigs decided to put their brick house up for sale and make a fresh start in a different part of Fairytale Forest. They purchased a lovely gingerbread house, and after watching some inspiring baking shows, they decided to open their very own bake shop! Now the Big Bad Wolf can head to their place for cupcakes and scones rather than pork. It's a win for everyone!

Build an adorable gingerbread house with a chimney and candy decorations on the roof. This is definitely a creation you'll want to keep and display!

KEY ELEMENTS

1—16 x 16 tan plate for the base
Various brown bricks, 1 stud wide
5—1 x 4 x 3 white windows with lattice panes
10—1 x 2 white slopes
1—1 x 1 x 3 white brick with two clips
1—door, 1 x 4 x 6 round top with window and keyhole
28—1 x 2 dark tan bricks, modified with brick lines
8—1 x 1 dark tan bricks
2—1 x 2 dark tan slopes, inverted
2—1 x 1 dark tan slopes, 30 degree
2—8 x 8 medium nougat plates
2—1 x 2 hinge bricks with a 2 x 2 hinge plate
24—2 x 2 round tiles in various bright colors
2—2 x 3 brown plates
8—2 x 4 brown bricks
4—2 x 4 tan tiles
1—1 x 1 brown brick with a stud on the side
2—1 x 2 brown plates with a clip on the end
1—1 x 4 brown antenna
1—1 x 2 brown plate
1—2 x 3 tan plate
2—pink cones (Part ID: 35574)
Food items—cookies, croissants, treats, etc.

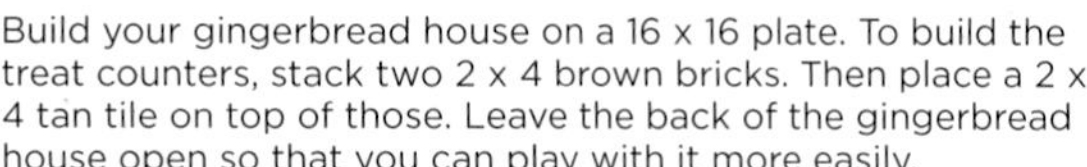

Build your gingerbread house on a 16 x 16 plate. To build the treat counters, stack two 2 x 4 brown bricks. Then place a 2 x 4 tan tile on top of those. Leave the back of the gingerbread house open so that you can play with it more easily.

Build a sloped roofline on the front of the house. Use five 1 x 2 white slopes on each side and fill in with brown bricks. Each side of the gingerbread house has a 1 x 2 gap that is one plate deep. This leaves a space where you will later attach the top pieces of the roof.

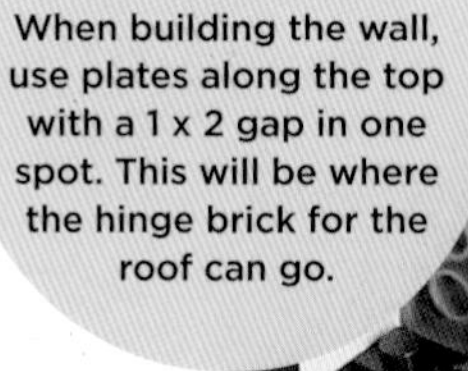

BUILDING TIP

When building the wall, use plates along the top with a 1 x 2 gap in one spot. This will be where the hinge brick for the roof can go.

The door is attached to a 1 x 1 x 3 white brick that has two clips. Use a 1 x 6 x 2 brown arch to make the opening for the door. Build the chimney with 1 x 2 dark tan bricks that have brick lines and 1 x 1 dark tan bricks. If you don't have bricks with brick lines, just use regular bricks in tan, gray or red. The chimney has a notch in it to accommodate the roof.

Build the roof out of 8 x 8 plates decorated with 2 x 2 round tiles in fun colors. If you don't have tiles, use 2 x 2 round plates. In fact, you can use any colorful plates or tiles to decorate the roof. You might want to use 2 x 2 round bricks to look like gumdrops!

Attach a 1 x 2 hinge brick with a 2 x 2 hinge plate to each roof panel. Then add a 2 x 3 brown plate to each one in the positions shown.

Attach the roof so that the hinge brick sits in the 1 x 2 space on the wall. Do this on both sides.

Pivot the roof pieces toward each other until the brown plates on the underside of each one meet to hold the roof in place.

Then design a cute sign for the front of the bake shop. Attach two 1 x 2 brown plates with a clip on the end to a 2 x 3 tan plate. Then add tiles decorated like cookies and treats. A 1 x 4 brown antenna will allow you to attach the sign to a stud on the side of the gingerbread house.

Add pink cones topped with 1 x 1 white plates with a swirl to decorate the front of the gingerbread house. Or design your own decorations!

Place some trees around the gingerbread house to create a forest scene. Then your Bake Shop is ready to open for business!

JACK'S COTTAGE

CREATIVE CHALLENGE

Jack and his mother live in a tiny cottage in Fairytale Forest. Sadly, they are very poor. One day, Jack's mother sends him to town to sell the family's cow so that he can get some money to buy some food. Jack instead meets a peddler along the road and trades the cow for a seed. A magic seed! Build a fairytale cottage with a garden where Jack can plant his magic seed. You can design the cottage in any color you like, and then make a yard with a garden. Then build the giant beanstalk that grows from the seed!

KEY ELEMENTS

2—green 16 x 16 plates

Various tan bricks, 1 stud wide

About 20—1 x 2 medium nougat bricks, modified with brick lines, or substitute regular bricks

24—2 x 4 red slopes

16—2 x 2 red slopes

2—2 x 4 red tiles

2—2 x 2 brown plates

4—1 x 4 x 3 brown windows with lattice panes

1—1 x 4 x 6 door

1—1 x 2 x 2⅔ window with a rounded top and a lattice pane

FLOWERS

Various plants and trees

White fence bricks

BEANSTALK

About 12—2 x 2 green round bricks (substitute other colors like yellow, lime green or brown if needed)

About 20—1 x 1 green round plates with three leaves (if you don't have leaves, use 1 x 2 green plates as leaves)

About 6—1 x 1 green round bricks for the sprouting beanstalk

STOVE

1—2 x 4 black brick

1—2 x 4 black plate

4—1 x 1 black cones

2—1 x 1 black round bricks

1—1 x 1 black slope, 30 degree

1—1 x 1 white round tile, printed with an egg

Frying pan

TABLE AND CHAIRS

1—4 x 6 brown plate

4—1 x 6 brown tiles

4—1 x 1 brown round bricks

4—1 x 1 brown cones

2—2 x 2 brown round bricks

2—2 x 2 brown round plates

Build a cozy little kitchen inside the cottage with a table and a woodburning stove for Jack's mother to cook on.

Build the stove with a 2 x 4 black brick and a 2 x 4 black plate. Substitute 1 x 1 bricks for the cone legs of the stove if needed.

A 4 x 6 brown plate is the perfect size for a table. Cover the table with 1 x 6 tiles, or you can leave it with the studs exposed. Each table leg is built with one 1 x 1 brown round brick and one 1 x 1 brown cone. You can easily substitute 1 x 1 bricks if you want. Since Jack and his mother are very poor, their chairs are simple logs cut from trees in the forest (2 x 2 round bricks with a 2 x 2 round plate on top).

Try building a peddler's cart. There's no wrong way to build one! Fill it with food items, pots, pans and any other accessories you'd like. Then pretend that Jack is meeting the peddler along the road into town.

The peddler assured Jack that the bean would sprout into an amazing magical plant that would make all of their dreams come true. Jack's mother, however, was more interested in food to eat than in dreams and wishes.

In spite of his mother's frustration, Jack planted the seed in the garden. He covered it with dirt and watered it and then waited to see what would grow.

Before long, a plant sprouted and began to grow. It quickly became taller than all the other plants in the garden!

In no time at all, the bean plant stretched nearly to the sky. Jack decided to climb the beanstalk and see what he could see from the top!

CASTLE IN THE CLOUDS

CREATIVE CHALLENGE

At the top of Jack's beanstalk lay a beautiful castle in the clouds. The castle was ruled by a king and queen who presented Jack with a gift. It was a goose that could lay golden eggs! With the gold, Jack and his mother would never go hungry again.

Build your fairytale castle on a base of white bricks to make it look like it's in the clouds. Give it towers and places for knights to stand and guard the castle. Then add flags as a finishing touch!

KEY ELEMENTS

1—16 x 16 plate in any color

Various white bricks and plates

Various light gray bricks, 1 stud wide

1—door, 1 x 4 x 6 round top with window and keyhole

2—1 x 2 x 2⅔ brown windows with a rounded top

1—6 x 16 light gray plate

1—8 x 8 light gray plate

1—6 x 6 light gray plate

3—1 x 6 light gray arch bricks

6—1 x 4 x 2 light gray arch bricks

About 15—1 x 2 light gray bricks, modified with brick lines (optional)

2—white 1 x 4 antennas

2—gold flags

2—1 x 2 light gray bricks with a clip for holding lanterns

4—2 x 2 bricks, modified facet

2—brown minifigure telescopes (lanterns)

2—flames

Optional—tiles for the floor of the castle

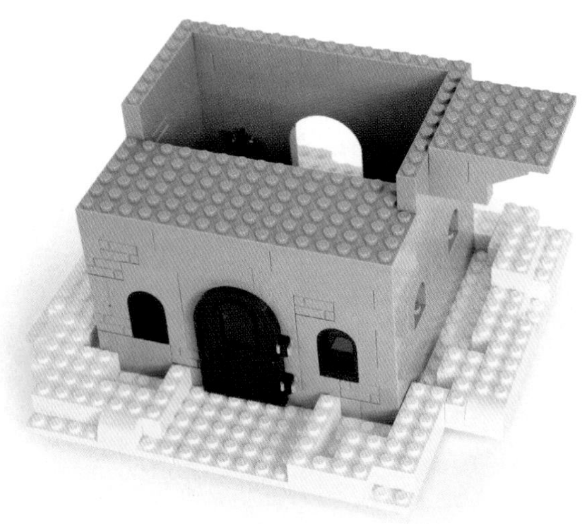

Build your castle on a 16 x 16 plate or use a larger 32 x 32 baseplate. Cover the base with white plates and add bricks around the edges to look like clouds. Then build the outline of your castle out of light gray bricks. Use arches to create medieval windows.

Make the supports for a tower by building a couple of 1 x 4 bricks into the walls so that they stick out on the side.

Place a 2 x 6 light gray brick and two 2 x 3 light gray inverted slopes on top of the tower supports. Then add a 6 x 6 plate on top to make a base for the tower. Add a 6 x 16 light gray plate on the front of the castle. Build another row of light gray bricks on the side of the castle.

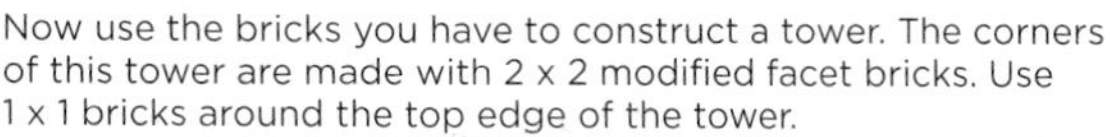

Now use the bricks you have to construct a tower. The corners of this tower are made with 2 x 2 modified facet bricks. Use 1 x 1 bricks around the top edge of the tower.

Then design the front of the castle. In addition to basic bricks, the bricks shown are 1 x 6 arches, 2 x 2 x 3 slopes and 2 x 2 x 3 slopes (double convex).

BUILDING TIP

Making the two towers different heights from each other will give your castle an interesting design! Try adding a third tower if you have enough bricks.

Add a tall tower on the left side of the castle. This tower is built on an 8 x 8 light gray plate and supported by the lower castle walls. Use slope bricks to create a roof for the tower. Then add flags in your choice of color.

This view from the back of the castle shows how the tall tower attaches to the lower story.

Once inside the castle, Jack met the kind king and queen. They listened to his tale of the peddler, the magic bean and his trip up the beanstalk.

"We have just the thing for you," the king announced.
The queen presented Jack with a goose that would lay golden eggs!

Jack scurried down the beanstalk with the goose in his arms. At first, his mother was confused.

BUILDING TIP

Use some white bricks to build a goose.

But Jack's mother quickly changed her tune when the goose laid one of its golden eggs! She couldn't wait to take that gold to town to buy food and supplies. Their fortunes had changed thanks to Jack planting the magic seed, finding the castle and bringing home the goose!

TERRIBLE FOREST TROLLS

STEP-BY-STEP

Deep in Fairytale Forest lurk the ugliest and most terrible trolls. These creatures possess an abundance of size and an astonishing lack of brains. Many a forest traveler has discovered with dread that they have managed to cross paths with one of these trolls and has trembled in fear! However, due to their bumbling ways, the trolls are too uncoordinated to pose an actual threat. Build your trolls with one eye or two, in your choice of color, and with a terrible expression. Then give them clubs and spears and send them off to cause mischief!

PARTS LIST

LIME GREEN BRICKS

2—2 x 6 plates
3—2 x 4 plates
2—2 x 3 plates
1—2 x 2 plate
8—1 x 2 plates
2—2 x 2 round plates
1—1 x 2 tile
2—1 x 6 bricks
3—2 x 4 bricks
7—2 x 2 bricks
9—1 x 2 bricks
5—2 x 2 slopes
2—2 x 2 slopes, inverted
1—1 x 2—2 x 2 bracket, inverted
4—1 x 1 bricks with a stud on the side

BROWN BRICKS

2—2 x 6 plates
1—2 x 6 brick
6—2 x 2 round bricks
4—1 x 1 cones
4—1 x 1 slopes (30 degree)

ASSORTED BRICKS

2—1 x 2 light gray plates with a socket on the end
2—1 x 2 dark gray plates with a ball on the side
2—1 x 2 dark gray plates with a clip on the end
2—1 x 2 dark gray plates with a ball and a socket
1—2 x 2 white round tile with open stud
1—1 x 2 red slope, 30 degree
1—1 x 1 black round plate
2—4 x 4 x 2 light gray cones with an axle hole
1—2 x 2 light gray round brick
2—black Technic pins with friction ridges
1—1 x 4 light gray antenna

STEP 1: Let's build a one-eyed troll! The troll shown has lime green skin, but you can use any color of bricks. First, find a 2 x 4 plate, a 2 x 2 brick, two 2 x 2 inverted slopes, a 1 x 2 brick and a 1 x 2 red slope (30 degree).

STEP 2: Attach a 2 x 2 brick and two 2 x 2 inverted slopes to the 2 x 4 plate.

STEP 3: Add the 1 x 2 red slope (30 degree) and place a 1 x 2 brick behind it. This will be the troll's mouth.

STEP 4: Attach a 2 x 2 brick on each side of the mouth. Then find the bricks shown.

STEP 5: Attach a 2 x 6 plate above the mouth. Then place two 2 x 2 bricks, a 2 x 2 slope and a 1 x 2 brick on top of the 2 x 6 plate. The slope sticks out to make the troll's nose.

STEP 6: Place a 1 x 2 plate and a 1 x 2 tile on top of the nose. Then find the bricks shown.

STEP 7: Attach a 1 x 2 brick and a 1 x 2 plate to the 1 x 2—2 x 2 inverted bracket. Attach a 1 x 1 black round plate to a 2 x 2 white round tile with one stud. This will be the eye.

STEP 8: Attach the 2 x 2 plate to the front of the bracket. Then add the eye and attach the whole assembly to the head just above the nose.

STEP 9: Find two 2 x 2 slopes, two 1 x 2 bricks and four 1 x 1 bricks with a stud on the side.

STEP 10: Place a 1 x 2 brick and two 1 x 1 bricks with a stud on the side on each side of the head. Then add a 2 x 2 slope on each side. Give your troll funny hair! Attach brown cones and slopes to a 2 x 4 plate. Find two 2 x 2 round plates to be the ears.

STEP 11: Attach the hair and the ears, and the troll's head is complete!

STEP 12: Find the bricks shown for building the troll's body.

STEP 13: Stack the two 2 x 6 brown plates and the 2 x 6 brown brick. Then add the lime green bricks on top of that, or any color that you are using for the body.

STEP 14: Add a 2 x 4 plate and two 1 x 2 bricks to the top of the body. Then find a 2 x 4 brick, a 2 x 6 plate and two 1 x 2 dark gray plates with a ball on the side.

STEP 15: Place the 2 x 4 brick in the center of the body, and then add a 1 x 2 dark gray plate with a ball on the side on each shoulder. Place a 2 x 6 plate on top to hold everything in place.

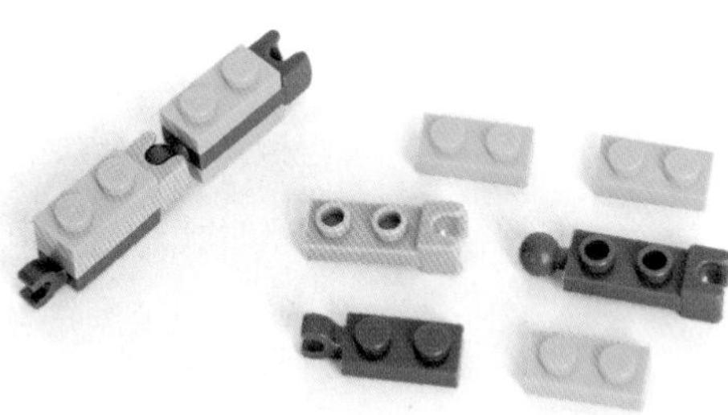

STEP 16: Now it's time to build the arms. Each arm has a 1 x 2 dark gray plate with a ball and socket, a 1 x 2 light gray plate with a socket on the end, a 1 x 2 dark gray plate with a clip on the end, and three 1 x 2 plates.

STEP 17: Attach the head and the arms to the troll's body.

STEP 18: Build the legs and feet. Each leg has three 2 x 2 round bricks, but you can substitute regular 2 x 2 bricks if you prefer. Build each foot with a 2 x 3 plate, a 2 x 2 slope and a 1 x 2 brick.

STEP 19: Attach the legs to the troll's body. Your troll is complete! Now it's time to build a big club for him to carry.

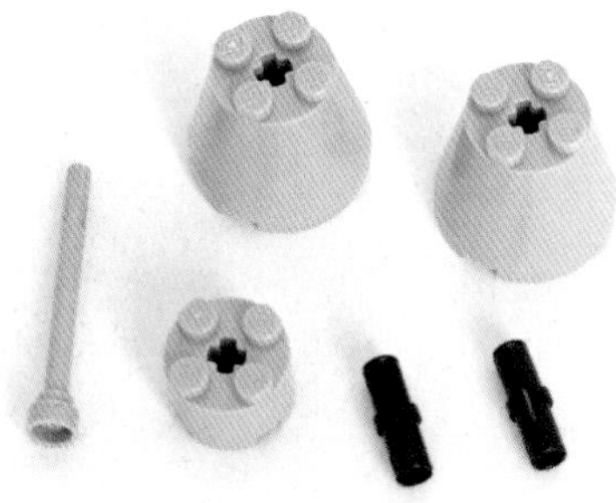

STEP 20: Gather the bricks shown for building the club.

STEP 21: Insert two black pins in the underside of one of the 4 x 4 x 2 light gray cones.

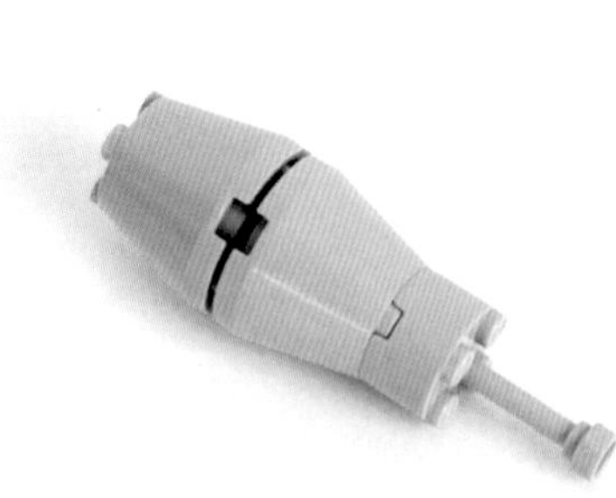

STEP 22: Use the pins to connect two 4 x 4 x 2 light gray cones. Attach the 2 x 2 light gray round brick. Then insert a 1 x 4 antenna into the round brick and cone. This makes the perfect handle for the troll to hold.

Now your troll is ready to go after some innocent forest inhabitants with his club! If he doesn't trip over his own two feet, that is . . .

Use the pictures to create other types of trolls! This one has feet with toes. Use 1 x 2 plates with three claws to make the toes. His mouth is built from two 1 x 2 slopes that face each other. Give him a vest by using 1 x 2 tan bricks on the front of his body. Behind those, there are red bricks across his back.

The ears are made from 1 x 2 plates with one stud on top (jumper plates). Attach the ears to a 1 x 1 brick with a stud on the side.

This ugly troll has a funny underbite! The bottom of his head is deeper than the top, making the teeth stick out in front. Give him a big belly with slope bricks.

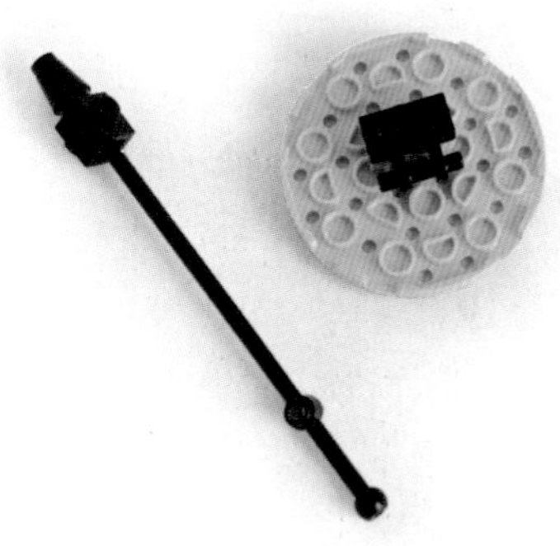

Make a spear and shield for your troll. The long piece in the spear is a bar (12 studs long), sometimes used as a boat mast.

Experiment with your bricks to make a round club or design your own weapons.

Now set up your knights riding through the forest. They're galloping along when suddenly they notice three ugly trolls with big weapons standing right in their path!

The knights are paralyzed by terror for a moment, but they quickly snap out of it and think of a clever plan.

The knights race off to the Three Little Pigs Bakery to pick up some sweets to use as a distraction. Trolls are suckers for treats!

And it works! The trolls set down their weapons and begin licking their lollypops!

Thanks to some creative thinking, the knights ride away unscathed.

MAGICAL UNICORNS

STEP-BY-STEP

Fairytale Forest would not be complete without some colorful and magical unicorns! Experiment with the colors in the mane until you get just the look you want. Once your unicorns are complete, build a majestic waterfall for the perfect magical scene. This project is fun to play with and also amazing to display.

PARTS LIST

WHITE BRICKS

1—2 x 6 plate
1—2 x 3 plate
3—2 x 2 plates
1—2 x 6 brick
1—2 x 2 brick
1—1 x 2 brick
1—1 x 2 brick with two studs on the side
4—1 x 1 bricks with a stud on the side
1—1 x 2—2 x 2 bracket
2—1 x 2 plates with one stud on top (jumper plates)
4—1 x 1 round bricks
4—1 x 1 cones

ASSORTED BRICKS

1—1 x 2 black plate
4—1 x 1 black round plates
1—1 x 1 gold cone
2—eyes
8—1 x 1 slopes, 30 degree, in the colors of your choice for the mane
1—1 x 2 plate in your choice of color for the tail

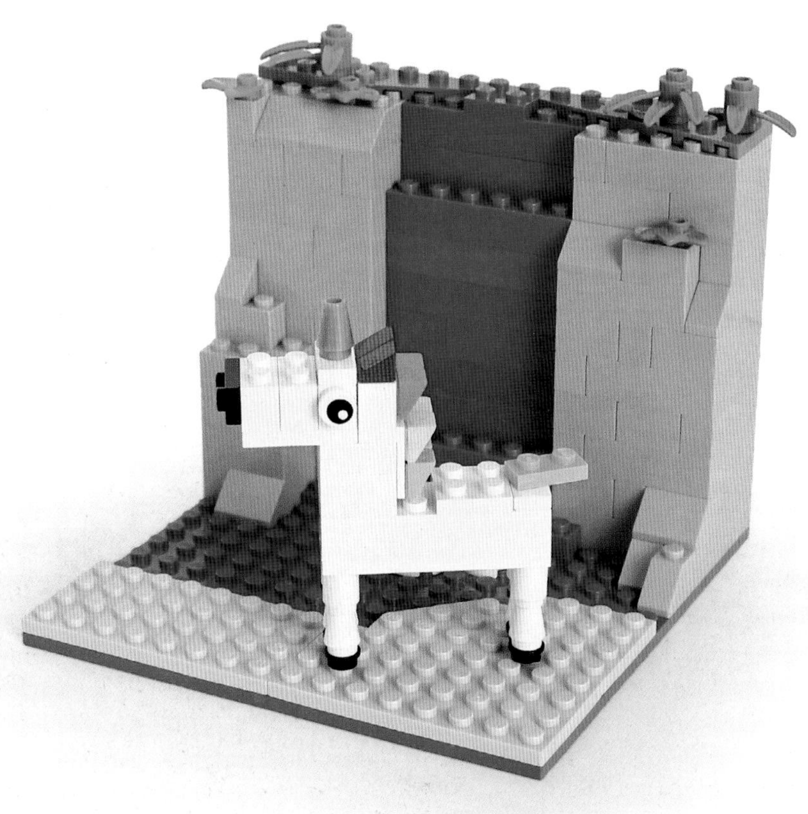

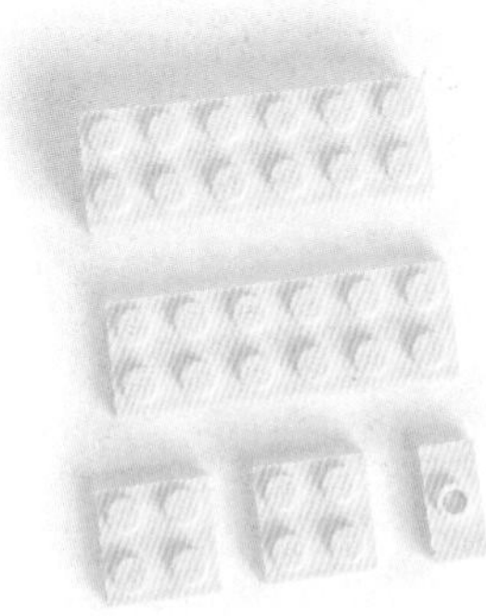

STEP 1: Find a 2 x 6 white brick, a 2 x 6 white plate, two 2 x 2 white plates and a white 1 x 2 plate with one stud on top (jumper plate).

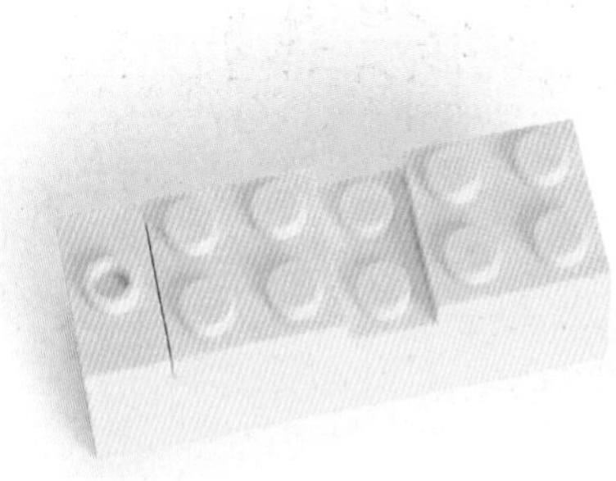

STEP 2: Attach the 2 x 6 white plate to the 2 x 6 white brick. Then add the 2 x 2 plates and the 1 x 2 jumper plate on top as shown.

STEP 3: Add a 2 x 2 white brick and a 2 x 2 white plate to build the unicorn's neck.

STEP 4: Attach a 1 x 2—2 x 2 white bracket to the top of the neck.

STEP 5: Gather the bricks shown for building the unicorn's head.

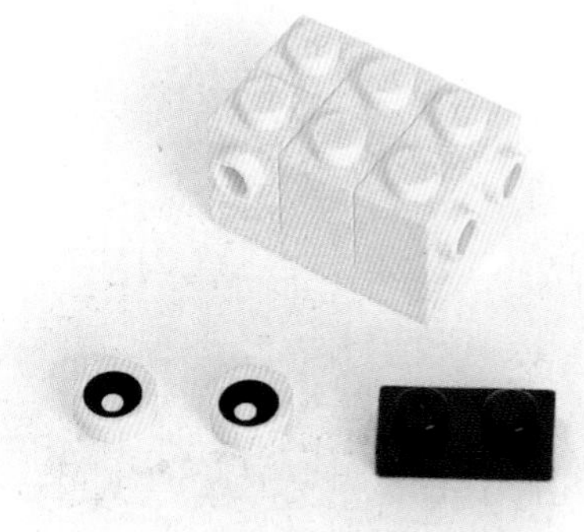

STEP 6: Attach a 1 x 2 white brick with two studs on the side, a 1 x 2 white brick and two 1 x 1 white bricks with a stud on the side to a 2 x 3 white plate.

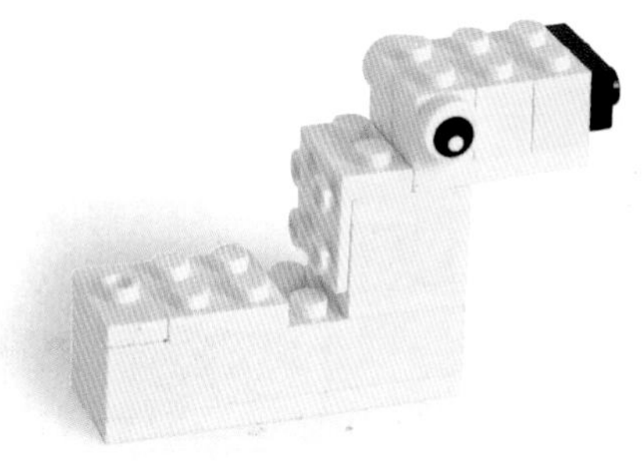

STEP 7: Add the eyes and the 1 x 2 black plate for a nose. Then attach the head to the unicorn's neck.

STEP 8: Place two 1 x 1 bricks with a stud on the side on the back of the head. Add a 1 x 2 white plate with one stud on top (jumper plate) just above the eyes.

STEP 9: Make the horn by adding a 1 x 1 gold cone. Add eight 1 x 1 slopes (30 degree) to make the unicorn's mane.

STEP 10: Finish up the unicorn by adding a 1 x 2 plate as the tail. Then build four legs. Each leg has a 1 x 1 white round brick, a 1 x 1 white cone and a 1 x 1 black round plate.

Try making more unicorns with different colors for the mane and tail!

Grab a blue 16 x 16 plate and make a waterfall scene for your unicorn! Build a mountain with light gray bricks. Make the center of the mountain out of blue bricks to look like water flowing down. Then add white round bricks and plates to make foam at the bottom of the waterfall.

THE WITCH'S TREEHOUSE LAIR

CREATIVE CHALLENGE

In the deepest, darkest part of Fairytale Forest lives a scheming and conniving witch. She mostly keeps to herself, but you can guarantee that if she is out and about in the forest, she is up to no good! For example, she might be stealing a baby dragon (page 140) or helping herself to some of the treats at the Three Little Pigs Bakery.

Build a spooky home for the witch in an old hollowed-out tree. This project can be completed with almost any shape of brick. Get creative with the bricks you have to create an old knobby tree with branches sticking out in every direction.

KEY ELEMENTS

1—16 x 16 bright green plate

Various brown bricks—use all types of shapes and sizes

About 4—1 x 5 x 4 brown arches

About 5—1 x 3 x 3 brown arches

Leaves—leaves shown are LEGO ID 2423 and 10884

About 12—1 x 2 light gray bricks, modified with brick lines or use regular light gray bricks

Light gray bricks, 1 stud wide

1 x 3 and 1 x 2 brown plates to make logs for the fire

Flames

Build your treehouse lair on a 16 x 16 plate. Make the house an irregular shape if you want so that it looks like a real tree. Use tiles for the floor, or just leave the green plate showing. Construct a fireplace and place it inside the house.

Here's a close-up look at the fireplace. You can also build a table for storing potion bottles. Use 1 x 1 round bricks or cones in translucent colors for the bottles. A 1 x 1 round tile makes a good lid.

Build up the sides of the treehouse and add branches and leaves. The door is made from an assortment of brown plates with a 4 x 4 round corner plate at the top. A 1 x 5 x 4 brown arch fits perfectly over the curve of the door.

BUILDING TIP

Use bricks with studs on the side and bricks with clips as you build the walls of your treehouse. These will allow you to attach leaves and vines to the house.

As you build your treehouse, use any shapes of brown bricks that you have! Combine round bricks and slope bricks along with regular bricks to give your tree an interesting design.

AMAZING IDEA

You may want to add a chimney to your tree house! Use red bricks to make it look like a brick chimney, or try using gray or brown bricks.

The door has a 1 x 2 plate with a handle on the end that is connected to a 1 x 1 brick with a clip. This allows the door to open and close.

Once you've completed your treehouse lair, add an outdoor cooking fire for the witch. Use light gray bricks to build a fire ring, and then place brown plates inside the ring to be logs. Add some trees and plants if you have them.

Now pretend that the witch has stolen a baby dragon! No one is sure what she plans to do with it, but it certainly can't be good. Jack and his mother have alerted the knights that a rescue is desperately needed!

When the knights arrived, the witch was busy at her cooking fire. They quietly hid just out of sight, and once she headed into the house, it was time to free that dragon!

Using their swords and all the strength they could muster, the knights began to pull down the bars on the dragon's cage.

In just a few minutes, the dragon was free! The knights grabbed the dragon and took off through the forest on horseback.

WISE OLD WIZARD

STEP-BY-STEP

Whenever anyone in Fairytale Forest is facing a challenge and doesn't know what to do, they are sure to visit the Wizard of Marshy Bog. He knows the forest like the back of his hand, and he knows quite a bit about those terrible trolls (page 115), too! Build your wizard with a classic wizard's hat, a raven for a companion and a staff that contains magical powers.

PARTS LIST

DARK GRAY BRICKS

1—2 x 4 brick
1—2 x 2 brick
3—1 x 4 bricks
2—2 x 2 corner bricks
7—1 x 1 bricks
2—2 x 2 x 2 slopes
3—2 x 2 slopes
2—1 x 2 Technic bricks
1—1 x 1 Technic brick
1—2 x 2 slope, inverted
1—4 x 2 wedge, triple left
1—1 x 2 plate
1—4 x 4 round plate
1—1 x 1 plate with a horizontal clip
1—1 x 1 slope, 30 degree

LIGHT GRAY BRICKS

1—1 x 4 brick
1—1 x 2 x 2 brick
2—1 x 1 bricks
2—1 x 1 round bricks
2—1 x 4 antennas
1—Technic pin
1—Technic pin, half length with 2-stud long bar extension (flick missile)

WHITE BRICKS

1—2 x 3 brick with a curved end
1—1 x 2 brick
1—1 x 2 brick with two studs on the side
1—2 x 2 plate
3—1 x 2 plates
2—1 x 2—2 x 2 brackets
1—1 x 2 slope, 30 degree

TAN BRICKS

1—1 x 2 brick
2—1 x 1 bricks with a stud on the side
1—1 x 2—2 x 2 bracket
1—1 x 2 plate with one stud on top (jumper plate)
1—1 x 1 tan slope, 30 degree

BLACK BRICKS

3—1 x 1 bricks
2—1 x 2 slopes
2—1 x 1 bricks with a stud on two opposite sides
2—1 x 2 plates
1—1 x 2 plate with two fingers
1—1 x 2 plate with one finger
1—Technic pin with friction ridges
1—1 x 1 slope, 30 degree

ASSORTED BRICKS

4—eyes
1—1 x 1 yellow plate
1—1 x 1 bright light orange plate with a horizontal tooth
1—1 x 1 translucent blue round plate
1—1 x 1 translucent light blue round plate

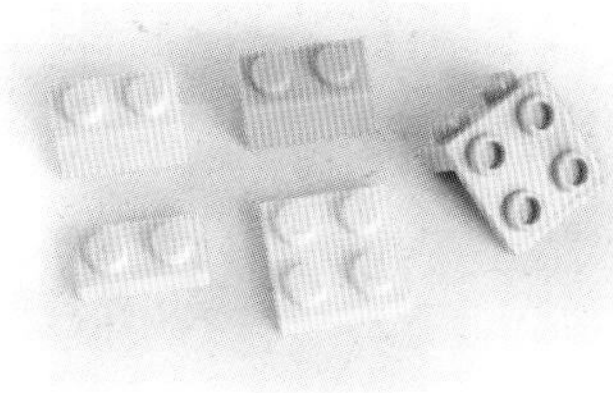

STEP 1: Gather the bricks shown for beginning the wizard's head.

STEP 2: Stack a 1 x 2 white plate and a 1 x 2 white brick and attach them to a 2 x 2 white plate. Then add a 1 x 2 tan brick.

STEP 3: Place a 1 x 2—2 x 2 tan bracket on top of the tan brick.

STEP 4: Create the wizard's hair by attaching two 1 x 2—2 x 2 brackets to the head. Then find the bricks shown to make his face.

STEP 5: Attach a 1 x 2 plate with one stud on top (jumper plate) to the tan bracket. Then add a 1 x 1 tan slope for the nose. Attach the eyes.

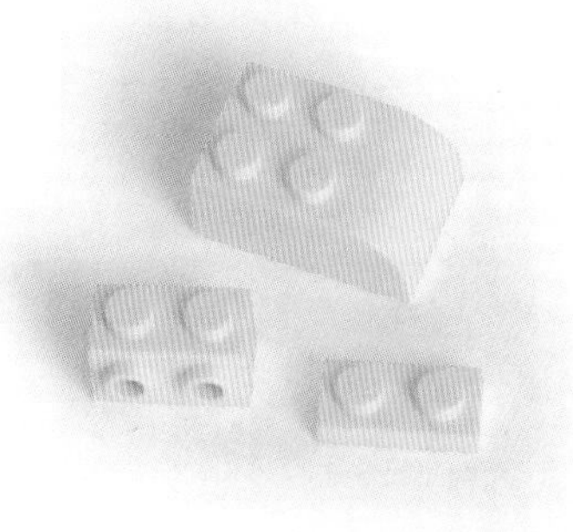

STEP 6: Find a 2 x 3 white brick with a curved end, a 1 x 2 white brick with two studs on the side, and a 1 x 2 white plate for building the wizard's beard.

STEP 7: Attach the studs on the side of the 1 x 2 white brick to the underside of the 2 x 3 white brick with a curved end. Then add the 1 x 2 plate on top of the 2 x 3 brick.

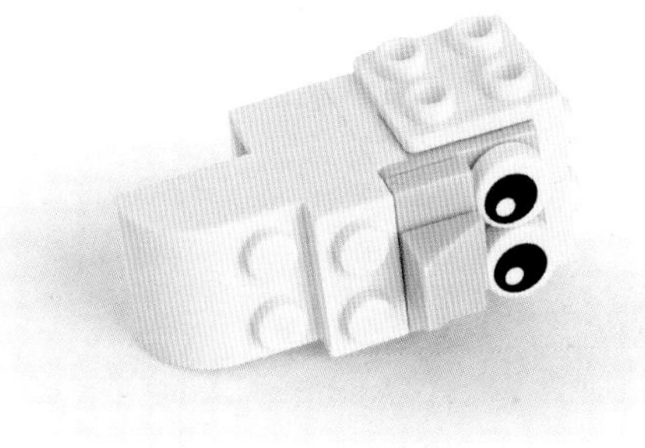

STEP 8: Use the studs on top of the 1 x 2 brick to attach the beard to the wizard's head.

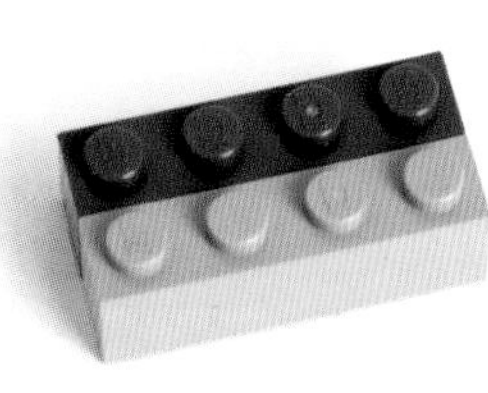

STEP 9: Let's make the wizard's body. Line up a 1 x 4 dark gray brick and a 1 x 4 light gray brick as shown.

STEP 10: Connect the two 1 x 4 bricks with two 2 x 2 dark gray corner bricks.

STEP 11: Add a 1 x 2 x 2 light gray brick, two 1 x 1 dark gray bricks and a 1 x 4 dark gray brick.

STEP 12: Continue building the wizard's body by adding a 2 x 4 dark gray brick, a 2 x 2 dark gray brick and two 1 x 2 dark gray Technic bricks.

STEP 13: Place two 2 x 2 dark gray slopes on top of the body.

STEP 14: Attach the wizard's head to the body as shown.

STEP 15: Give the wizard longer hair by adding a 1 x 2 white plate and a 1 x 2 white slope (30 degree) to the back of his head.

STEP 16: Build the wizard's legs. Each one has a 1 x 2 black slope, a 1 x 1 black brick and a 1 x 1 light gray brick. Then find two 2 x 2 x 2 dark gray slopes. Connect them with a 1 x 4 dark gray brick to make the bottom of the robe.

STEP 17: Add the legs and the bottom of the wizard's robe to his body.

STEP 18: Find a 1 x 1 dark gray Technic brick, two 1 x 1 dark gray bricks, a 1 x 2 dark gray plate, a 1 x 1 dark gray slope (30 degree) and a 1 x 1 tan brick with a stud on the side.

STEP 19: Attach the 1 x 1 Technic brick and the 1 x 1 slope (30 degree) to the 1 x 2 plate.

STEP 20: Then add the two 1 x 1 dark gray bricks and a 1 x 1 tan brick with a stud on the side. Attach the tan brick by using the stud on the side. Find a black pin with friction ridges.

STEP 21: Insert the black pin into the wizard's body, and then connect his left arm.

STEP 22: Find two 1 x 1 dark gray bricks, a 1 x 1 tan brick with a stud on the side, and a 1 x 1 dark gray plate with a horizontal clip.

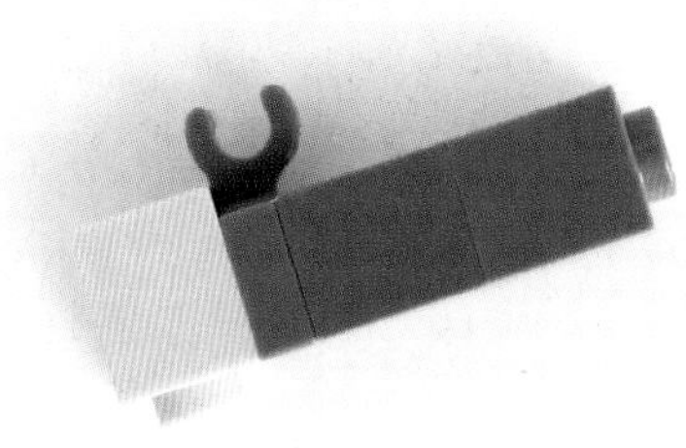

STEP 23: Attach the 1 x 1 dark gray plate with a clip to the stud on the side of the 1 x 1 tan brick. Then add the two 1 x 1 dark gray bricks.

STEP 24: Attach the wizard's right arm by inserting the stud of the dark gray brick into the hole in the Technic brick on the body.

STEP 25: Now build the wizard's hat. Attach a 2 x 2 dark gray slope to a 4 x 4 dark gray round plate. Then find the bricks shown.

STEP 26: Complete the hat by adding a 2 x 2 dark gray inverted slope. Then attach a 4 x 2 dark gray wedge (triple left). Place a 1 x 1 dark gray brick under the end of the wedge.

STEP 27: Place the hat on top of the wizard's head.

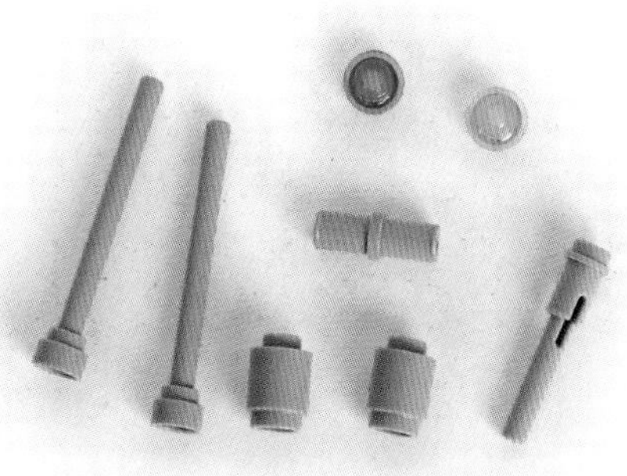

STEP 28: Build a staff for your wizard. Find the bricks shown.

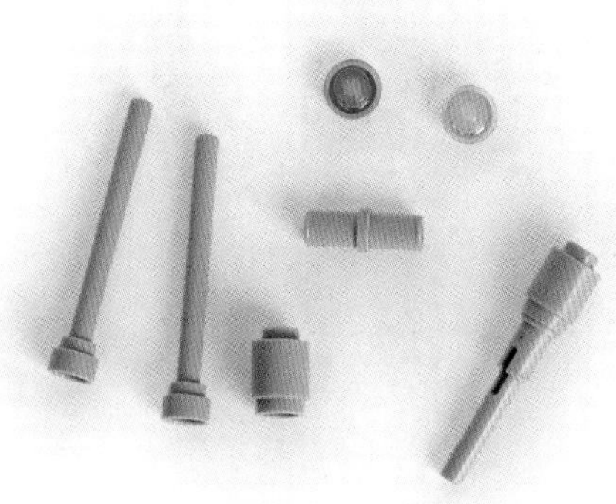

STEP 29: Attach a 1 x 1 light gray round brick to a flick missile.

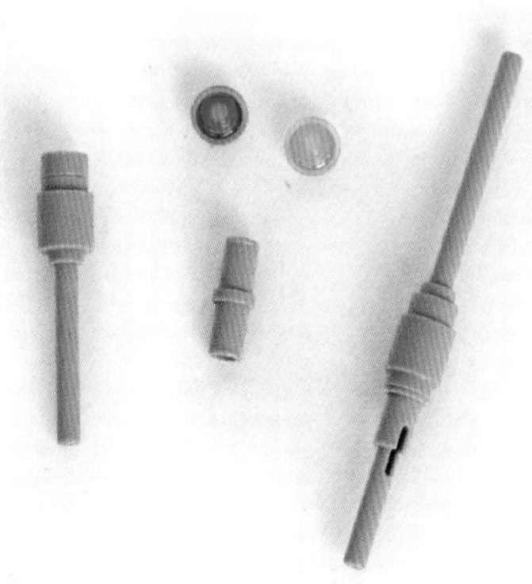

STEP 30: Then attach a 1 x 4 antenna to the top of the round brick. Slide a second 1 x 1 light gray round brick onto another antenna.

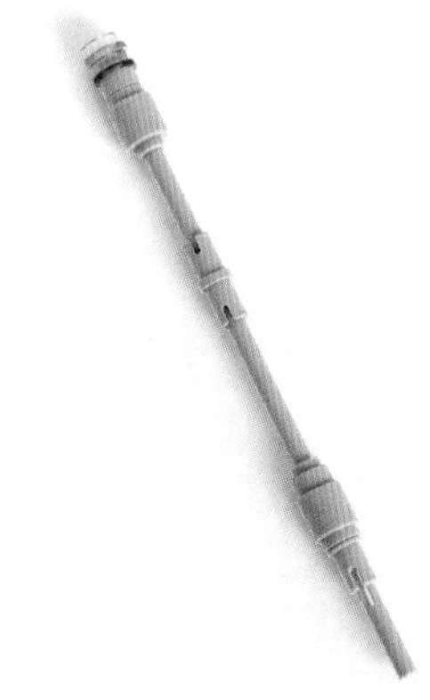

STEP 31: Use a light gray pin to attach the two parts of the staff. Then place a 1 x 1 translucent light blue round plate and a 1 x 1 translucent blue round plate on the top. The staff is complete!

Now try building a raven as a companion for your wizard. See if you can use the picture to build the raven's body. Attach a 1 x 3 black plate on each side of the body to make the wings. A 1 x 1 bright light orange plate with a horizontal tooth makes a great beak!

The raven can perch on the wizard's hand. It attaches to the stud on the tan brick on his hand. Your wizard is complete! Pretend that he is hiking through the forest in search of the unicorns (page 122). Or send him on an expedition to find a magical stone. His staff will protect him from any evil creatures that he might encounter on the way!

GRIFFIN

STEP-BY-STEP

One of the most majestic creatures in Fairytale Forest is the griffin. A griffin has the head and wings of an eagle and the body and legs of a lion, which makes it a powerful and beautiful flying creature. The griffin is a noble animal that is known for its ability to guard treasure and ward off enemies.

PARTS LIST

WHITE BRICKS

2—2 x 4 plates

2—2 x 3 plates

2—2 x 2 plates

1—2 x 3 wedge plate, right

1—2 x 3 wedge plate, left

1—1 x 3 plate

2—1 x 2 plates with three claws

2—1 x 1 plates with a horizontal tooth

2—1 x 1 plates

2—1 x 2 plates with a clip on the end

1—1 x 4 curved slope

1—1 x 2 tile

1—1 x 1 slope, 30 degree

1—1 x 1 round plate

TAN BRICKS

1—2 x 8 plate

1—2 x 4 plate

2—2 x 2 plates

2—1 x 2 plates

1—2 x 3 brick

3—1 x 2 bricks

10—1 x 1 bricks

2—1 x 2 Technic bricks

2—2 x 2 curved slopes

2—1 x 2 slopes, 30 degree

2—1 x 1 slopes, 30 degree

1—1 x 2 tile

1—2 x 2 round plate with rounded bottom

BROWN BRICKS

1—1 x 2 plate

1—2 x 3 plate

1—2 x 2 x ⅔ plate with two studs on the side

2—1 x 2 Technic bricks

1—2 x 2 slope

2—1 x 1 bricks with a stud on the side (headlight)

1—2 x 2 slope, inverted

3—1 x 2 plates with one stud on top (jumper plates)

2—1 x 1 slopes, 30 degree

ASSORTED BRICKS

2—1 x 2 light gray plates with a pin hole on the bottom

1—1 x 2 light gray plate with a handle on the side

1—1 x 2 light gray plate with a handle on both ends

2—1 x 2 dark gray plates with a pin hole on top

1—1 x 2 dark gray plate with a clip on the end

1—1 x 2 dark gray plate with one finger

1—1 x 2 dark gray plate with two fingers

2—eyes

1—1 x 2 yellow plate

1—1 x 1 yellow plate

1—1 x 2 dark brown curved slope

4—black Technic pins with friction ridges

1—1 x 2 bright light orange curved slope

STEP 1: Find a 2 x 3 brown plate, a 2 x 2 brown inverted slope and a 2 x 2 brown slope.

STEP 2: Attach both slope bricks to the 2 x 3 brown plate.

STEP 3: Add a 2 x 2 x ⅔ brown plate with two studs on the side. Then find two 1 x 1 brown bricks with a stud on the side (headlight), two eyes and two 1 x 1 brown slopes (30 degree).

STEP 4: Attach the two 1 x 1 bricks with a stud on the side (headlight) to the head, and then add the eyes. Place the two 1 x 1 slopes (30 degree) on the 2 x 2 x ⅔ plate with two studs on the side. Then find the bricks shown.

STEP 5: Place a 1 x 2 brown plate with one stud on top (jumper plate) on top of the eyes. Add a 1 x 2 brown plate and a 1 x 2 brown jumper plate behind the eyes.

STEP 6: Add a 1 x 2 dark brown curved slope on top of the griffin's head. Then find the bricks shown.

STEP 7: Place a 1 x 2 brown plate with one stud on top (jumper plate) in front of the eyes. Then build the beak by attaching a 1 x 1 yellow plate and a 1 x 2 bright light orange curved slope to a 1 x 2 yellow plate.

STEP 8: Attach the beak to the head as shown.

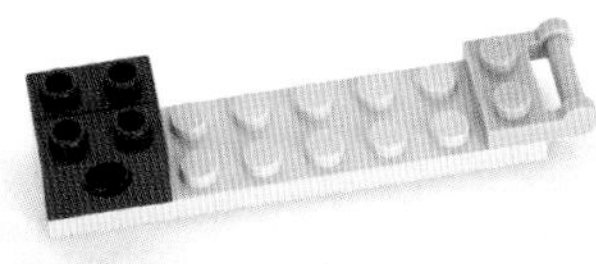

STEP 9: Start building the griffin's body. Attach two 1 x 2 brown Technic bricks to one end of a 2 x 8 tan plate and attach a 1 x 2 light gray plate with a handle on the side to the other end.

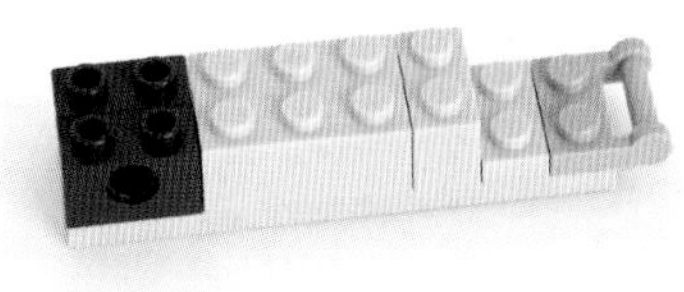

STEP 10: Add a 2 x 3 tan brick, a 1 x 2 tan brick and a 1 x 2 tan plate.

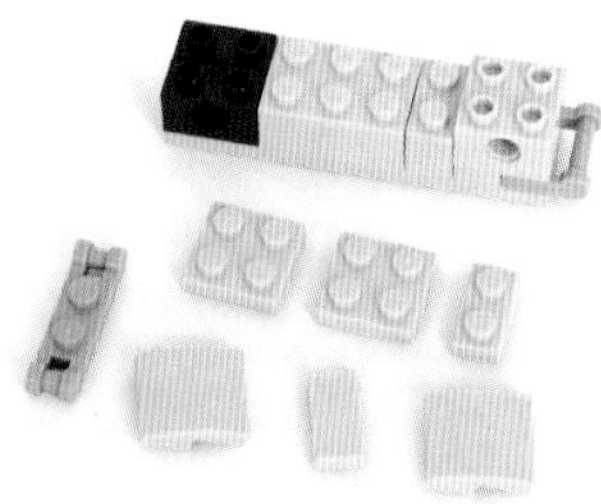

STEP 11: Place two 1 x 2 tan Technic bricks on the body. Then gather the bricks shown.

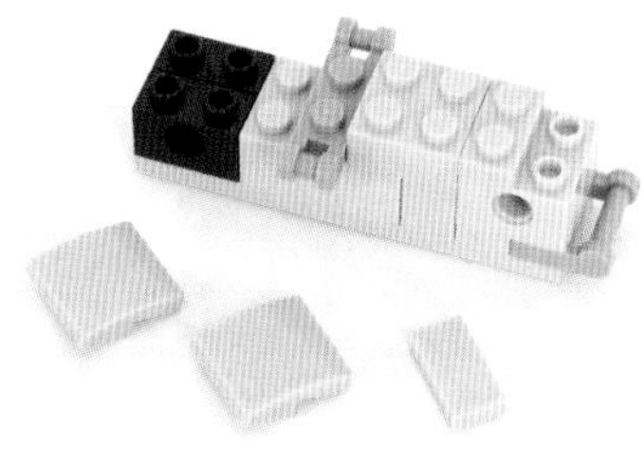

STEP 12: Add (from left to right) a 1 x 2 light gray plate with a handle on both ends, two 2 x 2 tan plates and a 1 x 2 tan plate.

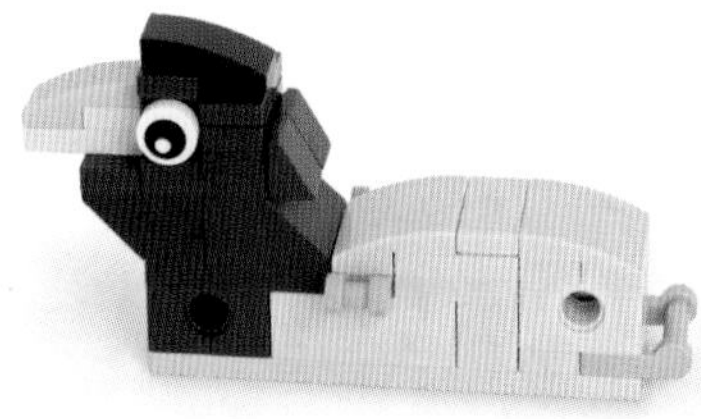

STEP 13: Turn the body around. Finish up the body by adding two 2 x 2 tan curved slopes and a 1 x 2 tan tile. Then attach the head to the griffin's body.

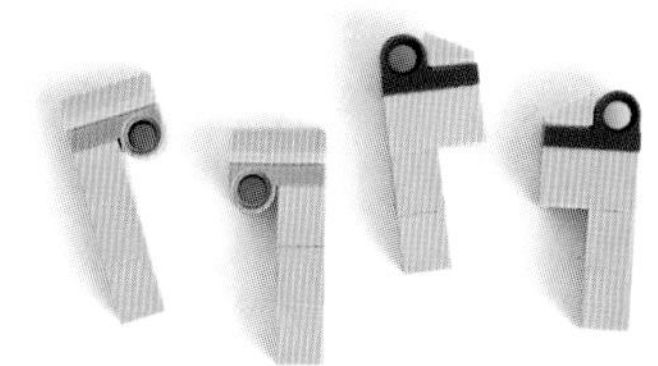

STEP 14: Build the legs. Each front leg has a 1 x 2 light gray plate with a pin hole on the bottom, three 1 x 1 tan bricks and a 1 x 2 tan slope (30 degree). Each back leg has a 1 x 2 dark gray plate with a pin hole on top, a 1 x 2 tan brick, two 1 x 1 tan bricks and one 1 x 1 tan slope (30 degree).

STEP 15: Add a 2 x 4 tan plate and a 2 x 2 tan plate with a rounded bottom to the underside of the griffin's body.

STEP 16: Insert a black pin with friction ridges into each of the Technic bricks on the body.

STEP 17: Attach the legs to the black pins.

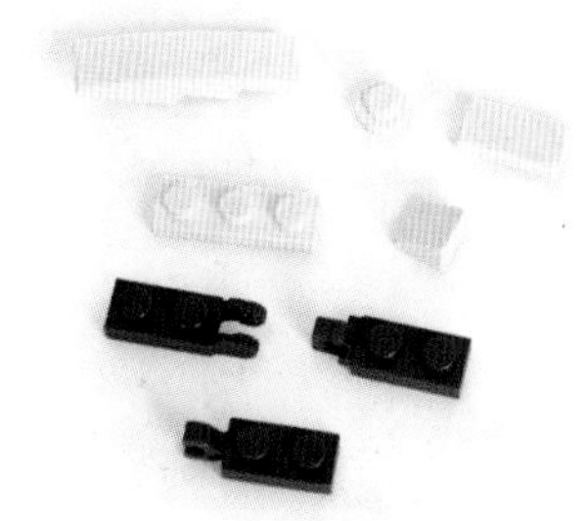

STEP 18: Find a 1 x 4 white curved slope, a 1 x 1 white round plate, a 1 x 2 white tile, a 1 x 3 white plate, a 1 x 1 white slope (30 degree), a 1 x 2 dark gray plate with two fingers, a 1 x 2 dark gray plate with one finger and a 1 x 2 dark gray plate with a clip on the end for building the tail.

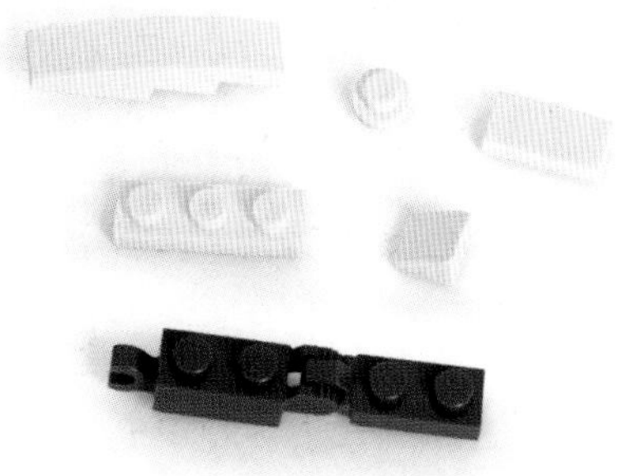

STEP 19: Place a 1 x 2 dark gray plate with two fingers on top of a 1 x 2 dark gray plate with a clip on the end. Then connect a 1 x 2 dark gray plate with one finger.

STEP 20: Attach a 1 x 3 white plate, a 1 x 1 white slope (30 degree) and a 1 x 2 white tile. Then add a 1 x 1 white round plate and a 1 x 4 white curved slope to finish up the tail.

STEP 21: Clip the tail to the griffin's body.

STEP 22: Build the wings. Attach a 2 x 3 white wedge plate and a 2 x 2 white plate to the underside of a 2 x 4 white plate.

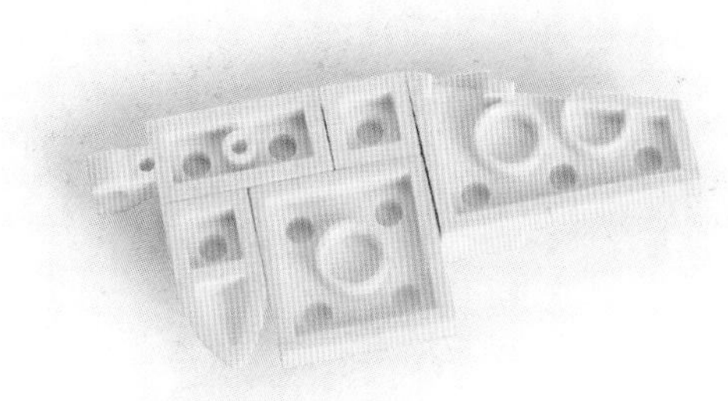

STEP 23: Add a 1 x 2 white plate with a clip on the end, a 1 x 1 white plate and a 1 x 1 white plate with a horizontal tooth.

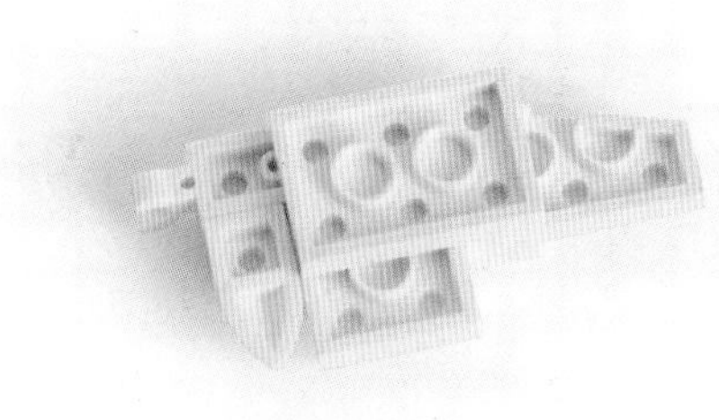

STEP 24: Secure the plates by adding a 2 x 3 white plate.

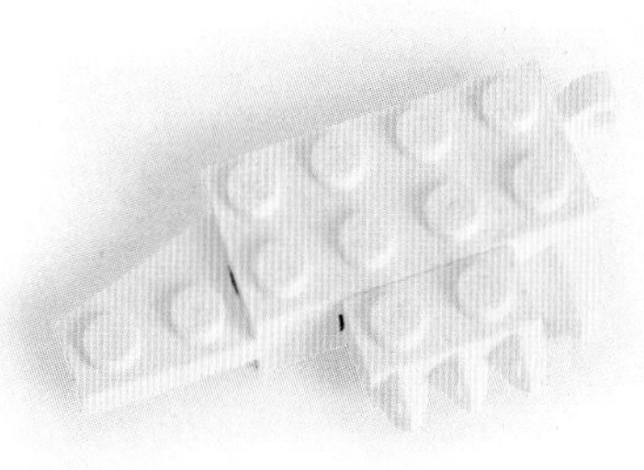

STEP 25: Turn the wing over and add a 1 x 2 white plate with three claws.

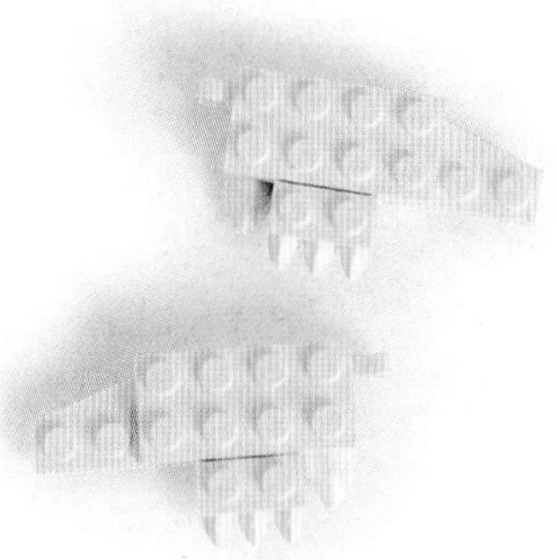

STEP 26: Build a second wing that is a mirror image of the first.

STEP 27: Attach the wings to the handles on the side of the body, and your griffin is complete!

BUILDING TIP

A minifigure can ride on the back of the griffin. They can't attach to the griffin, but they can sit on top. If you want them to attach to the griffin's back, you can replace a tan curved slope in step 13 with a plate.

The griffin and the terrible witch are, of course, enemies. Pretend that your griffin is defending the baby dragons from the witch and her schemes!

FAIRYTALE CREATURES

CREATIVE CHALLENGE

Fairytale Forest is full of all sorts of creatures, both big and small. Grab your bricks and create some adorable baby dragons with a nest. You can make them any color you choose! Create a funny baby troll, and then build a little owl and the cutest tiny mouse. Build a frog and add a crown to make him the frog prince. Which fairytale creature will be your favorite?

BABY DRAGONS

KEY ELEMENTS

DRAGON BODY

Note: The bricks shown are red, but you can use any color.

1—2 x 3 plate
2—1 x 4 plates
3—1 x 2 plates
2—1 x 2 plates with one stud on top (jumper plate)
1—2 x 2 plate
1—1 x 1 brick
1—2 x 3 wedge plate, right
1—2 x 3 wedge plate, left
1—1 x 4 curved slope
1—1 x 1 brick with two studs on opposite sides
2—1 x 2 plates with one finger
2—eyes
2—1 x 1 white round plates

NEST

Various brown plates
Various brown bricks, 1 stud wide

EGG

2—2 x 2 white slopes, inverted
2—2 x 2 x 2 white slopes
1—2 x 4 white plate
1—2 x 2 white plate

Build a nest with dragon eggs! Use large brown plates for the bottom of the nest, and then build the sides with brown bricks and plates that are 1 stud wide.

A tiny dragon has hatched from one of the eggs!

And now there are two baby dragons! Build your dragons from any color you like.

Find the bricks shown for building a baby dragon. Green, lime green, red and blue make great dragon colors. You can also use gray or even a mix of colors.

Attach a 1 x 2 plate with one stud on top (jumper plate), a 1 x 2 plate and a 1 x 4 plate to the top of a 2 x 3 plate.

Add a 2 x 2 plate, and then attach a 1 x 1 brick to the jumper plate.

Just behind the 1 x 1 brick, add a 1 x 4 plate and another jumper plate.

Build the tail by attaching a 1 x 4 curved slope to the jumper plate. Then attach a 2 x 3 wedge plate on each side to make the wings.

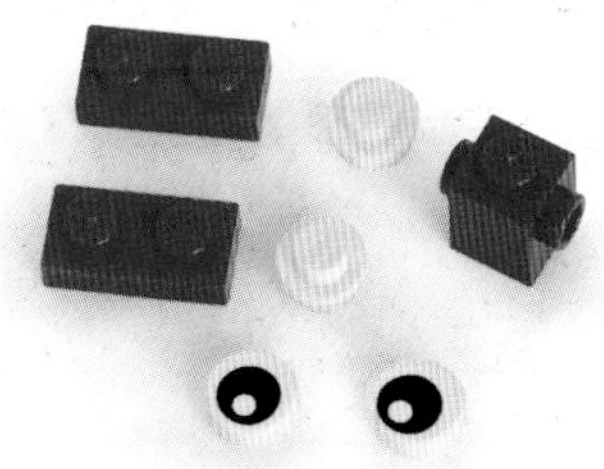

Find the bricks shown for building the baby dragon's head.

Attach a 1 x 1 brick with two studs on opposite sides and a 1 x 1 white round plate to a 1 x 2 plate.

Add a second 1 x 1 white round plate to the underside of a 1 x 2 plate. Attach this to the top of the head, and then add the eyes.

Attach the head to the body and find two 1 x 2 plates with one finger to make the feet. You can also use regular 1 x 2 plates or 1 x 2 plates that have a clip on the end.

Connect the feet to the underside of the 1 x 4 plate on each side of the body. Your baby dragon is complete! Now you'll want to build another one to fill up the dragon nest!

BABY TROLL

KEY ELEMENTS

GREEN BRICKS

5—2 x 3 plates
1—2 x 2 plate
2—1 x 3 plates
2—1 x 2 plates
2—1 x 2 slopes
2—1 x 2 curved slopes
1—1 x 3 brick
2—1 x 2 bricks
3—1 x 1 bricks
1—1 x 1 brick with a stud on the side (headlight)

WHITE BRICKS

2—2 x 3 plates
2—1 x 1 Technic bricks
1—1 x 1 brick
1—1 x 3 brick
1—1 x 1 plate

ASSORTED BRICKS

1—eye
6—1 x 1 brown round plates

Trolls may be huge and scary, but every now and then, you'll come across a baby troll in Fairytale Forest! These bumbling babies can only break twigs instead of trees, and they're quite cute . . . in an ugly sort of way.

See if you can use the pictures to build the troll's head and body. The feet are 1 x 2 slope bricks. Attach the stud on top of the slope brick to the hole in a 1 x 1 white Technic brick.

Green bricks are perfect for building baby trolls, but you can also use lime green or tan bricks.

OWL

KEY ELEMENTS

1—2 x 2 tan slope
2—1 x 2 tan bricks with two studs on the side
2—1 x 1 tan bricks with a stud on the side
1—1 x 2 tan plate with one stud on top (jumper plate)
2—1 x 1 tan slopes, 30 degree
2—eyes
1—2 x 3 brown wedge plate, right
1—2 x 3 brown wedge plate, left
1—1 x 1 bright light orange slope, 30 degree
2—1 x 1 bright light orange plates with a horizontal tooth

To build the owl's body, start with a 2 x 2 tan slope. Add two 1 x 1 tan bricks with a stud on the side. Place the bricks with the studs facing outward. Then add a 1 x 2 tan brick with two studs to hold the beak. Use two 1 x 1 bright light orange plates with a horizontal tooth to make the owl's feet. Substitute with brown, white or gray if you need to! A brown owl or a white snowy owl would look great.

The wings are made from 2 x 3 brown wedge plates. Attach each wing to the stud on the side of the body. A 1 x 1 slope (30 degree) is the perfect size for the beak. Attach it to a 1 x 2 tan plate with one stud on top (jumper plate). Now your owl is ready to perch in a tree or sit on the top of a cottage in the forest.

MOUSE

KEY ELEMENTS

DARK GRAY BRICKS

2—2 x 2 bricks

1—2 x 2 slope, inverted

1—2 x 2 slope

2—1 x 2 plates with one stud on top (jumper plates)

2—2 x 2 round plates

1—1 x 2 plate

2—1 x 2—1 x 2 brackets, inverted

4—1 x 1 round plates

ASSORTED BRICKS

2—eyes

1—1 x 1 black round plate

1—1 x 1 white cone

1—white barb/claw/horn (LEGO ID: 53451)

2—blue Technic pins, half length

4—1 x 1 light gray round tiles

Use the pictures to create the cutest mouse with an adorable face. The eyes are attached to the 2 x 2 round plates used as ears. Give him a little black nose attached to a 1 x 2 plate with one stud on top.

Build the mouse's body. Each leg is a 1 x 1 dark gray round plate and a 1 x 1 light gray round tile. The legs are attached to 1 x 2—1 x 2 inverted brackets with the smooth side of the tile facing downward.

FROG

KEY ELEMENTS

GREEN BRICKS

2—2 x 4 plates

1—2 x 2 plate

1—1 x 2 plate

1—1 x 2 brick

1—1 x 2 plate with one stud on top (jumper plate)

4—2 x 2 corner plates

2—2 x 1 x 1⅓ curved slopes with a recessed stud

2—1 x 2 curved slopes

1—2 x 2 slope, inverted

1—2 x 3 brick with a curved end

2—1 x 1 bricks with a stud on the side (headlight)

ASSORTED BRICKS

2—eyes

1—pearl gold crown (optional)

Use the pictures to build an adorable little Frog Prince! The Frog Prince is a human prince who was turned into a frog by the terrible witch of Fairytale Forest. He needs a princess minifigure to come along and kiss him so that he can turn back into a person again!

Use 2 x 2 corner plates for the frog's hands and feet. His legs are built from curved slope bricks.

A little minifigure crown will fit perfectly on the frog's head. Attach the crown in the center of the frog's head by adding a 1 x 2 plate with one stud on top (jumper plate) to the head.

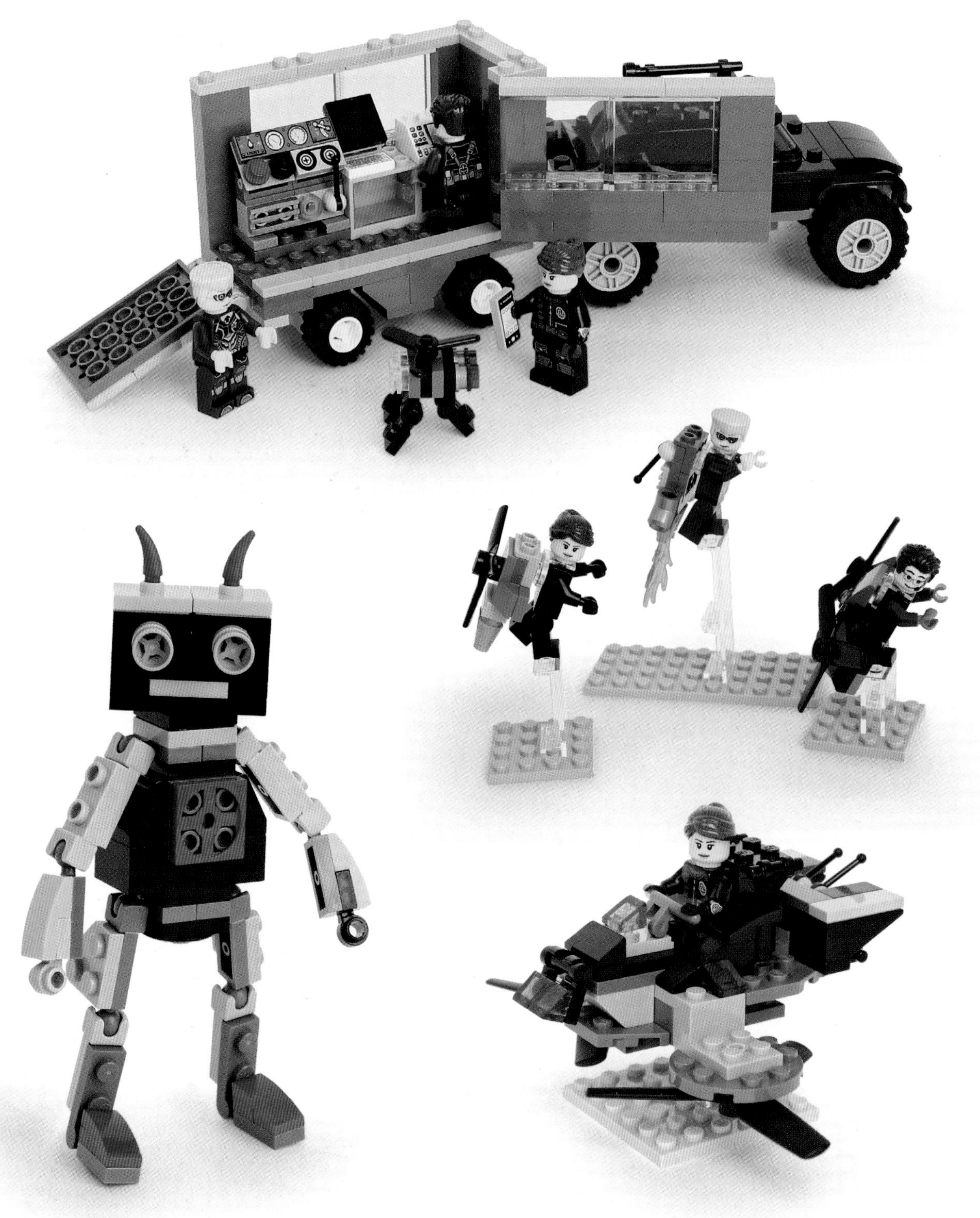

TEK AGENTS AND THE VILLAIN BOT

When there are villains, especially devious and destructive villains, someone has got to stop them. And before those villains can be stopped, someone has to have information. You know, the inside scoop on what's going on. Then they'll need to make a plan and get the right equipment for the job. Thankfully, there are TEK Agents!

TEK Agents are masters of surveillance and geniuses of defeat. With their agile drones, state-of-the-art surveillance equipment and powerful gadgets, they can go up against any villain—and come out on top!

Build the TEK Agents' headquarters, which is equipped with computers, tools and gadgets. Then design hovering speeders and jet packs for zooming around action scenes. Build a station for launching drones and an awesome surveillance trailer. With the support of their devices, the TEK Agents will be well-prepared to defeat the villain group SPYDER and their terrible Villain Bot.

AGENT HEADQUARTERS

CREATIVE CHALLENGE

TEK Agent Headquarters is the place for agents to invent gadgets, fix equipment and monitor villain activity with powerful cameras and computers. Build a workbench stocked with tools and create an area with large computer screens and keyboards. Give your headquarters a secure sliding door that opens when you turn a knob. This is the perfect home base for defeating the worst villains!

KEY ELEMENTS

2—16 x 16 tan plates

Various dark gray bricks, 1 stud wide

5—1 x 4 x 3 translucent light blue panels

1—black Technic bevel gear, 20-tooth

1—axle, 3 studs long

1—2 x 2 light gray round brick with ridges

1—1 x 2 dark gray Technic brick

2—1 x 6 light gray tiles

1—1 x 4 dark gray tile

10—2 x 4 tiles for the tops of the work surfaces

2 x 3 x 2 containers for building cabinets

Various tools

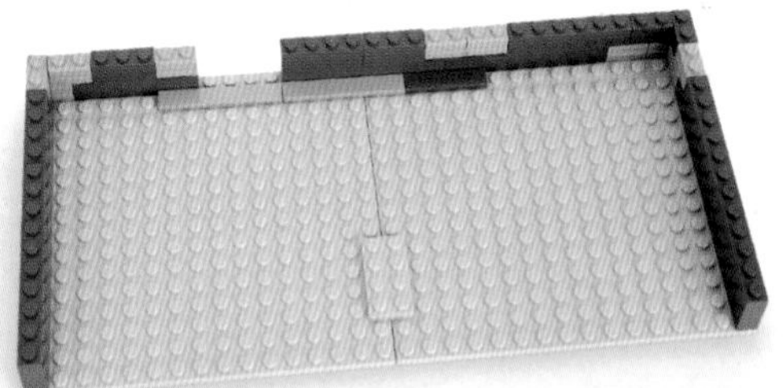

Begin building your agent headquarters by grabbing two 16 x 16 tan plates. Build walls on three sides of the building, leaving a space 4 studs wide for the door. Place two 1 x 6 tiles and one 1 x 4 tile in front of the door and to the side of the door as shown. These tiles will allow the door to slide easily.

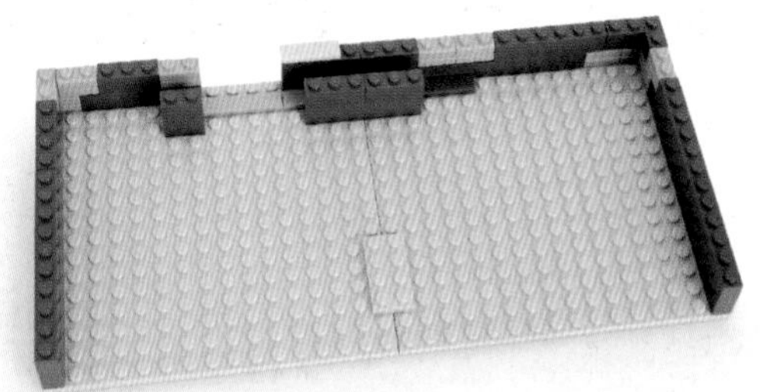

Place bricks on the other side of the tiles as shown, continuing to leave an open space for the doorway. These bricks will stabilize the door as it slides.

Build the door. The door should be six bricks high with two 1 x 4 light gray gear racks on top. If you want to build an ID scanner on the outside of the door, build a 1 x 2—1 x 2 yellow inverted bracket into the door. A simple 1 x 1 slope (30 degree) looks like an ID scanner. You can pretend that the 1 x 1 translucent light blue round tile next to it is a light that lights up when the ID scan is successful and the door has been unlocked!

For the mechanism on the door, you'll need a 20-tooth bevel gear, an axle (3 studs long), a 1 x 2 dark gray Technic brick and a 2 x 2 light gray round brick. If you have one with ridges on it, that will look awesome.

Slide the gear, the Technic brick and the 2 x 2 round brick onto the axle.

Build up the walls of the agent headquarters. Put the door in place on its track of tiles. Attach the gear assembly to the wall behind the door so that the teeth of the gear mesh with the teeth on the gear racks. The wall that holds the gear assembly needs to be seven bricks and one plate high. Add windows to the building if you want.

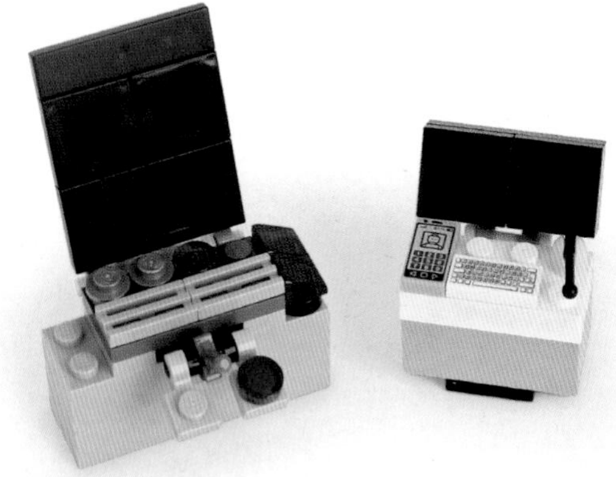

As you build the walls, build a 1 x 4 dark gray brick with four studs on the side into the wall. This will hold the tools for the workbench. If you have enough tiles, it looks great to add a row of tiles around the top of the building.

Once your building is complete, start constructing a computer station. The large screen can be used for video conferences with agents in remote locations. Gather fun accessories to add to your computer area, such as tiles with computer keyboards, buttons and dials.

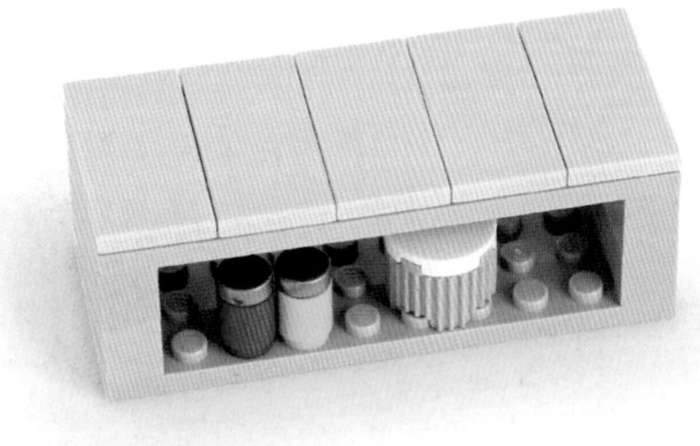

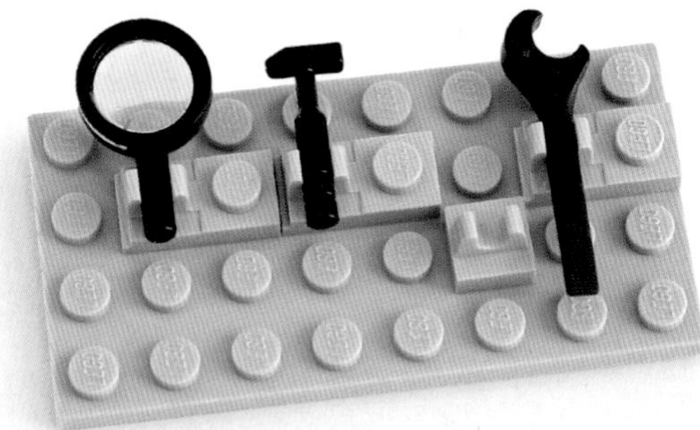

Make a workbench with a shelf underneath for supplies. If you have enough 2 x 4 tiles, cover the workbench with tiles. If not, it works just fine to leave it with the studs exposed. The workbench is built from two 4 x 10 light gray plates. There are two 1 x 4 bricks on each side.

Use a 4 x 8 plate as a pegboard for tools. Gather wrenches, hammers and even a magnifying glass, if you have one. Plates with clips are perfect for holding the tools.

Make swivel chairs for the TEK agents to sit in while they work. Attach a chair to a 2 x 2 turntable. Then place these on top of a 2 x 2 black round brick and a 2 x 2 black round plate.

Containers (2 x 3 x 2) make great cabinets for holding extra supplies! Grab some 1 x 1 round bricks to use as bottles. You can also use the cabinets to store small tools.

Once you have your agent headquarters set up, it's time for the agents to get to work! Today, they are repairing the EYE-Cam 75-X so that it's ready for its next mission. Of course, they are also watching the computers for any messages that come in over the agent network.

Turn the knob and the teeth on the black bevel gear mesh with the gear racks that are on the top of the door. This causes the door to slide open!

DRONE LAUNCH STATION

STEP-BY-STEP

TEK Agents rely on their high-tech drones to make important deliveries and to obtain audio and visual surveillance. Their current target is SPYDER, a highly-skilled villain group attempting to destroy key buildings and cause general mayhem. In order to defeat SPYDER, the TEK Agents are going to have to find out what SPYDER is up to. Create an awesome drone and a launch station for the agents to use as they gather information!

PARTS LIST

DARK GRAY BRICKS

1—8 x 16 plate

1—2 x 4 plate

2—1 x 2 plates with one stud on top (jumper plate)

1—2 x 2 plate

4—1 x 1 dark gray slopes (30 degree)

LIGHT GRAY BRICKS

1—4 x 6 plate

1—6 x 10 plate

1—2 x 4 plate

1—2 x 4 brick

2—1 x 2 hinge bricks with a 2 x 2 hinge plate

1—1 x 2 tile, printed with gauges

1—1 x 1 tile, printed with a white and red gauge

BLACK BRICKS

1—2 x 2 tile

1—1 x 2 plate with one stud on top (jumper plate)

2—1 x 2 black plates with handles on ends

4—1 x 2 black plates with a clip on the end

1—2 x 2 black tile with pin

1—propeller

ASSORTED BRICKS

1—2 x 2 dark tan plate

2—1 x 2 dark tan plates

2—2 x 2 dark tan plates with one stud on top

1—2 x 2 tan plate with one stud on top

2—1 x 2 dark red plates

1—1 x 2 tile, printed with a keyboard

1—yellow antenna

1—1 x 2 translucent red plate

1—2 x 4 brown plate

2—1 x 2 brown bricks, log

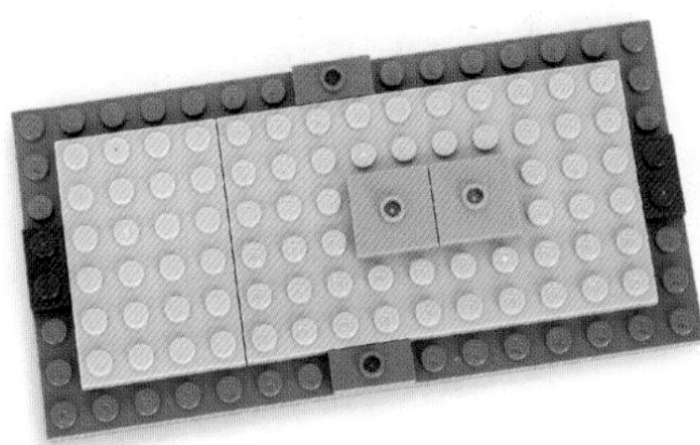

STEP 1: Use an 8 x 16 dark gray plate as the base for your drone launch station. Add a 4 x 6 light gray plate and a 6 x 10 light gray plate. Place two 1 x 2 dark red plates and two 1 x 2 dark gray plates with one stud on top (jumper plate) around the perimeter for decoration. Or substitute with any other bricks you like. Place two 2 x 2 dark tan plates with one stud on top on the light gray plate as shown.

STEP 2: Build the launch control center. Start with a 2 x 4 light gray brick. Add two 1 x 2 hinge bricks with a 2 x 2 hinge plate. Place a 2 x 2 black tile on one of them to make a computer screen. Cover the other one with tiles printed with gauges and an antenna.

STEP 3: Gather the bricks shown for building the drone.

STEP 4: Place a 2 x 2 dark gray plate and two 1 x 2 black plates with handles on the ends on top of a 2 x 4 dark gray plate.

STEP 5: Place a 1 x 2 translucent red plate on one of the black plates and a 1 x 2 black plate with one stud on top (jumper plate) on the other one.

STEP 6: Add a 2 x 2 black tile with a pin. Then look for a propeller that has a pin hole.

STEP 7: Attach the propeller to the pin. Then build the four legs of the drone. Each leg is a 1 x 2 black plate with a clip on the end and a 1 x 1 dark gray slope (30 degree).

STEP 8: Connect the legs to the body of the drone.

STEP 9: Build a package for the drone to carry. Start with a 2 x 4 brown plate. Add two 1 x 4 brown bricks (log type) and then a 2 x 4 light gray plate. Finish the top of the package with two 1 x 2 dark tan plates, a 2 x 2 dark tan plate and a 2 x 2 tan plate with one stud on top.

The drone can easily attach to the top of the package.

The drone sits on top of the two 2 x 2 dark tan plates with one stud on top. It's very easy to remove the drone and package since they are only attached by two studs.

Now it's time to launch! This package is carrying classified information to agents that are working right outside the SPYDER home base. TEK Agents have picked up signals that SPYDER is building a dangerous machine. It's imperative that they find out exactly what this machine is!

For this task, they'll launch the EYE Cam 75-X. This little drone is quick, agile and unlikely to be seen. It can detect conversations through brick and metal walls and can take high-definition video from 100 feet away. Build this mini drone using the picture as a guide. The propeller is attached to a 1 x 2 plate with a wheel holder. Agent Cody directs the EYE Cam 75-X to the roof of SPYDER's headquarters where the leaders are meeting right now.

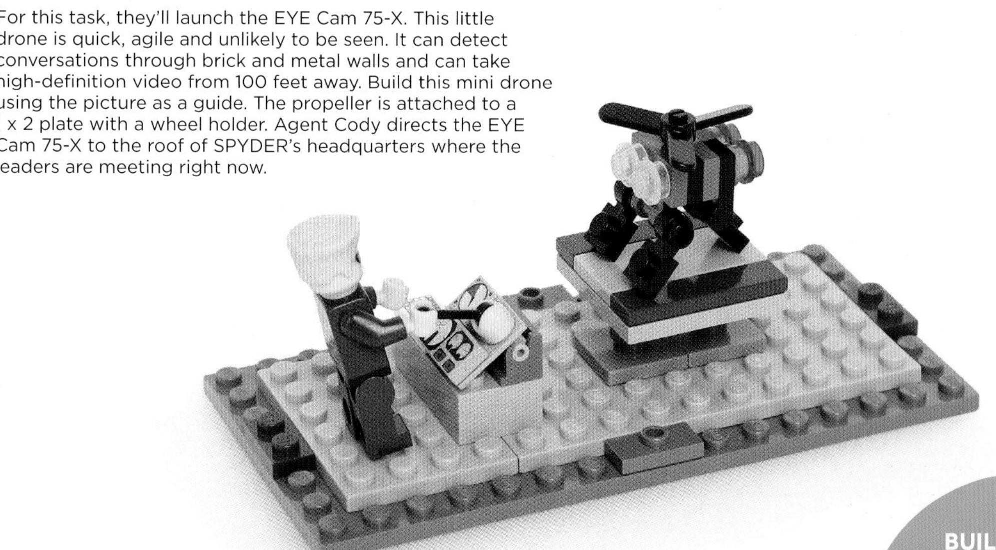

BUILDING TIP

It's easy to make a platform for the smaller drone! Attach two 1 x 1 dark gray round bricks to the dark tan plates. Then add a 4 x 4 plate. Cover the plate with tiles.

Once the drone has landed, Flora and Mitchell keep their eyes on its information screen. Apparently, SPYDER is building a highly-skilled robot. And it's a destructive robot too!

AGENT SURVEILLANCE TRAILER

STEP-BY-STEP

In addition to their drones, the TEK Agents use a lot of high-tech equipment. When they need to bring their devices to the job site, they rely on their state-of-the-art surveillance trailer to get them there. Build an awesome trailer equipped with computers, recording equipment and plenty of places to store extra gear. Then design a rugged SUV to tow the trailer and send your agents on their way!

The door of the surveillance trailer opens to make a ramp, and the side of the trailer swings open to make it easy to access the equipment inside.

PARTS LIST

DARK GRAY BRICKS

1—6 x 12 plate
1—4 x 6 plate
1—2 x 6 plate
2—2 x 4 plates
2—1 x 8 plates
2—1 x 6 plates
1—1 x 4 plate
7—1 x 2 plates
1—1 x 8 brick
2—1 x 6 bricks
5—1 x 4 bricks
3—2 x 4 bricks
1—1 x 3 brick
2—1 x 2 x 2 bricks
4—1 x 2 bricks
3—2 x 2 corner bricks
5—1 x 1 bricks
2—1 x 4 hinge plates with swivel top
4—1 x 2 slopes, inverted
2—1 x 2 grills
1—2 x 2 dish
1—1 x 1 plate with a light attachment
2—1 x 2 hinge bricks with a 2 x 2 hinge plate
1—1 x 4 tile, printed with gauges

LIGHT GRAY BRICKS

1—6 x 12 plate
1—2 x 4 plate
4—2 x 2 plates with a wheel holder
1—1 x 6 plate
1—1 x 4 plate
1—1 x 2 plate
2—1 x 2 plates with a handle on the side
2—1 x 2 plates with clips on the side
1—1 x 4 brick with four studs
1—1 x 2 hinge brick with a 2 x 2 hinge plate
2—2 x 4 tiles
1—1 x 6 tile
1—1 x 4 tile
1—1 x 2 tile
4—1 x 4 plates with two studs
1—2 x 2 dish
1—4 x 4 dish
1—pneumatic T piece
1—2 x 2 plate with a tow ball socket
1—1 x 2 tile, printed with black tape reels

ASSORTED BRICKS

2—2 x 3 x 2 lime green containers
4—1 x 4 x 3 translucent light blue panels
2—1 x 4 medium azure tiles
1—1 x 2 medium azure tile
2—1 x 2 dark tan plates with one stud on top (jumper plate)
1—1 x 4 yellow tile
1—1 x 2 pearl dark gray grill
1—2 x 2 white slope, printed with a computer screen
1—1 x 2 white tile, printed with a keyboard
1—2 x 2 black tile
1—1 x 1 black round plate
2—2 x 2 bright light orange plates
2—1 x 1 translucent orange round plates
1—1 x 1 red round plate
1—1 x 1 translucent green round tile
1—yellow antenna
4—wheels

PERISCOPE

1—1 x 1 dark gray brick with studs on opposite sides
1—1 x 1 dark gray brick with a stud on the side
1—1 x 1 dark gray brick
2—1 x 1 light gray plates
2—1 x 1 clear round tiles
1—light gray pneumatic T piece

STEP 1: Begin building the trailer by finding a 6 x 12 dark gray plate and three 2 x 4 dark gray bricks.

STEP 2: Turn the plate upside down and attach the three 2 x 4 bricks as shown.

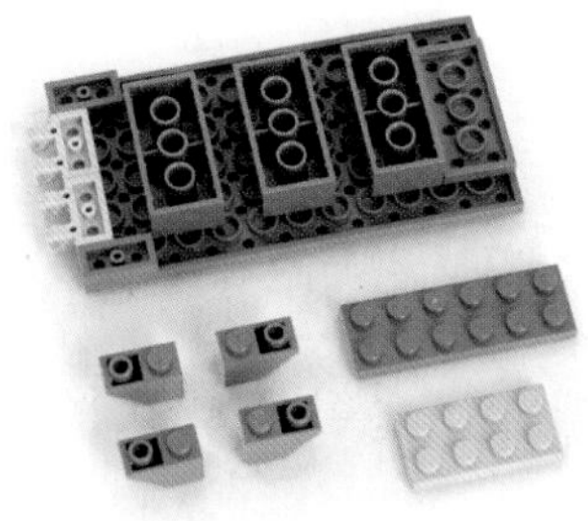

STEP 3: Add two 1 x 2 dark gray plates and two 1 x 2 light gray plates with clips on the side on the back end of the trailer. Add a 2 x 4 dark gray plate on the front end. Then find the bricks shown.

STEP 4: Place two 1 x 2 inverted slopes on each side of the trailer. Then attach a 2 x 6 plate to the underside of them. Add a 2 x 4 light gray plate at the front of the trailer. Then find a 1 x 6 light gray plate and a 2 x 2 light gray plate with a tow ball socket.

STEP 5: Use the 1 x 6 light gray plate to secure the plates on the back end of the trailer. Add the 2 x 2 plate with a tow ball socket on the front end.

STEP 6: Assemble the wheels. Use a 2 x 2 bright light orange plate to connect two 2 x 2 light gray plates with a wheel holder. Attach the wheels. Then build a second set of wheels.

STEP 7: Attach the wheels to the dark gray 2 x 4 bricks on the underside of the trailer.

STEP 8: Turn the trailer right side up. Add one 1 x 2 medium azure tile and two 1 x 4 medium azure tiles as shown. Or substitute any color tiles.

STEP 9: Place two 1 x 2 dark gray plates next to the tiles. Then add dark gray bricks on the front and side of the trailer.

STEP 10: Find two 1 x 8 dark gray plates, one 1 x 2 dark gray plate and a 1 x 4 hinge plate for building the opening side door of the trailer.

STEP 11: Attach the plates and hinge plate as shown. Then find a 1 x 4 dark gray brick, two 1 x 6 dark gray plates and two 1 x 2 dark gray plates.

STEP 12: Add the 1 x 4 brick to the side door. Then add two 1 x 6 plates next to it. Place two 1 x 2 plates on top of the end of the hinge plate. Find a 1 x 4 dark gray plate and another 1 x 4 dark gray hinge plate.

STEP 13: Fill in the door by adding the 1 x 4 dark gray plate and the hinge plate.

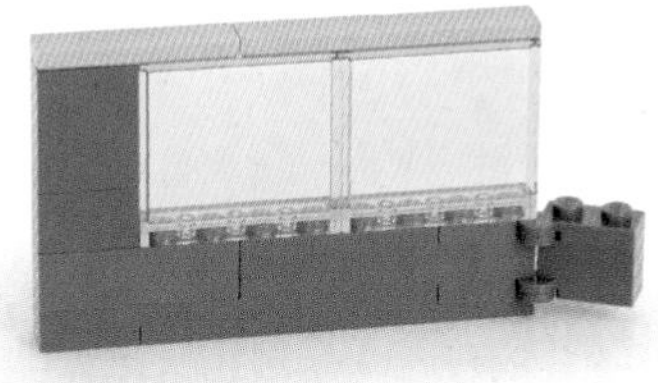

STEP 14: Add two 1 x 4 x 3 translucent light blue panels to the door. Then add a 1 x 2 dark gray brick and a 1 x 2 x 2 dark gray brick. Place a row of light gray tiles across the top. These will allow the side door to easily swing open.

STEP 15: Attach the side door to the surveillance trailer.

STEP 16: Finish building the other two walls so that they match the height of the side door. Place four 1 x 4 light gray plates with two studs around the top of the trailer. These will make it possible to attach the roof and also remove it easily for play.

STEP 17: Now it's time to build some equipment to go inside the trailer. Find a 2 x 4 dark gray plate and place one 1 x 2 dark tan plate with one stud on top (jumper plate) on either end. Then find the bricks shown.

STEP 18: Place a 1 x 4 light gray brick with four studs on top of the dark tan plates. Then add two 1 x 2 hinge bricks with a 2 x 2 hinge plate.

STEP 19: Add tiles printed with gauges, a lever and 1 x 1 round plates to look like lights. Get creative with the tiles and pieces you have.

STEP 20: Place your surveillance equipment inside the trailer. Add two 2 x 3 containers and place computers on top of them.

STEP 21: Gather the bricks shown for building the back door.

STEP 22: Attach two 2 x 4 light gray tiles and one 1 x 4 yellow tile to the 4 x 6 plate. Then add two 1 x 2 light gray plates with a handle on the side. Place two 1 x 1 translucent orange round tiles and a 1 x 2 light gray tile on top of them.

STEP 23: Use the clips on the trailer to attach the door.

STEP 24: Place a 6 x 12 light gray plate on the top of the trailer as the roof. You'll need to add a 1 x 4 light gray plate on the underside of the roof to fill in the gap at the top of the back door. Place two 1 x 2 dark gray grills on the roof.

STEP 25: Gather the bricks shown for building a satellite dish on top of the trailer.

STEP 26: Attach a 1 x 1 dark gray plate with a light attachment to a 1 x 1 dark gray brick. Insert a pneumatic T piece into the hole on the plate.

STEP 27: Slide a 2 x 2 light gray dish onto the T piece. Then attach a 2 x 2 dark gray dish to the center of a 4 x 4 light gray dish.

STEP 28: Attach the larger dish to the 2 x 2 light gray dish.

STEP 29: Place the satellite dish on the roof of the surveillance trailer, and your trailer is complete!

Now design a vehicle to pull your trailer. It can be anything you like! A rugged SUV is a great choice since it will have the towing power to pull the trailer. Use the pictures to build an SUV like this one or create your own design.

Be sure to add a 2 x 2 plate with a tow ball on the back of your vehicle so that you can hook up the trailer. Also make sure that the height of the tow ball matches the height of the socket on the trailer.

Here's another fun accessory to build for your surveillance trailer. Make a periscope! A periscope is a device that lets agents see over the tops of walls or around corners.

Gather the bricks shown for building the periscope.

Insert the T piece into one of the studs on a 1 x 1 dark gray brick with studs on opposite sides.

Place a 1 x 1 light gray plate on the top of the dark gray brick. Then add a 1 x 1 clear round tile. Attach a 1 x 1 dark gray brick to the stud on the opposite side of the dark gray brick.

Finish up the periscope by adding a 1 x 1 dark gray brick with a stud on the side. Add a 1 x 1 light gray plate and a 1 x 1 clear round tile. Your agents can hang onto the T piece to use the periscope.

HOVER SPEEDERS

STEP-BY-STEP

When an emergency situation is unfolding, TEK Agents don't have time for vehicles that are confined to the road. Zooming through the city on a hover speeder is a much better option! Build some awesome hover speeders with handlebars like a motorcycle and powerful rocket engines.

PARTS LIST

DARK GRAY BRICKS

1—4 x 6 wedge plate, cut corners
1—2 x 8 plate
1—2 x 6 plate
2—4 x 4 round plates
1—2 x 4 wedge plate
1—1 x 4 tile
1—2 x 4 brick
1—1 x 2 plate with bar handles
1—handlebars

LIGHT GRAY BRICKS

2—5 x 2 x 1⅓ brackets
1—2 x 2 slope, inverted
1—1 x 2 plate with a clip on top
2—1 x 3 tiles
1—1 x 2 plate with door rail
2—antennas
2—Technic pins without friction ridges

BLACK BRICKS

1—2 x 2 plate
2—1 x 2 plates
5—1 x 2 plates with a handle on the side, free ends
1—1 x 2 plate with a handle on the side
2—2 x 3 slopes, inverted
2—2 x 2 slopes, inverted
1—1 x 2 plate with clips on the side
2—1 x 2 plates with one stud on top, jumper plate
1—1 x 2—1 x 2 bracket, inverted
2—1 x 2 curved slopes
2—1 x 3 slopes
1—1 x 2 brick
2—1 x 1 round bricks
1—1 x 2 slope, 30 degree
2—propellers, 9-stud diameter

ASSORTED BRICKS

2—1 x 2 dark red tiles
3—1 x 1 translucent black slopes, 30 degree
2—1 x 1 translucent red slopes, 30 degree
2—1 x 1 translucent red round plates
1—1 x 2 translucent red grill
1—1 x 2 translucent yellow plate
3—1 x 1 translucent yellow plates

STEP 1: Gather the bricks shown for building the base of the hover speeder.

STEP 2: Place a 2 x 2 black inverted slope, two 1 x 2 black plates, a 2 x 4 dark gray brick and a 2 x 4 dark gray wedge plate on top of a 2 x 6 dark gray plate.

STEP 3: Add a 1 x 2 dark gray plate with bar handles and a 2 x 2 light gray inverted slope.

STEP 4: Place two 5 x 2 x 1⅓ light gray brackets on the speeder. Then add a 4 x 6 dark gray wedge plate.

STEP 5: Attach a 2 x 8 dark gray plate so that it runs down the center of the speeder. Then find the bricks shown.

STEP 6: Place two 1 x 2 black plates with one stud on top (jumper plates) and a 1 x 1 black plate with clips on the side on the front of the speeder. Then add a 1 x 2 light gray plate with a clip on top and a 1 x 2 black slope (30 degree).

STEP 7: Attach handlebars to the light gray clip. Then add a 1 x 1 translucent yellow plate and a 1 x 1 translucent black slope (30 degree).

STEP 8: On each side of the speeder, add a 1 x 2 black plate with a handle (free ends), a 1 x 1 translucent yellow plate and a 1 x 3 black slope.

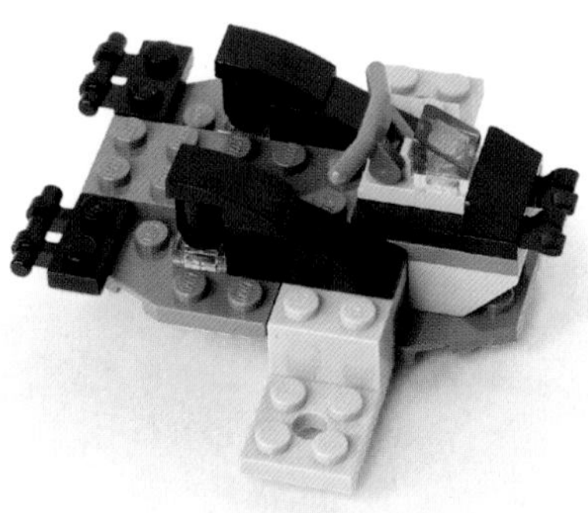

STEP 9: Place a 1 x 1 black round brick and a 1 x 2 black curved slope on each side of the speeder.

STEP 10: Place a 1 x 2 black brick just behind the driver's seat. Then place a 1 x 2 light gray plate with door rail on the back of the speeder.

STEP 11: Find a 1 x 4 dark gray tile, a 1 x 2 black plate with a handle (free ends), a 2 x 2 black plate and two light gray antennas.

STEP 12: Place the 1 x 2 plate with a handle on top of the 2 x 2 plate. Then add the 1 x 4 dark gray tile and two antennas.

STEP 13: Place two 2 x 3 black inverted slopes on the back of the speeder. Add the antenna assembly in between them. Then gather the bricks shown.

STEP 14: Add two 1 x 3 light gray tiles and two 1 x 2 dark red tiles to the back of the speeder. Place a 1 x 1 translucent red slope (30 degree) on each side. Then gather the bricks shown.

STEP 15: Place a 2 x 2 black inverted slope on the speeder just behind the driver's seat. Then place two 1 x 2 black plates with a handle (free ends) on top of it. Then gather the bricks shown.

STEP 16: Attach two 1 x 1 translucent black slopes (30 degree) to a 1 x 2 black plate with a handle on the side. Connect this to the clips on the front of the speeder. Build the propellers by using a light gray pin to connect a propeller (9-stud diameter) to a 4 x 4 dark gray plate.

STEP 17: Connect the 4 x 4 dark gray round plate to the light gray bracket on the speeder. The pin should go through the hole in the bracket. Build one of these propellers on each side of the speeder.

STEP 18: Gather the bricks shown for building taillights on the speeder.

STEP 19: Attach two 1 x 1 translucent red round plates to the underside of a 1 x 2—1 x 2 black inverted bracket. Then add a 1 x 2 translucent yellow plate and a 1 x 2 translucent red grill.

STEP 20: Turn the speeder upside down and connect the taillights to the underside of the 4 x 6 dark gray wedge plate. Your hover speeder is complete!

When a call comes in, Agent Flora is ready to zoom off to assess the situation!

BUILDING TIP

Make your speeder look like it's flying by elevating it with two 1 x 2 clear bricks.

Now use the photos to construct Agent Mitchell's speeder. Build it in gray, black and orange, or chose your own favorite colors.

This speeder has adjustable fins on either side as well as an adjustable tail. Use black mechanical arms on the back to create engines.

The base of this speeder is a 2 x 6 plate. Build 1 x 2 plates with a handle on the side into your speeder so that you can attach the adjustable fins. Then your speeder is ready to fly! It's an awesome way to get around town, especially when every second counts!

TEK AGENT JET PACKS

CREATIVE CHALLENGE

Your agents can fly high in the sky if they travel by jet pack! These personal transportation devices are useful for emergency situations where speed and elevation are extremely important. Use your creativity and the bricks you have to design cool jet packs with rocket engines, propellers, levers, buttons and more!

KEY ELEMENTS

2—1 x 2 black plates with a handle on the end

2—1 x 1 black plates with a clip

1—1 x 2 black plate

2—2 x 2 black tiles with a pin

2—black propellers, 5-stud diameter

1—2 x 2 dark gray curved slope

1—2 x 3 dark gray wedge plate, right

1—2 x 3 dark gray wedge plate, left

1—1 x 1 translucent green round plate

1—1 x 1 translucent red round plate

1—clear minifigure neck bracket with two back studs

STEP 1: Let's build a double propeller jet pack! Place two 1 x 1 black plates with a clip on top of a 1 x 2 black plate. Then find two 1 x 2 black plates with a handle on the end.

STEP 2: Attach the plates with handles to the clips. Then add a 2 x 2 dark gray curved slope.

STEP 3: Use a 2 x 2 black tile with a pin to attach a 2 x 3 dark gray wedge plate to each wing.

STEP 4: Attach a propeller to each black pin. Then add a 1 x 1 translucent green round plate and a 1 x 1 translucent red round plate.

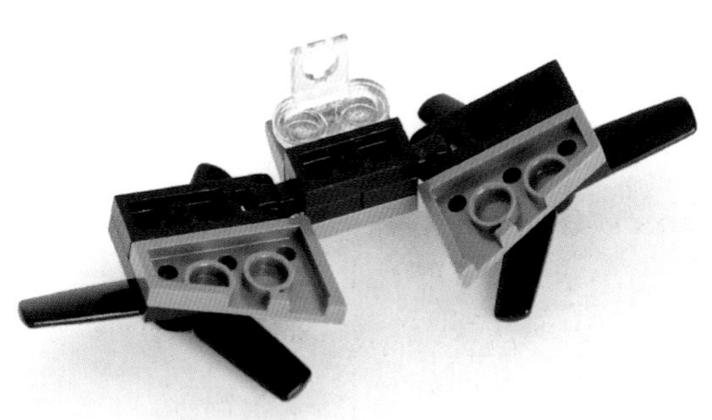

STEP 5: Turn the jet pack over and attach a clear minifigure neck bracket with two back studs. To attach it to the minifigure, you'll need to remove their head, slide the neck bracket over their neck post and then attach the head again.

The completed jet pack has a lot of power for long-distance flights!

Now try building a rocket engine jet pack.

Gather the bricks shown for building the jet pack.

Attach a 2 x 2 dark gray plate to two 1 x 2—1 x 2 dark gray inverted brackets. Add a 1 x 4 plate with angled tubes.

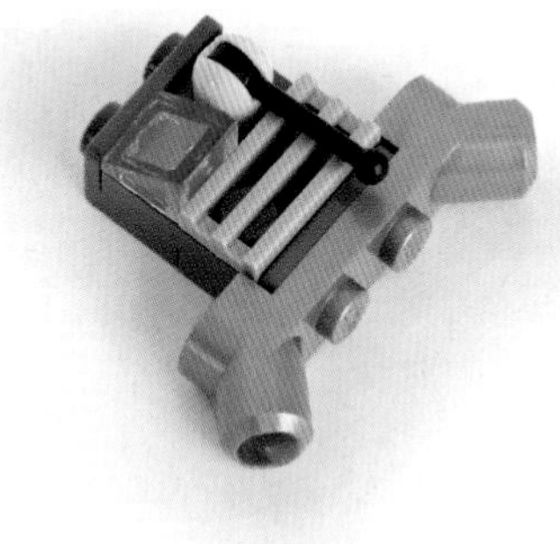

Finish up the jet pack by adding a 1 x 2 light gray grill, a 1 x 1 translucent light blue slope (30 degree) and a yellow antenna.

Add some rocket engines with flames to your jet pack! Use 1 x 1 orange cones to hold the flames.

Now try modifying the design! This jet pack has a similar base to the rocket engine jet pack. Add a 1 x 2 dark gray plate and a 1 x 4 blue plate to two 1 x 2 light gray inverted brackets. Then add a 2 x 2 blue tile with a pin and attach a propeller.

THE VILLAIN BOT

STEP-BY-STEP

The TEK Agents knew that SPYDER was up to no good, and they were certainly right about that. The tech team at SPYDER had been creating a terrible Villain Bot capable of exploding cars and destroying buildings! Build a posable Villain Bot with an impressive laser gun. Then create crazy scenes with your bot causing havoc around the city!

PARTS LIST

BLACK BRICKS

1—2 x 4 brick

3—2 x 4 plates

3—2 x 2 plates

1—1 x 4 plate

3—1 x 2 plates

2—2 x 2 plates with a wheel holder

1—2 x 2 plate with rounded bottom

1—1 x 1 plate with a light attachment

2—1 x 2 tiles with bar handle

1—2 x 2 turntable

DARK GRAY BRICKS

1—2 x 2 brick

1—1 x 2—2 x 2 bracket

1—1 x 2—1 x 2 bracket, inverted

4—1 x 2 plates with a ball on the side

2—1 x 2 plates with a ball on the end

2—1 x 2 plates with a ball and a socket

2—1 x 2 plates with a handle on the end

2—1 x 2 plates with a clip on the end

1—1 x 2 plate

1—2 x 2 corner plate

1—1 x 2 plate with one stud on top (jumper plate)

LIGHT GRAY BRICKS

6—1 x 2 plates with a socket on the end

1—2 x 2 plate

2—2 x 2 wedge plates, cut corner

1—1 x 1 plate with a light attachment

2—wheels with a hole for a wheel holder

2—2 x 2 plates with a wheel holder

1—bar, 1 stud long with 1 x 1 round plate with hollow stud

ASSORTED BRICKS

2—2 x 2 lime green plates with one stud on top

2—1 x 2 lime green curved slopes

1—1 x 2 lime green plate

2—1 x 1 red plates

2—1 x 2 red curved slopes

2—red horns

1—2 x 2 red turntable base

1—1 x 1 translucent red round plate

1—2 x 2 translucent red dish

1—1 x 1 silver cone

1—2 x 2 white plate

1—1 x 1 white round brick

1—1 x 2 translucent blue tile

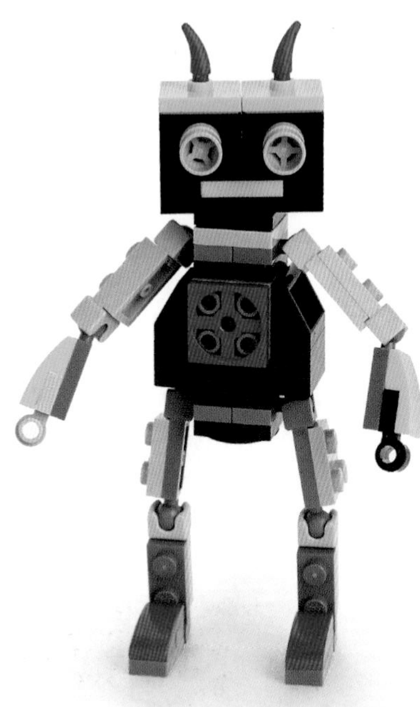

STEP 1: Build the robot's head. Place three 1 x 2 black plates and a 1 x 2 lime green plate on top of a 2 x 4 black plate.

STEP 2: Find a 2 x 4 black plate, a 1 x 4 black plate and two 2 x 2 black plates with wheel holders.

STEP 3: Place the 2 x 4 black plate on the head, and then add the 1 x 4 black plate.

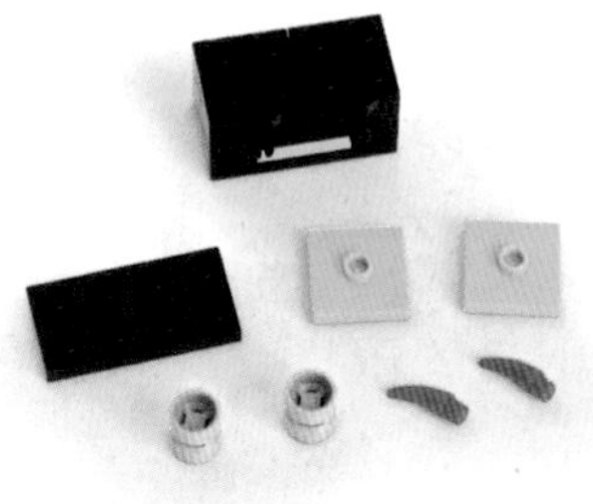

STEP 4: Attach two 2 x 2 black plates with wheel holders to the head. Then find a 2 x 4 black plate, two 2 x 2 lime green plates with one stud on top, two red horns and two light gray wheels with holes for wheel holders.

STEP 5: Place the two 2 x 2 lime green plates with one stud on top of the head. Use the studs to hold the red horns. Then attach the light gray wheels to the wheel holders. These will be the robot's eyes.

STEP 6: Gather the bricks shown for building the robot's body.

STEP 7: Attach a 2 x 2 dark gray brick and two 1 x 2 black tiles with a bar handle to a 2 x 4 black brick. Find a 1 x 2 dark gray plate, a 1 x 2—2 x 2 dark gray bracket and a 2 x 2 red turntable base.

STEP 8: Place the bracket on the body of the robot, and then place the 1 x 2 dark gray plate just behind it. Attach the 2 x 2 red turntable base to the bracket.

STEP 9: Add a 2 x 2 black plate to the body. Then add two 1 x 2 dark gray plates with a ball on the side. Find a 2 x 2 black turntable and a 2 x 2 light gray plate.

STEP 10: Place the 2 x 2 light gray plate and the 2 x 2 black turntable on top of the body. The turntable will allow the head to rotate.

STEP 11: Find two 1 x 2 dark gray plates with a ball on the side, two 2 x 2 black plates and a 2 x 2 black plate with a rounded bottom.

STEP 12: Place a 2 x 2 black plate on the underside of the body. Then add two 1 x 2 dark gray plates with a ball on the side and another 2 x 2 black plate. Lastly, add a 2 x 2 black plate with a rounded bottom.

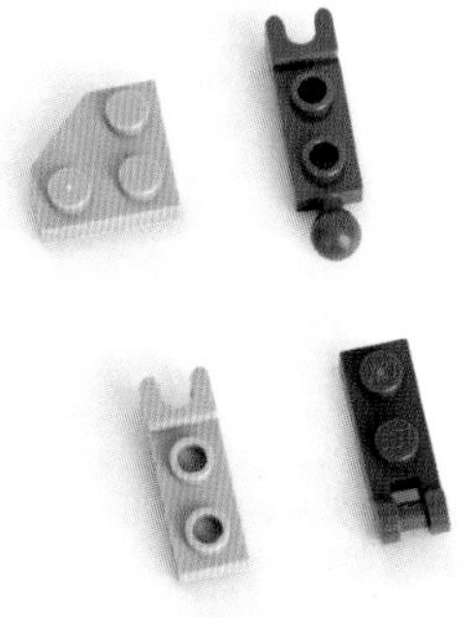

STEP 13: Gather the bricks shown for building one of the robot's legs.

STEP 14: Assemble the leg by attaching a 1 x 2 dark gray plate with a ball and a socket to a 1 x 2 light gray plate with a socket on the end. Add a 2 x 2 light gray wedge plate (cut corners) and a 1 x 2 dark gray plate with a handle on the end. Then build a foot by attaching a 1 x 2 red curved slope and a 1 x 1 red plate to a 1 x 2 dark gray plate with a clip on the end.

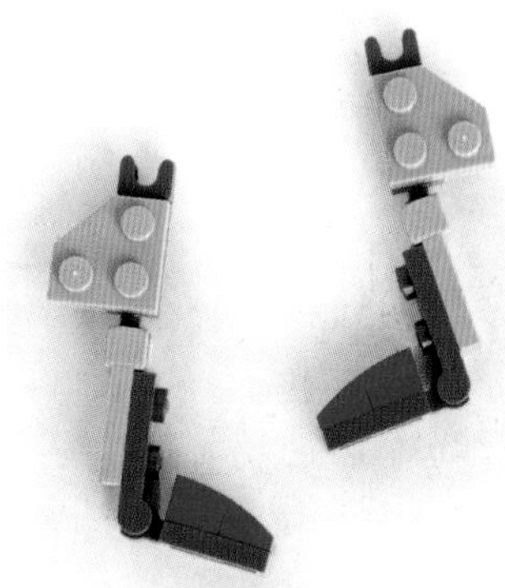

STEP 15: Repeat steps 13 and 14 again to build a second leg. Attach the feet to the legs using the clips.

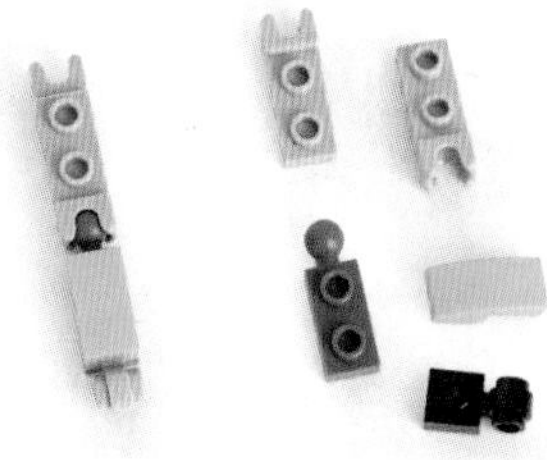

STEP 16: Build two robot arms. Each arm has two 1 x 2 light gray plates with a socket on the end, one 1 x 2 dark gray plate with a ball on the end, a 1 x 2 lime green curved slope and a 1 x 1 plate with a light attachment.

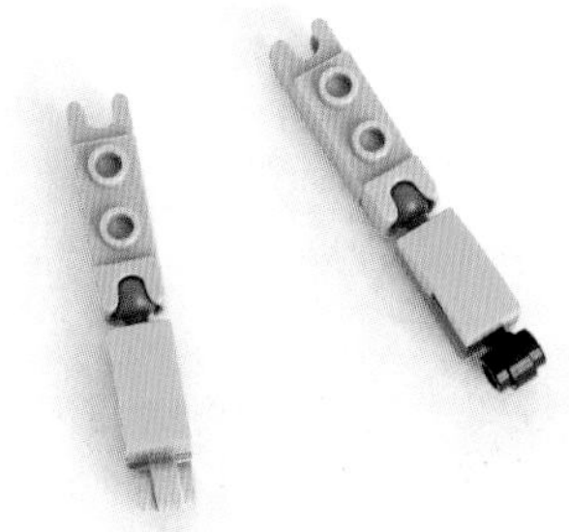

STEP 17: Assemble the arms as shown. The hands (the 1 x 1 plates with a light attachment) can be the same color as each other or use one gray and one black as pictured.

STEP 18: Attach the arms and legs to the ball joints, and your robot is complete!

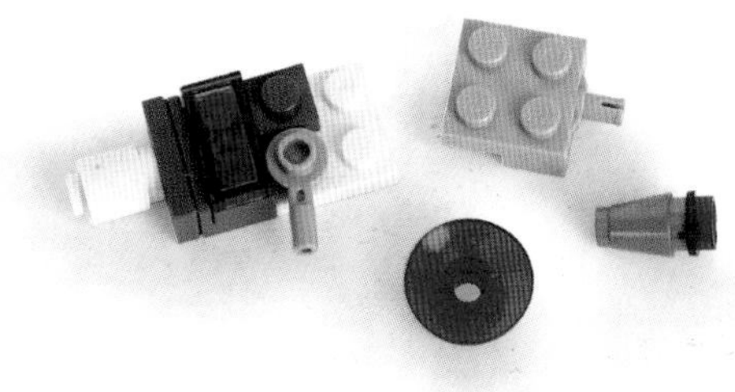

Now design a powerful gun for your robot! A light gray bar with a 1 x 1 round plate makes the perfect handle for your robot to hold onto. It can slide right into the opening in his hand.

Use a 2 x 2 translucent red dish and a 1 x 1 translucent red round plate to make the gun look like a laser. A 2 x 2 light gray plate with a wheel holder will keep the handle in place and also provide a way to attach the red dish and silver cone. Once you've got your weapon built, it's time to set up some scenes!

Mrs. Clark and her son Reid were eating a nice pizza lunch at Joe's Pizza Café. Little did they know that SPYDER had released their awful villain bot . . . and he was out in the street! Pointing his laser gun directly at their car!

Suddenly, they heard the terrible sound of an explosion. They gasped in horror as their car (what was left of it) went up in flames!

BUILDING TIP

Create the effects of an explosion by taking a car apart and adding flames! Use 1 x 1 translucent orange cones to hold the flames.

Mrs. Clark pulled out her phone and called the TEK Agents. She knew that whatever bizarre thing was going on, the TEK Agents would be able to solve it! Within minutes, agents were arriving by jet pack and hover speeder.

"We're already on this," Agent Cody assured them. "This is the work of SPYDER. We knew they were working on this villain bot . . . we just didn't know quite where they would release it. But don't worry, we'll take him down. And we'll get your car replaced too!"

AMAZING IDEA

Create more scenes with the Villain Bot! Try building a tall building, and then give it a huge, jagged hole in the side where the Villain Bot blasted it with his laser.

THE HERO BOT

CREATIVE CHALLENGE

Once the TEK Agents realized the magnitude of what they were up against with SPYDER's Villain Bot, they knew they had no other choice but to build their own bot. One that would be stronger, faster and capable of bringing that terrible robot down! Using some of the same building techniques as the villain bot, design your own hero bot. Then give him a powerful weapon for defeating the enemy!

KEY ELEMENTS

4—1 x 2 dark gray plates with a ball on the side

2—1 x 2 dark gray plates with a ball on the end

2—1 x 2 dark gray plates with a ball and a socket

2—1 x 2 dark gray plates with a clip on the end

6—1 x 2 light gray plates with a socket on the end

2—1 x 2 light gray curved slopes

2—1 x 1 light gray round plate

Various bricks and plates for customizing the robot's body

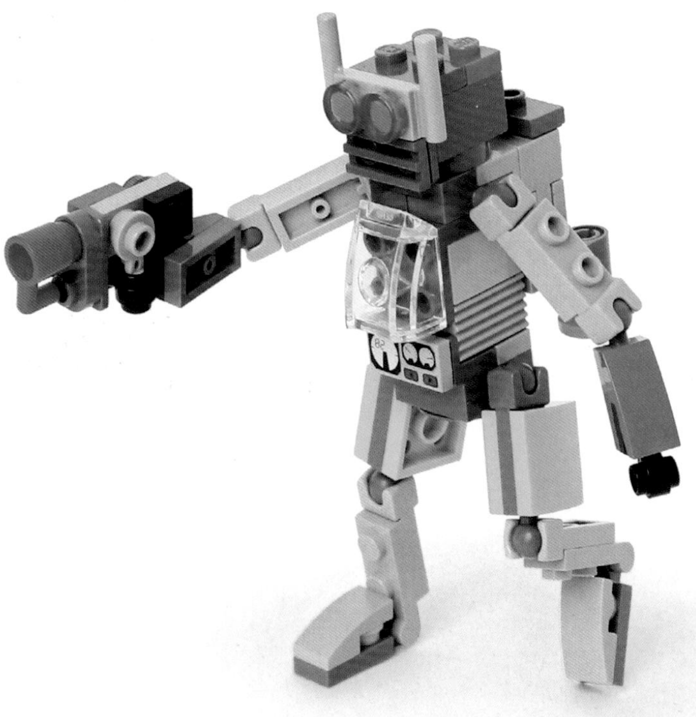

Use the pictures and what you learned about robots from the Villain Bot instructions (page 169) to create a Hero Bot! This robot has a built-in jet pack for quick getaways. Attach a 1 x 2—1 x 2 bracket to the back of the robot's neck. Then attach the jet pack to the bracket.

The Hero Bot needs a powerful gun, of course! Use common bricks in new ways to create an awesome-looking weapon. For example, the barrel of this gun is a coffee mug!

Like the Villain Bot, a light gray bar with a 1 x 1 round plate makes it easy for the robot to hold the gun.

Once your hero bot is complete, it's time for a showdown!

Well, well . . . what do we have here?

Thought you'd play along, huh? Well, it's too bad that your robot is just a TOY!

The TEK Agents intercepted a key piece of SPYDER communication, alerting them to the fact that SPYDER would be testing improvements to their robot at the old downtown parking lot at 7:00 pm. By 7:01, the TEK Agents were swooping in with their Hero Bot! Both bots instinctively knew it was time for battle.

Despite SPYDER's extreme confidence in their Villain Bot, the battle did not last long. And it was SPYDER, not the TEK Agents, who were carrying home their bot in pieces!

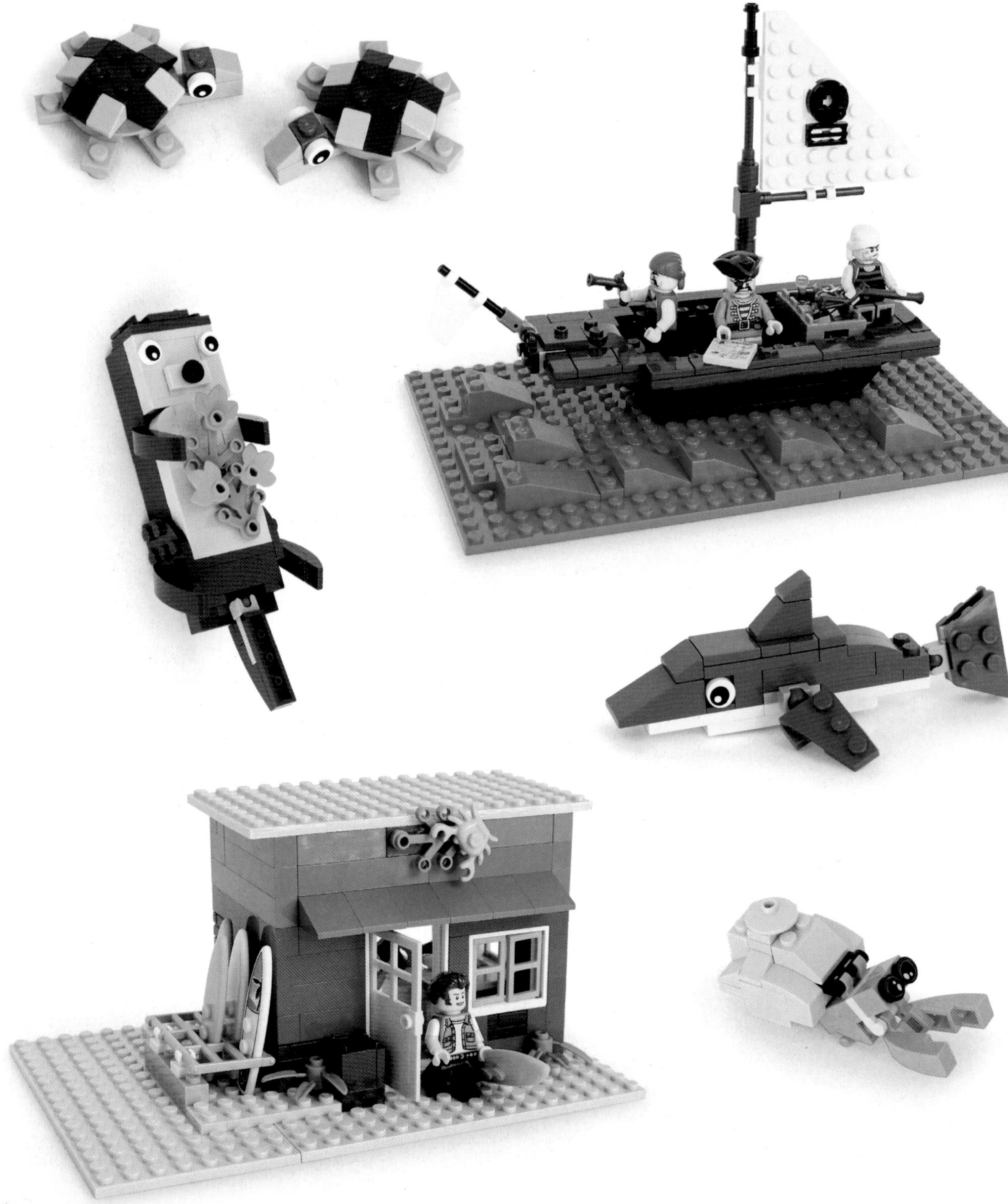

VACATION BY THE SEA

There is so much to love about going to the beach! Grab your bricks and create a seaside getaway. These projects explore all the great things about the sand and the sea. Build a day at the beach for your minifigures, complete with beach towels, sandcastles and a concession stand. Create a surf shop that supplies surfboards and life jackets. Make some ocean art by building a beautiful underwater scene with coral, fish, seaweed and more. Build a collection of ocean creatures, and then construct a pirate ship that is ready for a treasure-hunting adventure. Each of these projects will allow you to make creative changes with the bricks you have!

A DAY AT THE BEACH

CREATIVE CHALLENGE

Use your LEGO bricks to create a picture-perfect day at the beach! Your minifigures will enjoy building sandcastles, swimming in the ocean and relaxing by the shore. You can even build a fun concession stand with ice cream cones and hot dogs for sale.

KEY ELEMENTS

BEACH

1—32 x 32 tan baseplate

Various blue plates for building the water

Various 1 x 4 and 1 x 6 plates in any color for beach towels

Various tan bricks for sandcastles

Beach umbrella

2—chairs

1—4 x 4 dark gray round plate

1—2 x 2 lime green round brick

1—6 x 6 yellow inverted dish (table umbrella)

1—axle, 7 studs long

CONCESSION STAND—ASSORTED BRICKS

6—1 x 2 red slopes

6—1 x 2 white slopes

Various medium azure bricks

2—1 x 4 x 3 clear panels

1—1 x 1 lime green round tile

1—blue pin, half length

1—2 x 4 dark gray plate

1—1 x 4 dark gray brick

1—1 x 4 dark gray brick with four studs on the side

4—1 x 1 black round plates

4—1 x 2 black grills

2—1 x 2 x 3 tan slopes, inverted

1—1 x 2 brown brick

2—1 x 1 brown slopes, 30 degree

1—1 x 2 dark pink brick

2—1 x 1 dark pink slopes, 30 degree

Food items—hot dogs, ice cream cones, drinks, popsicles, etc.

CONCESSION STAND—LIGHT GRAY BRICKS

1—6 x 12 light gray plate

2—2 x 4 tiles

1—2 x 3 brick

1—1 x 2 brick

1—1 x 1 brick

1—1 x 2 x 2 brick

1—2 x 2 plate

1—1 x 1 cone

1—1 x 2 grill

1—1 x 1 brick with a stud on the side

2—1 x 1 round tiles

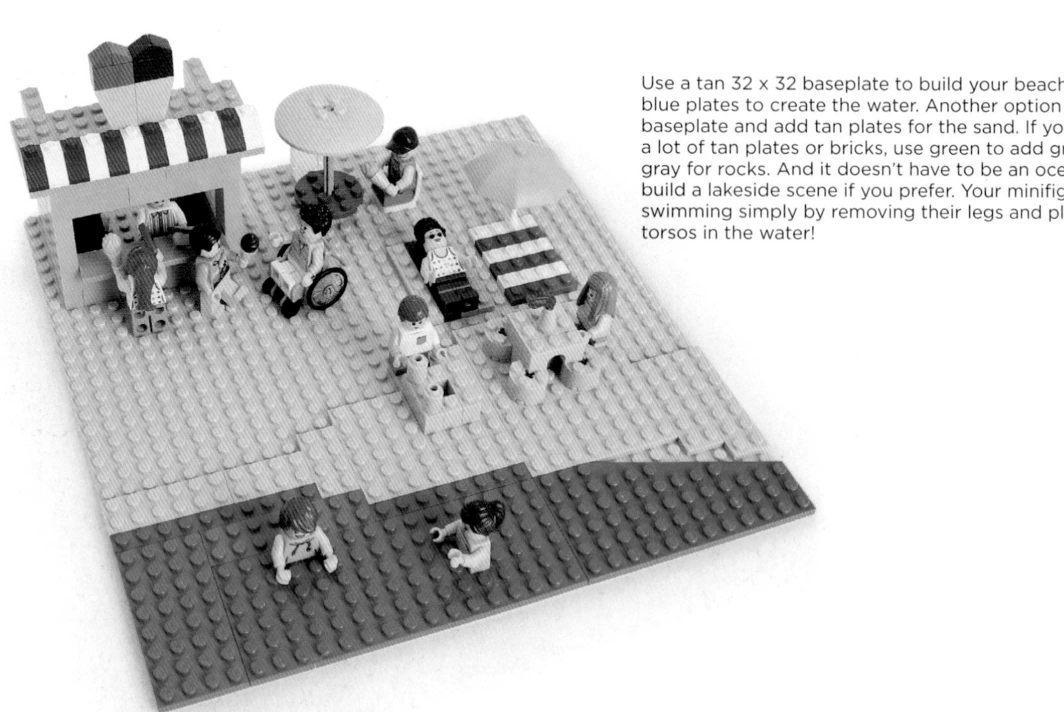

Use a tan 32 x 32 baseplate to build your beach scene. Add blue plates to create the water. Another option is to use a blue baseplate and add tan plates for the sand. If you don't have a lot of tan plates or bricks, use green to add grassy areas or gray for rocks. And it doesn't have to be an ocean! You can build a lakeside scene if you prefer. Your minifigures can go swimming simply by removing their legs and placing their torsos in the water!

Build a concession stand where your minifigures can grab some treats to eat! The building is a simple square. Leave the back open for play. Use a 6 x 12 plate for the roof, and then add red and white 1 x 2 slope bricks to create an awning, or use the colors that you have.

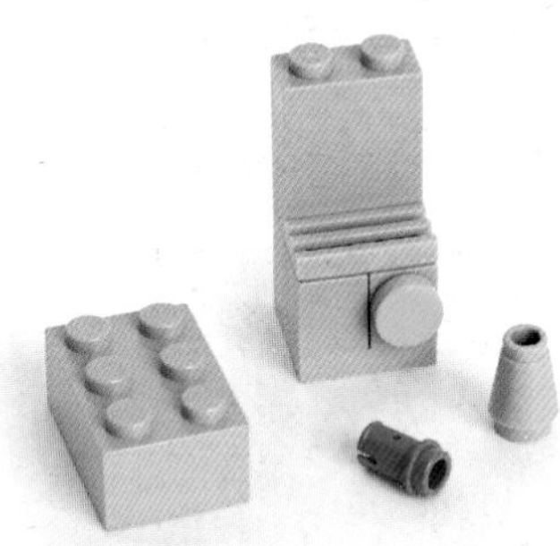

Use light gray bricks to create a soft-serve ice cream machine. Start with a 2 x 2 plate. Add a 1 x 2 brick, a 1 x 1 brick and a 1 x 1 brick with a stud on the side. Attach a 1 x 1 lime green round plate to the stud. Then add a 1 x 2 grill and a 1 x 2 brick (two bricks high).

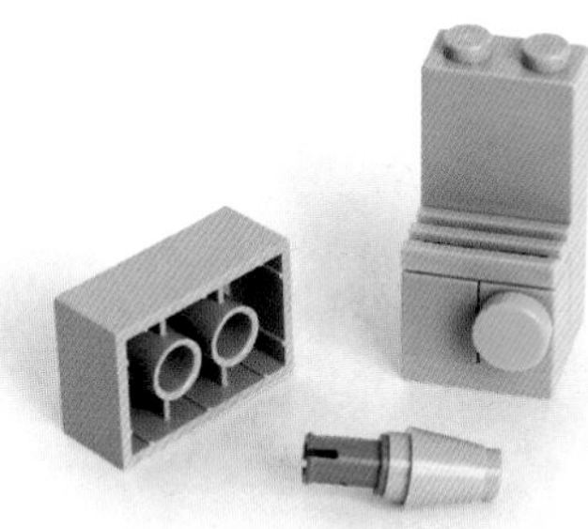

Insert a pin (half length) into a 1 x 1 cone.

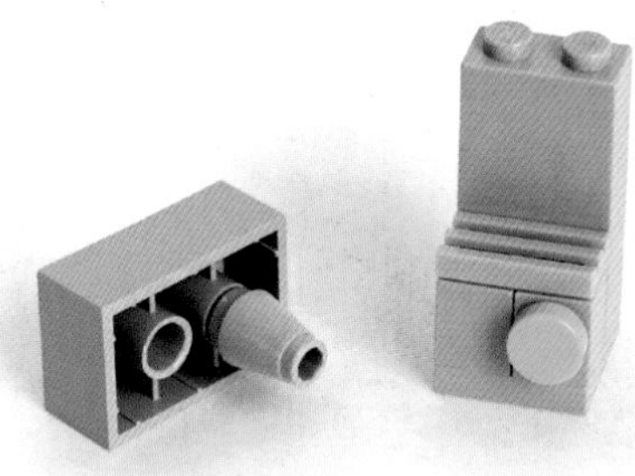

Then insert the pin into one of the holes on the bottom of a 2 x 3 brick. Place the 2 x 3 brick on the top of the ice cream machine, and it's ready to go.

Then build a grill. Start with a 2 x 4 dark gray plate. Add a 1 x 4 dark gray brick and a 1 x 4 dark gray brick with four studs on the side. Use 1 x 1 round tiles to make knobs on the front of the grill. Give the grill feet by placing a 1 x 1 black round plate under each corner. Place hot dogs on the grill, or other minifigure food items you have.

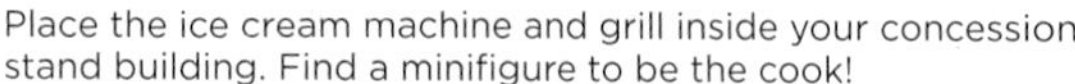

Place the ice cream machine and grill inside your concession stand building. Find a minifigure to be the cook!

Add some giant ice cream cones to the top of the concession stand building! Use 1 x 2 x 3 tan inverted slopes for the cones. Then build the ice cream part with a 1 x 2 brick and two 1 x 1 slopes (30 degree).

The concession stand is ready to open for business! One chocolate cone, please! You can serve whatever foods you have at the concession stand. Use accessories like popsicles, ice cream cones, pretzels or drinks.

Build a little table and chairs so that people have a place to sit while eating their treats. The table is made with a 2 x 2 round brick, a 4 x 4 round plate, an axle (7 studs long) and a 6 x 6 inverted dish. The axle slides into the X-shaped hole in the round brick, and the dish makes a great umbrella.

You can use 1 x 6 or 1 x 4 plates for beach towels. Make them striped towels by using a variety of colors. Then create sandcastles with tan bricks and cones. Everyone is having so much fun at the beach!

SURF SHOP

CREATIVE CHALLENGE

While some people are relaxing at the beach, others might be looking for more of an adventure! This surf shop is just the thing. Build a little shop where your minifigures can rent a surfboard and life jacket for the day. Then they'll be ready to catch a wave!

KEY ELEMENTS

1—16 x 16 tan plate
2—8 x 16 tan plates
2—1 x 4 x 3 windows
1—1 x 4 x 6 door
Various red and blue bricks, 1 stud wide
6—2 x 3 blue slopes
2 x 2 brown container
2—1 x 1 light gray bricks with a vertical clip
1—light gray Technic pin, half length with 2-stud long bar extension (flick missile)
4—1 x 4 tan bricks
2—2 x 4 tan tiles
1—bar 1 x 4 x 6 grille with end protrusions
2—1 x 1 white tiles with clips
1—1 x 4 red brick with four studs on the side
Accessories like plants and a crab for the sign
Surfboards
Life jackets
Fishing pole

Build a simple building for the surf shop and keep the back open for play. The dimensions of the shop are 8 studs by 14 studs. Use tan bricks and 2 x 4 tan tiles to make a counter. Build two 1 x 1 light gray bricks with a clip and a 1 x 1 red brick with a stud on the side into the walls so that you can use them to hang up life jackets, a surfboard and a fishing pole. Insert a light gray pin (flick missile) into one of the clips.

Use the flick missile pin for holding life jackets. The surfboard can be hung by attaching it to the red brick with a stud on the side. If you have a fishing pole, hang it from one of the clips.

As you complete your building, use 2 x 3 blue slopes to make an awning. Build a 1 x 4 red brick with four studs on the side into the front of the building.

Use an 8 x 16 tan plate for the roof of the surf shop. Attach a plant and a crab to the red brick with studs on the side to be a sign. You can also use a tile with a seashell printed on it.

A 1 x 4 x 6 bar grille is perfect for displaying the surfboards that are available to rent. Attach the bar grille to a 1 x 6 light gray brick by using two 1 x 1 white tiles with a clip.

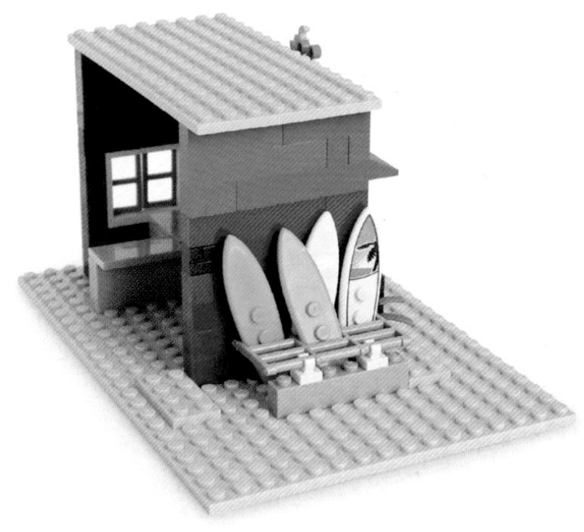

You can slide the surfboards down in between the bars.

It's a busy day at the surf shop! Customers are grabbing boards and life jackets for a day of riding the waves.

AMAZING IDEA

Grab a blue baseplate and construct a surfing scene! Use tan plates or bricks for the sandy beach. Then use small blue bricks and slopes to build waves, and then pose your minifigures riding the waves!

PIRATE SHIP

STEP-BY-STEP

Yo-ho-ho! What do we have here but a rugged and seaworthy pirate ship? Captain Blackheart is trying to direct the ship toward another stash of buried treasure, but clumsy first mate James the Howler keeps dropping gold and jewels over the side of the ship. Keep your hands out of the treasure, James, or it will be your LAST voyage!

Build your own pirate ship with a base of plates and inverted slope bricks. If you don't have enough brown, add in tan, black and gray bricks. The parts list for this project is truly flexible, meaning that the project can easily be modified based on what you have. Try building a sail with a skull on it and send your minifigures off on an expedition for gold. Treasure, ho!

PARTS LIST

BROWN BRICKS

1—4 x 10 plate
2—4 x 6 plates
1—4 x 4 plate
2—2 x 8 plates
1—2 x 12 plate
1—2 x 4 plate
24—2 x 2 slopes, inverted
4—2 x 2 slopes, double inverted convex
1—1 x 8 tile
4—1 x 6 tiles
4—2 x 2 corner tiles
7—1 x 2 tiles
1—1 x 2 plate with a handle on the side, free ends
1—2 x 2 plate with one stud on top
1—2 x 2 round brick
1—2 x 2 round plate
5—1 x 1 round bricks
1—2 x 2 curved slope with two studs and curved sides
3—bars, 6 studs long with a stop ring
1—1 x 1 brick with a stud on the side

ASSORTED BRICKS

1—1 x 2—1 x 2 light gray bracket
1—black bar, 4 studs long
1—2 x 2 white flag
1—dark gray bar holder with clip
1—dark brown telescope
1—8 x 8 white wedge plate, cut corner
2—1 x 2 white plates with clips on the side
1—2 x 2 black round plate
1—1 x 2 black grill
1—3 x 4 container
Jewels, bottles and gold pieces for treasure
Various blue plates for the ocean
About 7—2 x 3 blue slopes for waves

STEP 1: Start your ship with a 4 x 10 brown plate. Place 2 x 2 brown inverted slopes around all four sides. Find a 4 x 4 brown plate and a 4 x 6 brown plate.

STEP 2: Attach the 4 x 4 plate and 4 x 6 plate to the inverted slope bricks. Then add a second layer of inverted slopes around the ship.

STEP 3: Add a 4 x 6 plate at the front of the ship and add a row of plates that are 2 studs wide around the rest of the ship. Each plate should attach to the ship by one row of studs. Place a 1 x 2—1 x 2 light gray bracket at the bow of the ship.

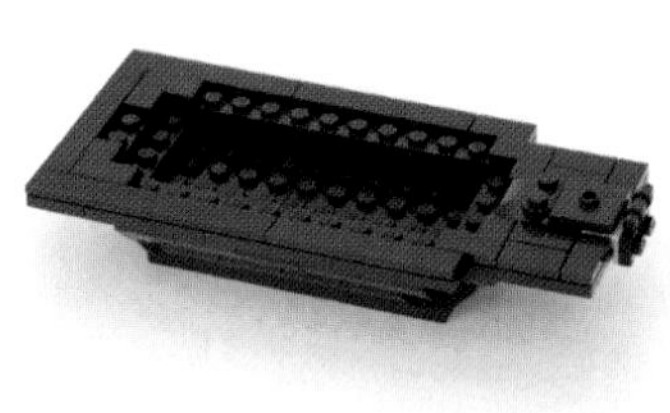

STEP 4: Now add brown tiles to finish off your ship. Place a 1 x 2 brown plate with a handle on the side (free ends) at the bow of the ship. This will hold a flag.

STEP 5: Build the flag. Insert a black bar (4 studs long) into a dark gray bar holder with clip. Then add a 2 x 2 white flag or substitute any flag you have.

STEP 6: Gather the bricks shown for building the mast and sail. Make a skull on the sail with a 2 x 2 black round plate and a 1 x 2 black grill.

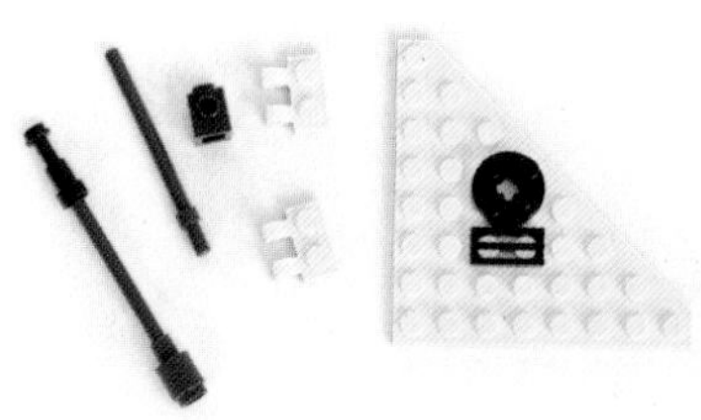

STEP 7: Slide a brown bar into a 1 x 1 brown round brick. Add a telescope to the top of the brown bar.

STEP 8: Attach the 1 x 1 brown round brick to a 1 x 1 brick with a stud on the side. Insert another brown bar into the hole in the stud. Attach two 1 x 2 white plates with clips on the side to the back of the sail.

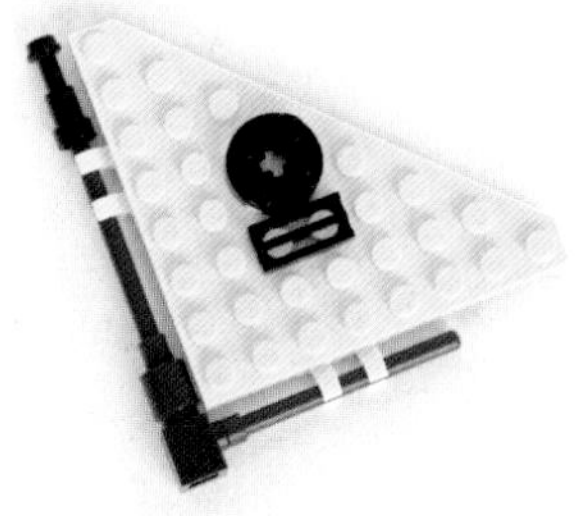

STEP 9: Clip the sail to the mast.

STEP 10: Gather the bricks shown for building the lower portion of the mast.

STEP 11: Slide four 1 x 1 brown round bricks onto a brown bar. The bar will keep the bricks from coming apart as you play with the ship.

STEP 12: Attach the round bricks to a 2 x 2 brown round brick and a 2 x 2 brown round plate. Place these inside the ship. Then add the top part of the mast and sail. Attach the flag to the handle at the front of the ship. Your pirate ship is ready for her maiden voyage!

Create a fun scene by building some ocean water for the ship to sail in. Use 2 x 3 blue slope bricks to build waves.

Then it's time for Captain Blackheart to command a voyage to a deserted island in search of treasure!

UNDER THE SEA DIORAMA

CREATIVE CHALLENGE

Use your bricks to construct a beautiful underwater scene! Build colorful corals, wavy seaweed and bright green ocean plants. Then create tropical fish to swim through the underwater landscape. This project can be easily customized with whatever bricks you have. Ocean water appears to change color as the waves roll and the light hits it in different ways, so you can combine different shades of blue as you build the water. Add any ocean creatures you have, such as crabs or sea turtles.

KEY ELEMENTS

1—16 x 16 tan plate

1—8 x 16 tan plate

Various shades of blue bricks

2 x 6 and 2 x 4 tan plates

Bricks, cones and slopes in bright colors for building coral and sea anemone

Diver minifigure, or any minifigure to be a swimmer

Sea animals—sea turtle, crab

1—clear minifigure utensil posing stand, bar with hollow stud

CLOWNFISH

2—1 x 2 orange slopes

2—1 x 1 orange slopes, 30 degree

1—1 x 2 orange plate

1—2 x 2 orange wedge plate, right

2—1 x 2 black plates

2—1 x 2 white plates

2—1 x 1 white bricks with a stud on the side

1—1 x 1 clear round tile with a bar and pin holder

BLUE TANG FISH

1—2 x 2 blue slope

1—2 x 3 blue slope

1—2 x 2 blue slope, inverted

1—2 x 3 blue slope, inverted

1—2 x 3 black plate

1—1 x 4 yellow plate

1—1 x 2 yellow plate with one stud on top (jumper plate)

1—2 x 1 x 1⅓ yellow curved slope with a recessed stud

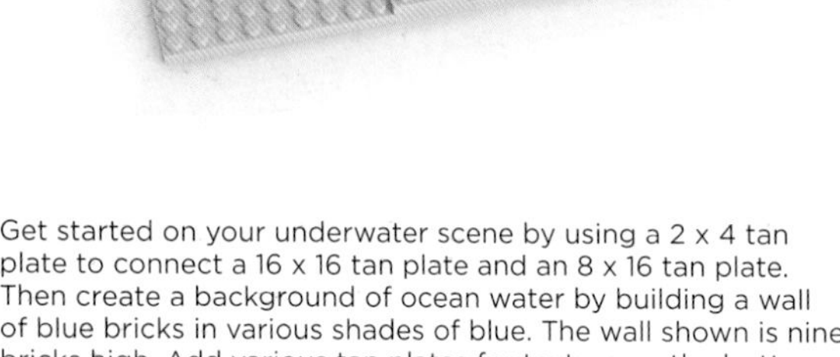

Get started on your underwater scene by using a 2 x 4 tan plate to connect a 16 x 16 tan plate and an 8 x 16 tan plate. Then create a background of ocean water by building a wall of blue bricks in various shades of blue. The wall shown is nine bricks high. Add various tan plates for texture on the bottom of the sea.

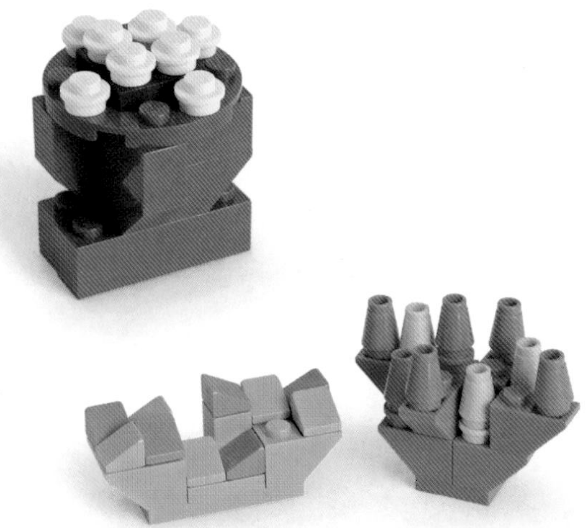

Design colorful corals and sea anemones with the bricks you have. You may want to start with inverted slope bricks on the bottom. Once you have the shape you like, decorate it with cones, 1 x 1 round plates or 1 x 1 slopes (30 degree).

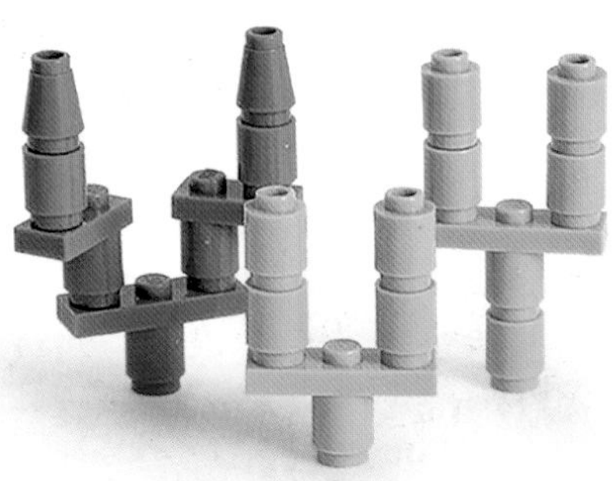

Build some seaweed in either green or lime green, or use a combination of both. Start with one or two 1 x 1 round bricks on the bottom. Add a 1 x 3 plate on top of that, and then make two leaves on the second layer by adding more round bricks. You may want to use cones at the top.

This little blue tang fish is easy to build with just a few bricks! The yellow fins on each side are made with a 1 x 4 yellow plate that runs through the fish's body. Place a 1 x 2 clear brick under the fish to make it look like it's swimming through the water.

A clownfish is easy to build. Start with two 1 x 2 orange slopes for the tail. Add layers of white, black and orange plates. Place two 1 x 1 white bricks with a stud on the side in the center of the fish so that one stud faces the bottom of the fish and one stud faces the side.

Use a 2 x 2 wedge plate for a fin. Then attach the fish to a 1 x 1 clear round tile with a bar and pin holder. This provides a way to mount the fish in the ocean display.

Arrange your fish, seaweed and corals inside your ocean diorama. Add a diver who is exploring the coral reef. You can attach a minifigure with a clear minifigure posing stand. If you have a crab or sea turtle, add those to your display.

BUILDING TIP

Clear bricks are very useful for posing objects to look like they are suspended in the water!

SEA CREATURES

Ocean animals are fascinating and beautiful to look at, and it's fun to create your own brick versions! Build a shark with posable fins and tail, and then construct some little sea turtles. Make a sea otter and a cute little hermit crab. These animals are perfect to use in ocean scenes, or display them on your desk or windowsill.

SHARK (STEP-BY-STEP)

PARTS LIST

DARK GRAY BRICKS

3—2 x 4 plates
1—2 x 3 plate
2—2 x 4 wedge plates
1—2 x 2 plate
1—1 x 2 plate
1—2 x 3 wedge plate, right
1—2 x 3 wedge plate, left
1—1 x 2 brick
2—1 x 1 bricks with a stud on the side (headlight)
1—1 x 2 slope
1—2 x 3 slope
2—1 x 2 curved slopes
1—1 x 2 slope, 30 degree
1—1 x 1 slope, 30 degree
2—1 x 2 plates with one stud on top (jumper plate)
3—1 x 2 plates with a ball on the side
1—2 x 2 tile
1—1 x 2 tile

ASSORTED BRICKS

3—1 x 2 light gray plates with a socket on the side
2—2 x 6 white plates
1—2 x 4 white plate
1—1 x 2 light gray plate
2—eyes

STEP 1: Begin the shark's body by finding a 2 x 4 white plate and two 2 x 6 white plates.

STEP 2: Attach one 2 x 6 plate and one 2 x 4 plate to a 2 x 6 plate.

STEP 3: Add (from left to right) a 1 x 2 dark gray plate with a ball on the side, a 2 x 3 dark gray plate, two 1 x 2 light gray plates with a socket on the side, a 1 x 2 dark gray brick, two 1 x 1 dark gray bricks with a stud on the side (headlight), and a 2 x 3 dark gray slope.

STEP 4: Place a 2 x 2 dark gray plate and a 2 x 4 dark gray plate on the back of the shark. Then gather the pieces shown.

STEP 5: Add a 2 x 4 dark gray plate just behind the 1 x 2 dark gray brick. Then add another 2 x 4 dark gray plate on top.

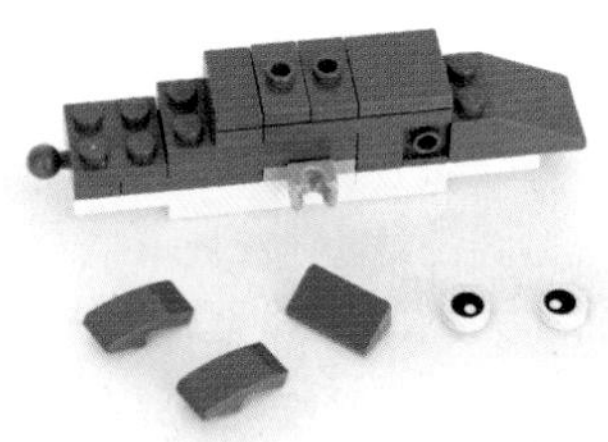

STEP 6: Attach a 1 x 2 dark gray plate just behind the second 2 x 4 plate added in step 5. Then add (from left to right) a 1 x 2 dark gray tile, two 1 x 2 dark gray plates with one stud on top, and a 2 x 2 dark gray tile. Find the bricks shown.

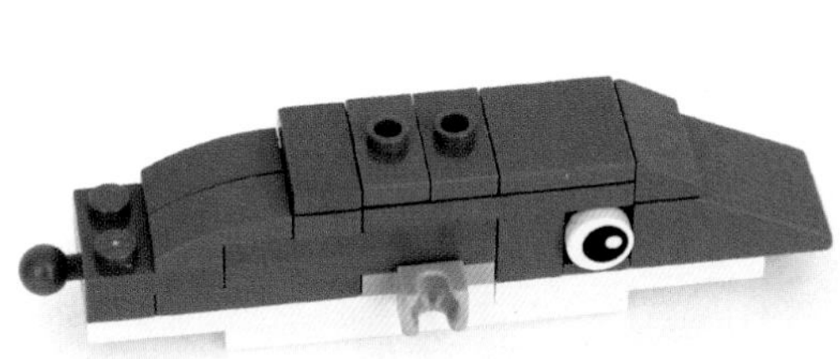

STEP 7: Place the eyes on the 1 x 1 dark gray headlight bricks and add a 1 x 2 dark gray slope (30 degree) in front of the eyes. Then place two 1 x 2 dark gray curved slopes on the back of the shark.

STEP 8: Build the shark's dorsal fin by adding a 1 x 2 dark gray slope and a 1 x 1 dark gray slope (30 degree). Then build the pectoral fins. Each one is a 1 x 2 dark gray plate with a ball on the side and a 2 x 3 dark gray wedge plate.

STEP 9: Attach the pectoral fins to the sides of the shark's body. Build the tail fin (called the caudal fin) with two 2 x 4 dark gray wedge plates, a 1 x 2 light gray plate and a 1 x 2 light gray plate with a socket on the side.

STEP 10: Connect the caudal fin to the body, and your shark is complete!

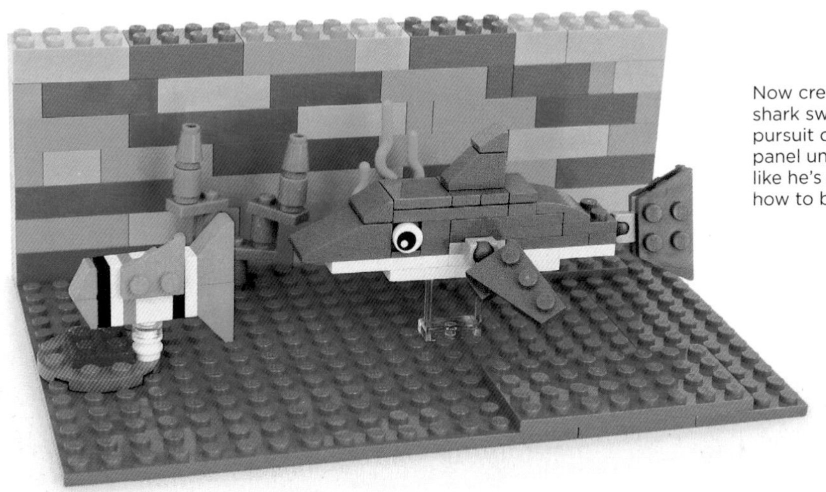

Now create an action scene with your shark swimming through the water in pursuit of a smaller fish! Place a clear panel under the shark to make it look like he's suspended in the water. See how to build the Clownfish on page 189.

SEA TURTLE (STEP-BY-STEP)

PARTS LIST

1—4 x 4 light gray round plate
2—2 x 2 brown plates
4—1 x 1 brown slopes, 30 degree
4—1 x 1 tan slopes, 30 degree
1—1 x 4 lime green plate
1—1 x 1 lime green plate
5—1 x 2 lime green plates
1—1 x 1 lime green slope, 30 degree
4—1 x 1 lime green round plates
1—1 x 1 dark gray brick with studs on opposite sides
2—eyes

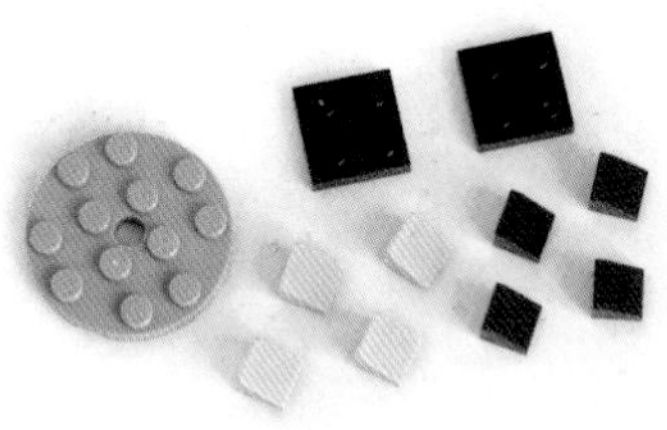

STEP 1: Find a 4 x 4 light gray round plate, two 2 x 2 brown plates, four 1 x 1 brown slopes (30 degree) and four 1 x 1 tan slopes (30 degree).

STEP 2: Attach the two 2 x 2 brown plates to the center of the 4 x 4 light gray round plate. Then add the 1 x 1 brown and tan slopes (30 degree) around the edge of the shell.

STEP 3: Gather the bricks shown for building the turtle's head.

STEP 4: Place a 1 x 1 dark gray brick with studs on opposite sides on a 1 x 4 lime green plate. Attach the eyes. Then add a 1 x 1 lime green plate and a 1 x 1 lime green slope (30 degree) to make the nose.

STEP 5: Attach the shell to the turtle's neck.

STEP 6: Flip the turtle over and add five 1 x 2 lime green plates to make legs and a tail. Place a 1 x 1 lime green round plate under each leg.

Your sea turtle is complete! If you have enough pieces, you'll want to build another one so that your turtle has a friend.

Then use blue and tan plates to build a tiny beach for your turtles to go swimming!

HERMIT CRAB (CREATIVE CHALLENGE)

KEY ELEMENTS

Various tan plates and slopes

1—4 x 4 tan plate

1—2 x 2 tan dish

1—1 x 2 black plate with a handle on the side

1—1 x 2 yellow plate with a handle on the side

2—1 x 1 orange plates with a vertical clip

1—1 x 2 orange plate with two clips on the side

2—1 x 3 orange curved slopes

1—2 x 2 orange slope, inverted

2—1 x 1 orange bricks

1—1 x 2 orange plate with a handle, free ends

2—1 x 1 black tiles with circular pattern

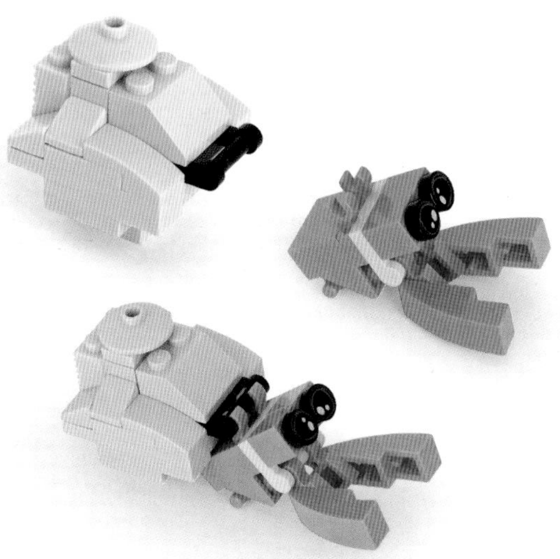

See if you can use the pictures to design your own little hermit crab. To build the shell, start with a 4 x 4 tan plate. Place bricks or inverted slopes under the 4 x 4 plate. Then design the top with a variety of tan plates and slope bricks. Be sure to work a 1 x 2 plate with a handle on the side into your shell so that you can attach the crab to the shell.

Then build the body and head of the crab. The 1 x 1 orange plates with clips will connect the crab to the shell. If you don't have the black eyes, you can substitute regular eyes. You may want to use 1 x 3 orange curved slopes for the crab's pincers, or you can create your own design.

SEA OTTER (STEP-BY-STEP)

PARTS LIST

TAN BRICKS

3—1 x 4 bricks
2—1 x 2 bricks
2—1 x 1 bricks
2—1 x 1 bricks with a stud on the side
1—1 x 2 brick with two studs on the side
4—1 x 4 plates
1—1 x 2 plate
2—1 x 1 plates
1—1 x 2 plate with one stud on top (jumper plate)
2—2 x 1 x 1⅓ curved slopes with a recessed stud

BROWN BRICKS

6—2 x 4 bricks
1—2 x 2 brick
2—1 x 4 bricks
1—1 x 2 brick
2—2 x 4 plates
4—1 x 4 plates
4—1 x 2 plates
5—1 x 1 plates
2—3 x 3 round corner plates
2—1 x 1 round plates
6—1 x 1 bricks with a stud on the side
2—2 x 2 slopes, inverted
1—1 x 2 slope, 30 degree
2—1 x 1 slopes, 30 degree
1—2 x 2 tile
1—1 x 4 curved slope
4—1 x 4 curved slopes, double

ASSORTED BRICKS

2—eyes
1—1 x 1 black round plate
1—1 x 2 dark gray plate with a ball on the side
1—1 x 2 light gray plate with a socket on the end

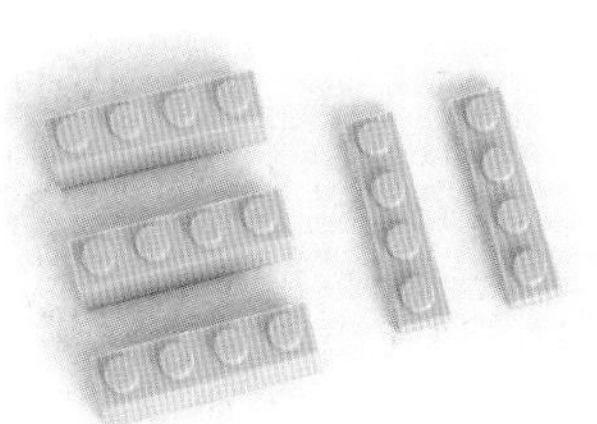

STEP 1: Start by building the otter's tan belly. Grab three 1 x 4 tan bricks and two 1 x 4 tan plates.

STEP 2: Stack the bricks and plates.

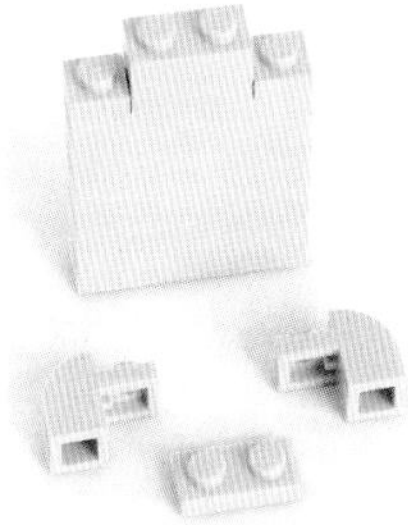

STEP 3: Add a 1 x 2 tan brick and two 1 x 1 tan plates at the top. Then find a 1 x 2 tan plate and two 2 x 1 x 1⅓ tan curved slopes with a recessed stud.

STEP 4: Place the two 2 x 1 x 1⅓ curved slopes on top of the tan bricks. Then add the 1 x 2 tan plate.

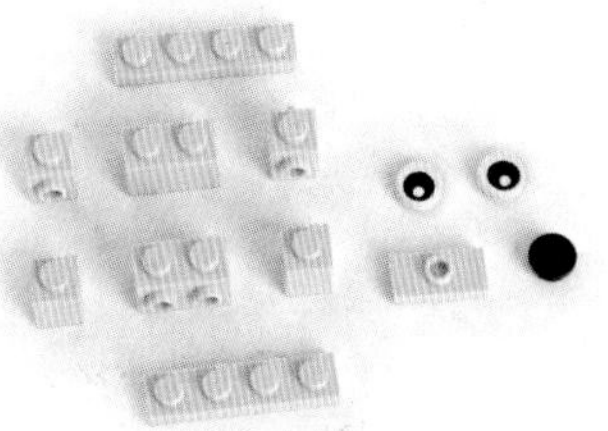

STEP 5: Gather the bricks shown for building the otter's head.

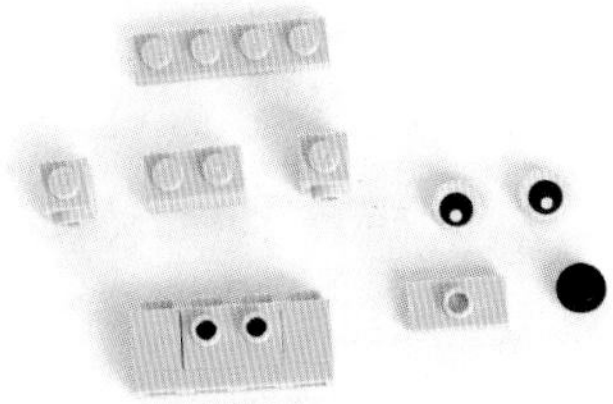

STEP 6: Attach a 1 x 2 tan brick with two studs on the side and two 1 x 1 tan bricks to a 1 x 4 tan plate.

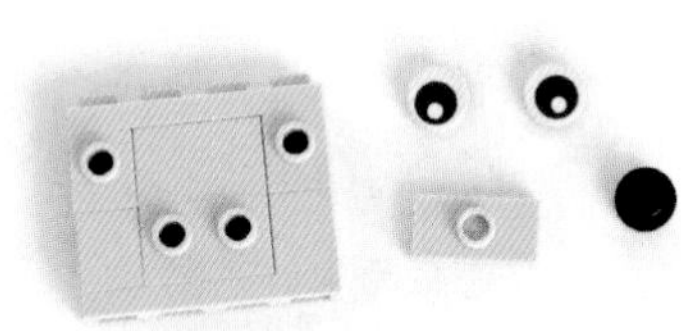

STEP 7: Add a 1 x 2 tan brick and two 1 x 1 tan bricks with a stud on the side. Then place a 1 x 4 tan plate on top of those.

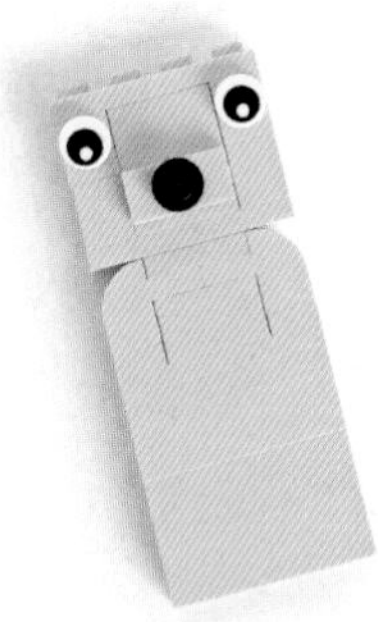

STEP 8: Attach a 1 x 2 tan plate with one stud on top (jumper plate) to the brick that has two studs on the side. Add a 1 x 1 black round plate for the nose. Then attach the eyes. Place the head on top of the tan belly.

STEP 9: Grab a 2 x 4 brown plate, a 1 x 4 brown plate, a 2 x 2 brown brick and four 1 x 1 brown bricks with a stud on the side for building the otter's body.

STEP 10: Use the 2 x 2 brick to connect the 1 x 4 and 2 x 4 plates. Then place two 1 x 1 bricks with a stud on the side on each side of the 2 x 2 brick.

STEP 11: Add three 2 x 4 brown bricks.

STEP 12: Place a 1 x 4 brown brick on the top of the body. Then add a 1 x 2 brown brick and two 1 x 1 brown bricks with a stud on the side.

STEP 13: Add three more 2 x 4 brown bricks to the body.

STEP 14: Attach the tan belly and head to the brown plate sticking out at the bottom of the body. Then find a 2 x 2 brown tile, a 2 x 4 brown plate, a 1 x 2 brown slope (30 degree) and two 1 x 1 brown slopes (30 degree).

STEP 15: Place the 2 x 4 brown plate and the 2 x 2 brown tile on top of the otter's head.

STEP 16: Add the 1 x 2 brown slope (30 degree) and two 1 x 1 brown slopes (30 degree) to the back of the head.

STEP 17: Find two 2 x 2 brown inverted slopes and a 1 x 4 brown plate.

STEP 18: Attach the two inverted slopes and the 1 x 4 plate to the bottom of the body. Then find the bricks shown.

STEP 19: Connect a 1 x 2 dark gray plate with a ball on the side to the 1 x 4 brown plate from step 18. Then place a 1 x 1 brown plate on either side of it. Add a 1 x 4 brown brick.

STEP 20: Secure the plate with a ball on the side by attaching a 1 x 4 brown plate. Then add a 1 x 1 brown plate on either end of the 1 x 4 brick.

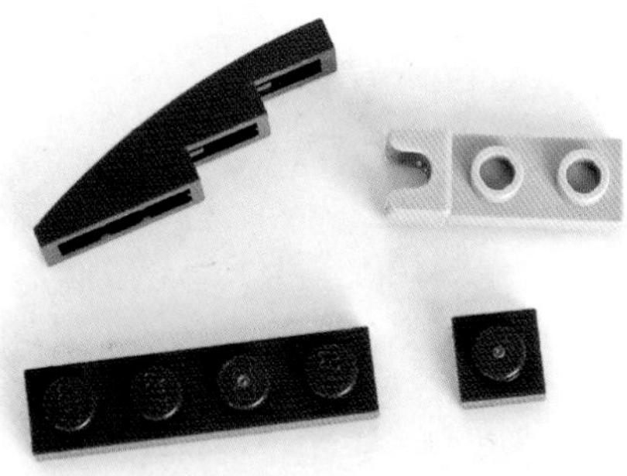

STEP 21: Build the otter's tail. Find a 1 x 4 brown plate, a 1 x 1 brown plate, a 1 x 4 brown curved slope and a 1 x 2 light gray plate with a socket on the end.

STEP 22: Attach the 1 x 2 light gray plate with a socket on the end to the 1 x 4 brown plate and add the 1 x 1 brown plate on top of it. Then add the 1 x 4 brown curved slope.

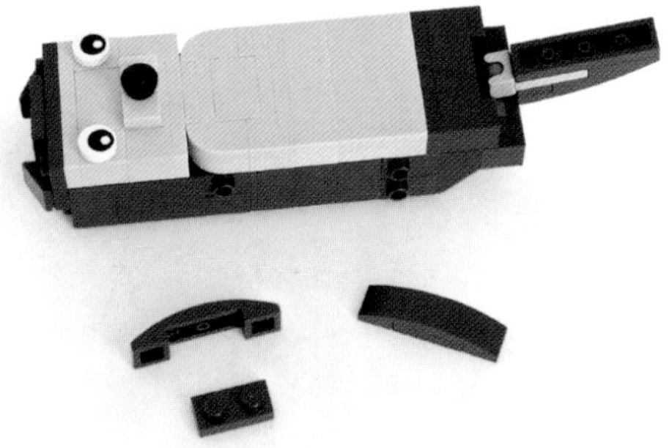

STEP 23: Connect the tail to the body by attaching it to the plate with a ball on the side. Build the otter's front legs by attaching 1 x 2 brown plates to the center of two 1 x 4 brown double curved slopes.

STEP 24: Attach the front legs to the studs on the sides of the otter's body. Then attach a 3 x 3 round corner plate to each side of the lower body.

STEP 25: Build two back legs in the same way that you built the front legs. In order to sit at the correct angle, each back leg will need to have a 1 x 1 brown round plate under it.

STEP 26: Attach the back legs to the round corner plates, and the otter is complete!

Create an ocean scene with your adorable otter! Use medium azure plates or blue plates to build the water and make your otter float on his back. Connect leaves together to make seaweed for the otter to hold.

AWESOME MINI BUILDS

Build cool LEGO creations on a tiny scale! These projects are small in size, but they are certainly not lacking detail. With all of the different tiny LEGO elements available, you can build some really awesome tiny projects. And once you start building these creations, you'll think of ideas for many more! Build a whole menagerie of miniature animals, and then construct vehicles on a tiny scale. Design little robots with wacky personalities and build tiny versions of things we use every day, such as a camera or a candy machine. Once you've built your projects, you'll definitely want to find a place to display them!

TINY VEHICLES

Build some awesome vehicles in miniature form. These cars, trucks and flying vehicles are too small for minifigures to fit inside, but they are pocket-sized and tons of fun! Make a tiny tractor with a wagon to pull, and then build a mini farm to go with it. Build some super-fast race cars and design awesome spaceships. Then create some miniature construction equipment. Which vehicle will you build first?

RACE CARS (STEP-BY-STEP)

PARTS LIST

NOTE: The colors listed are the colors shown, but you can choose any colors for this project!

BLUE BRICKS

2—2 x 6 plates
1—2 x 4 plate
1—2 x 2 plate
1—1 x 4 plate
1—1 x 2 plate
2—1 x 1 plates
1—2 x 2 curved slope
1—1 x 2 brick

ASSORTED BRICKS

1—2 x 2 clear slope
2—1 x 1 clear slopes, 30 degree
2—2 x 2 black plates with wheel holders
1—1 x 2 orange slope, 30 degree
1—2 x 2 orange tile
1—1 x 4 dark gray plate
1—1 x 2—1 x 2 dark gray bracket
2—1 x 1 dark gray slopes, 30 degree
4—wheels

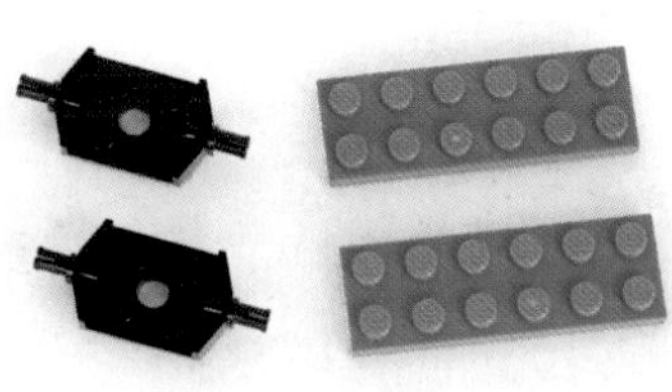

STEP 1: Find two 2 x 2 black plates with wheel holders and two 2 x 6 blue plates.

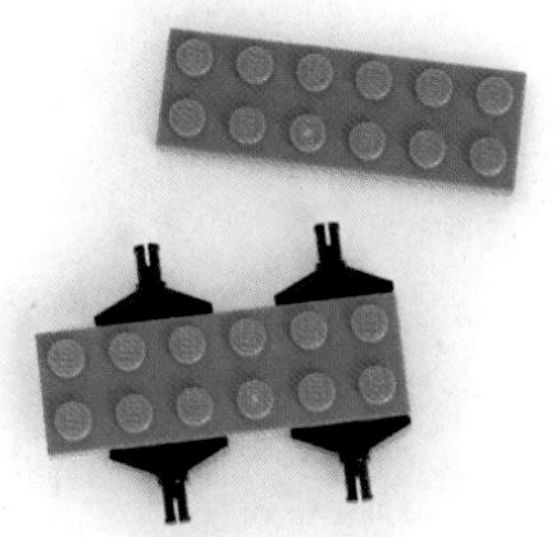

STEP 2: Attach the plates with wheel holders to the underside of a 2 x 6 plate.

STEP 3: Add the second 2 x 6 plate so that it hangs off the other 2 x 6 plate by one row of studs. Then find the bricks shown.

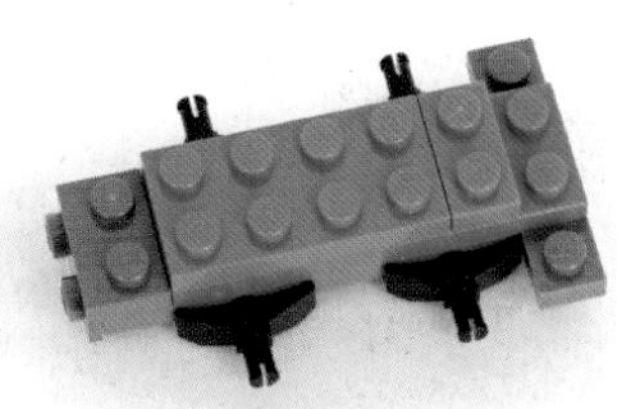

STEP 4: Place a 1 x 2—1 x 2 dark gray bracket on the back of the car. Then add a 2 x 4 blue plate and a 1 x 2 blue plate. Place a 1 x 4 dark gray plate under the blue plate at the front of the car.

STEP 5: Add a 2 x 2 clear slope for the windshield and a 2 x 2 blue curved slope for the hood of the car. Then add two 1 x 1 dark gray slopes (30 degree).

STEP 6: Find a 1 x 4 blue plate, a 2 x 2 blue plate, a 1 x 2 blue brick and two 1 x 1 clear slopes (30 degree).

STEP 7: Place a 1 x 2 blue brick behind the 2 x 2 clear slope. Add a 1 x 4 blue plate on the back of the car and put a 2 x 2 blue plate on top of it. Build the back windshield with two 1 x 1 clear slopes (30 degree).

STEP 8: Build a spoiler by placing a 1 x 2 orange slope (30 degree) on the back of the car. Then find two 1 x 1 blue plates.

STEP 9: Attach the two 1 x 1 plates to the underside of the 1 x 4 blue plate. Then add a 2 x 2 orange tile on the roof of the car. Attach wheels to the wheel holders and your race car is complete!

Once you've built one race car, you'll want to build more in other colors. You might want to build a racetrack as well!

SEMI-TRUCK AND TRAILER (CREATIVE CHALLENGE)

PARTS LIST

1—2 x 8 dark gray plate
1—1 x 2 dark gray plate
2—2 x 6 light gray bricks
1—2 x 6 light gray plate
2—2 x 2 red bricks
1—2 x 2 red plate
2—1 x 1 red bricks with a stud on the side (headlight)
1—1 x 2 light gray grill
3—2 x 2 light gray round plates, thin with wheel holder
1—1 x 2 clear brick
3—black skateboard wheels

This might be the smallest semi-truck ever built with LEGO bricks! The entire truck is built on a 2 x 8 dark gray plate and a 1 x 2 dark gray plate. Use three 2 x 2 light gray wheel holders and tiny skateboard wheels.

Build a tiny cab with two 2 x 2 bricks, two 1 x 1 bricks with a stud on the side (headlight type), a 1 x 2 clear brick and a 2 x 2 plate. Use red as pictured or choose another color.

The trailer for the truck is made with two 2 x 6 bricks and a 2 x 6 plate. Use light gray bricks or white bricks for the trailer. Then your truck will be ready to hit the road!

MINI CAR (STEP-BY-STEP)

PARTS LIST

GREEN BRICKS

1—2 x 4 brick
1—1 x 2 brick
1—2 x 3 brick with a curved end
1—2 x 2 slope
3—1 x 4 plates
1—2 x 2 plate
2—2 x 2 corner plates
4—1 x 1 plates
2—2 x 2 curved slopes
4—1 x 4 curved slopes, double

ASSORTED BRICKS

2—2 x 2 black plates with wheel holders
4—small wheels with a hole for a wheel holder
2—2 x 2 clear slopes
1—1 x 2 clear brick
2—1 x 1 translucent orange plates
2—1 x 1 translucent yellow round plates

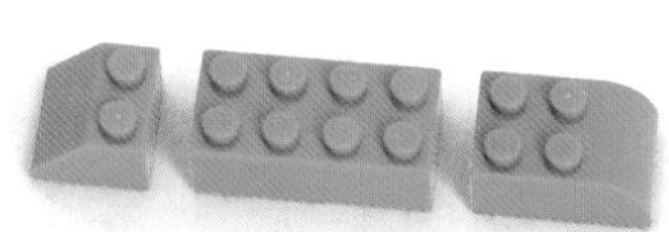

STEP 1: Grab a 2 x 2 green slope, a 2 x 4 green brick and a 2 x 3 green brick with a curved end.

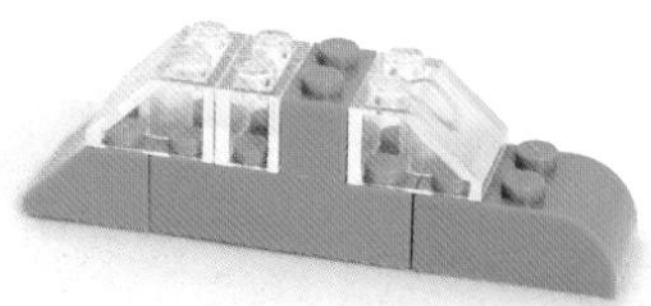

STEP 2: Connect the green bricks by adding a 2 x 2 clear slope, a 1 x 2 clear brick, a 1 x 2 green brick and a second 2 x 2 clear slope.

STEP 3: Place a 2 x 2 green plate on the top of the car. Then find two 2 x 2 green curved slopes.

STEP 4: Add both curved slopes to the top of the car to create a rounded roof.

STEP 5: Grab two 1 x 4 green plates, two 1 x 4 double curved slopes, two 1 x 1 green plates and two 1 x 1 translucent yellow round plates for building the front fenders.

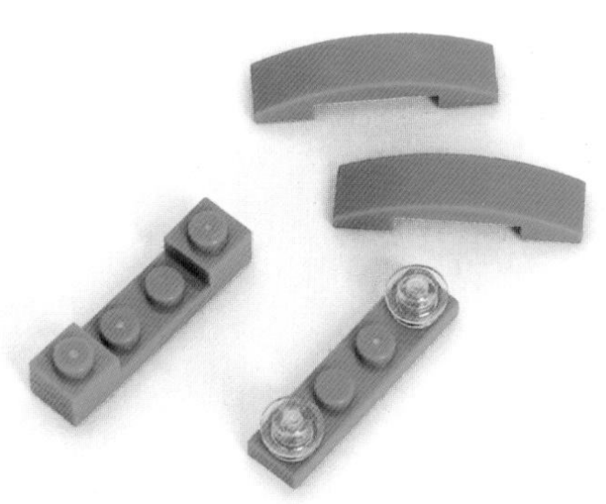

STEP 6: Place a 1 x 1 green plate on each end of a 1 x 4 green plate. Then place a 1 x 1 translucent yellow round plate on each end of another 1 x 4 green plate.

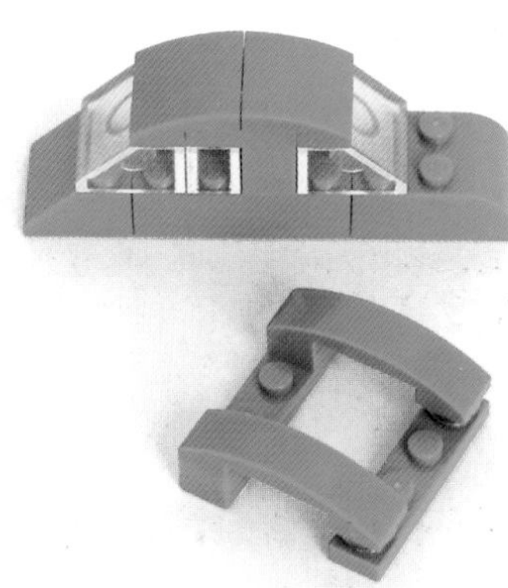

STEP 7: Connect the two 1 x 4 green plates by adding two 1 x 4 double curved slopes.

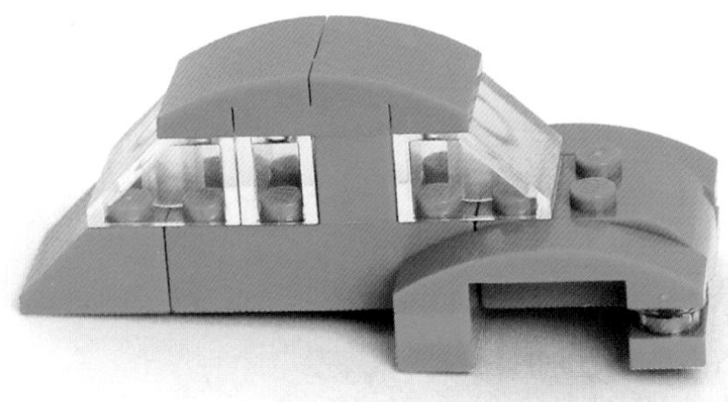

STEP 8: Attach the front fenders to the car.

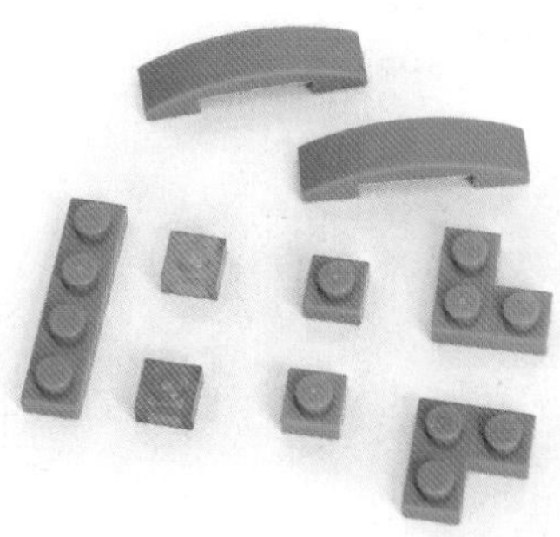

STEP 9: Find a 1 x 4 green plate, two 1 x 1 translucent orange plates, two 1 x 1 green plates, two 2 x 2 green corner plates and two 1 x 4 double curved slopes for building the rear fenders.

STEP 10: Place a 1 x 1 translucent orange plate on both ends of a 1 x 4 green plate. Then place a 1 x 1 green plate on both 2 x 2 green corner plates as shown.

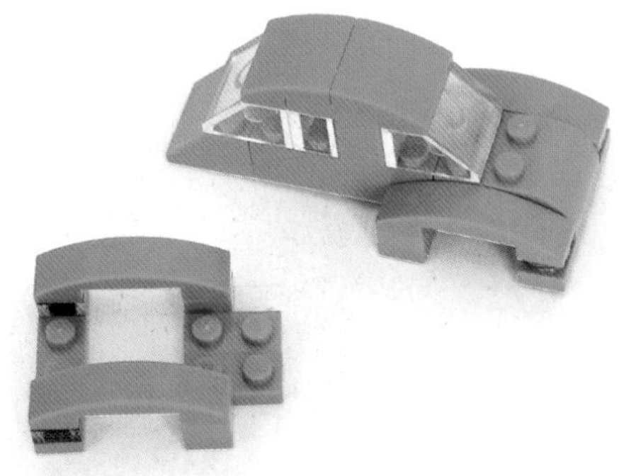

STEP 11: Connect the 1 x 4 green plate with the two 2 x 2 corner plates by attaching two 1 x 4 double curved slopes.

STEP 12: Attach the rear fenders to the car. Then find two 2 x 2 plates with wheels holders and four small wheels.

STEP 13: Add the wheels, and your mini car is complete!

TRACTOR AND WAGON (STEP-BY-STEP)

PARTS LIST

BLUE BRICKS

1—2 x 4 plate
1—2 x 3 plate
1—1 x 2 brick
1—2 x 2 tile
2—1 x 2 plates with one stud on top (jumper plates)

DARK GRAY BRICKS

1—2 x 4 plate
1—2 x 3 plate
1—1 x 2 grill
1—1 x 1 round plate
1—1 x 2 plate, rounded with open studs
1—1 x 2—1 x 2 bracket, inverted

LIGHT GRAY BRICKS

1—2 x 2 plate with pin holes
2—1 x 2 plates with a pin hole on the bottom
1—1 x 2 plate with a handle on the side, free ends
1—1 x 2 plate
4—1 x 1 x 1 corner panels
2—1 x 2 x 1 panels
1—1 x 2 plate with a clip on the side
4—Technic pins without friction ridges

ASSORTED BRICKS

1—2 x 2 black plate with wheel holders
1—1 x 2 x 1 clear panel
4—wheels with pin holes
2—small wheels with a hole for a wheel holder

STEP 1: Find the bricks shown for building the tractor.

STEP 2: Place a 2 x 3 blue plate and a 1 x 2 light gray plate with a handle on the side (free ends) on the underside of a 2 x 4 blue plate.

STEP 3: Add two 1 x 2 light gray plates with a pin hole on the bottom. These will hold the back wheels.

STEP 4: Gather the bricks shown.

STEP 5: Attach a 1 x 2—1 x 2 dark gray inverted bracket and a 1 x 2 light gray plate to a 2 x 2 black plate with wheel holders. Then attach a 1 x 2 dark gray grill to the bracket.

STEP 6: Attach the wheel holder and grill section to the tractor.

STEP 7: Add two 1 x 2 blue plates with one stud on top (jumper plates), a 1 x 2 x 1 clear panel and a 1 x 2 brick to the tractor. Then find the pieces shown.

STEP 8: Place a 1 x 2 dark gray plate (rounded with open studs) on the top of the tractor's hood. Then add a 1 x 1 dark gray round plate. Place a 2 x 2 blue tile on top of the cab. Find four wheels and two light gray pins.

STEP 9: Attach the wheels, and the tractor is complete!

STEP 10: Now build a wagon for the tractor to pull. Find a 2 x 4 dark gray plate, four 1 x 1 x 1 light gray corner panels and two 1 x 2 x 1 light gray panels.

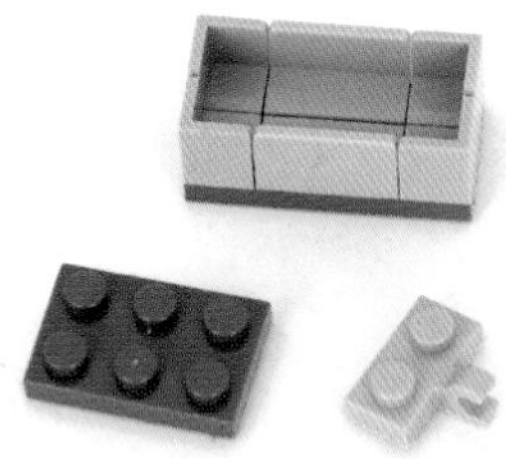

STEP 11: Attach the panels to the 2 x 4 dark gray plate to create the sides of the wagon. Then find a 2 x 3 dark gray plate and a 1 x 2 light gray plate with a clip on the side.

STEP 12: Place a 2 x 3 dark gray plate and a 1 x 2 light gray plate with a clip on the side on the underside of the wagon.

STEP 13: Add a 2 x 2 light gray plate with pin holes. Then find two wheels that have pin holes and two light gray pins.

STEP 14: Attach the wheels to the wagon, and your wagon is complete! Clip the wagon to the handle on the back of the tractor. Then fill the wagon with 1 x 1 brown round plates to look like dirt. You can also use 1 x 1 red round plates to look like a load of apples. You might want to build an entire tiny farm to go with your tractor and wagon!

EXCAVATOR (STEP-BY-STEP)

PARTS LIST

YELLOW BRICKS

3—2 x 4 plates
1—1 x 4 plate
1—1 x 4 tile
1—1 x 2 plate
1—1 x 2 plate with one clip on top
1—1 x 2 curved slope
1—1 x 2 plate with a clip on the end

LIGHT GRAY BRICKS

1—2 x 2 plate with pin holes
1—4 x 4 plate
2—1 x 2 plates with a handle on the end
1—1 x 2 plate with a clip on the end
1—1 x 1 plate with a handle

ASSORTED BRICKS

1—1 x 2 dark gray grill
1—1 x 2 dark gray plate
2—1 x 2 translucent black bricks
1—2 x 2 black tile
2—1 x 5 black Technic liftarms
2—black Technic pins with friction ridges

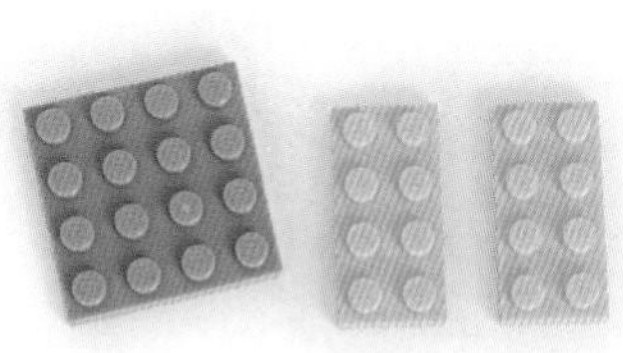

STEP 1: Find a 4 x 4 light gray plate and two 2 x 4 yellow plates.

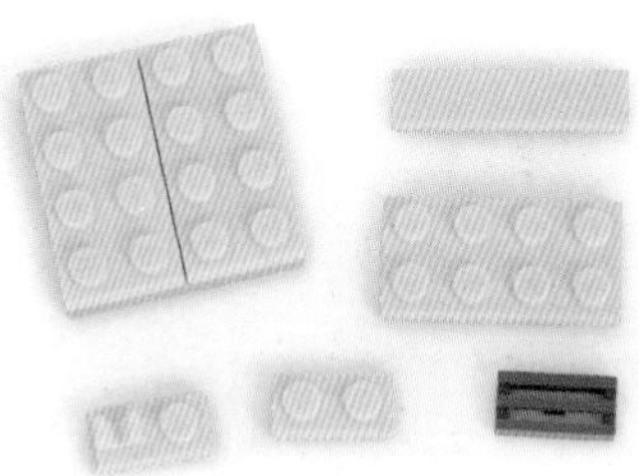

STEP 2: Place the two 2 x 4 yellow plates on top of the 4 x 4 light gray plate. Then find the bricks shown.

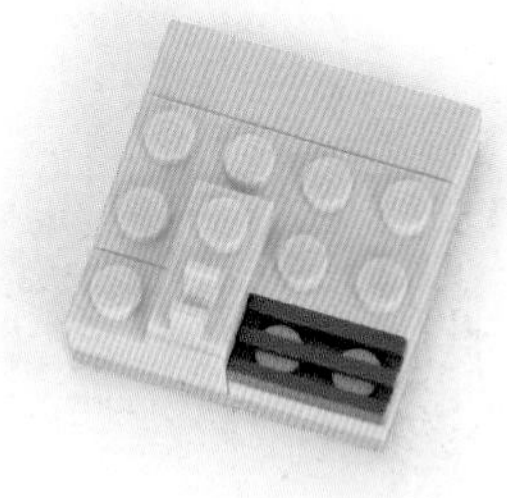

STEP 3: Place a 1 x 4 yellow tile, a 2 x 4 yellow plate, a 1 x 2 yellow plate and a 1 x 2 dark gray grill on top of the excavator. Then add a 1 x 2 yellow plate with one clip on top.

STEP 4: Build the cab by adding two 1 x 2 translucent black bricks. Place a 2 x 2 black tile on top of them.

STEP 5: Build the excavator's arm (also called the boom). Use a 1 x 4 yellow plate to connect two 1 x 2 light gray plates with a handle on the end. Attach a 1 x 2 yellow plate with a clip on the end and place a 1 x 2 light gray plate with a clip under that. Then find the pieces shown.

STEP 6: Build the digging bucket with a 1 x 1 light gray plate with a handle, a 1 x 2 yellow curved slope and a 1 x 2 dark gray plate.

STEP 7: Use the yellow clip on the body of the excavator to attach the arm.

STEP 8: Build the excavator's tracks. Find two 1 x 5 black liftarms, a 2 x 2 light gray plate with pin holes, and two black pins.

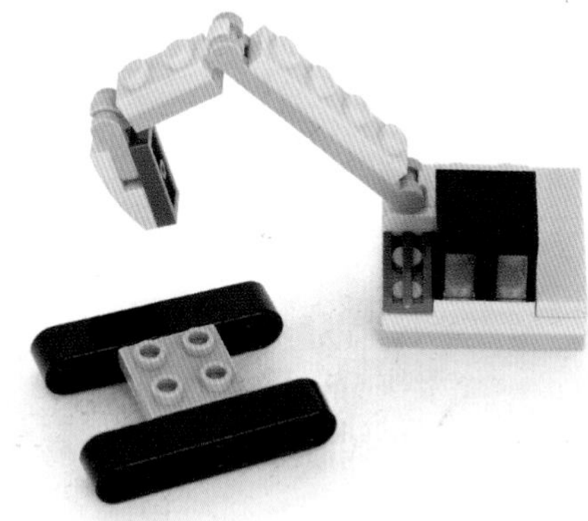

STEP 9: Use the pins to connect the liftarms to the 2 x 2 plate.

STEP 10: Attach the body of the excavator to the tracks, and your vehicle is complete!

The arm of the excavator is fully posable so that you can make it dig in the dirt. Set up scenes with the mini dump truck on page 209!

DUMP TRUCK (CREATIVE CHALLENGE)

PARTS LIST

DARK GRAY BRICKS

1—2 x 8 plate
1—4 x 6 plate
2—1 x 6 bricks
2—1 x 2 bricks

ASSORTED BRICKS

1—1 x 2 light gray plate
1—2 x 4 light gray plate
1—1 x 2 light gray grill
1—2 x 2 green brick
1—1 x 2 green brick
1—2 x 2 green plate
2—1 x 1 green bricks with a stud on the side (headlight)
1—1 x 2 clear brick
3—2 x 2 black plates with wheel holders
6—small wheels with a hole for a wheel holder

Begin your dump truck by grabbing a 2 x 8 dark gray plate. Add three sets of wheels attached to 2 x 2 black plates with wheel holders. Begin the cab with a 2 x 2 brick as shown. Then add two 1 x 1 green bricks with a stud on the side (headlight) and attach a 1 x 2 light gray grill to the studs. Finish up the cab with a 1 x 2 green brick, a 1 x 2 clear brick and a 2 x 2 green plate. Place a 2 x 4 light gray plate and a 1 x 2 light gray plate on top of the dark gray plate behind the cab.

Add a 4 x 6 dark gray plate for building the bed of the truck. Then grab two 1 x 6 dark gray bricks and two 1 x 2 dark gray bricks.

Build a border around the bed of the truck, and your dump truck is complete!

Set up a scene with an excavator (instructions on page 207) filling up the bed of the dump truck with dirt!

MINI SPACESHIPS (STEP-BY-STEP)

PARTS LIST

2—1 x 1 black bricks with studs on four sides

1—2 x 4 black tile

1—1 x 2 dark gray plate, rounded with open studs

2—1 x 2 dark gray tiles with bar handle

2—1 x 2 dark gray curved slopes

1—1 x 4 light gray plate with two studs

2—3 x 3 dark blue wedge plates, cut corners

4—1 x 1 translucent red round plates

1—1 x 1 translucent light blue round plate

2—1 x 1 gold cones

STEP 1: A great way to build a tiny spaceship is to start with a core of bricks that have studs on all sides. Then find a 2 x 4 black tile.

STEP 2: Attach the core of the ship to the studs on the underside of the 2 x 4 black tile. Then add a 1 x 2 dark gray plate (rounded with open studs).

STEP 3: Place a 1 x 4 light gray plate with two studs on top of the ship. Then add 3 x 3 dark blue wedge plates for wings. They will attach to the studs on the black bricks.

STEP 4: Once the wings are attached, add a 1 x 2 dark gray tile with a bar handle on each side of the ship.

STEP 5: Add a 1 x 2 dark gray curved slope on each side.

STEP 6: Turn the ship around and add two 1 x 1 gold cones to make rocket engines on the back of the ship. Then your mini spaceship is complete!

Now try using the pictures to build a spaceship with posable wings. Use wedge plates for the shape of the ship. The windshield is a 2 x 2 translucent black curved slope with a lip.

Build 1 x 2 plates with clips into the ship so that you can attach the wings. Each wing has a 1 x 2 plate with a handle on the side. Look for tiny pieces like 1 x 2 slopes with four slots to make your ship look really sharp.

The rocket engines on the back of the ship are 2 x 2 dark gray dishes. Attach them by inserting the studs on top of the 2 x 2 dark gray dishes into the holes on two 1 x 2 Technic bricks. Then it's time to zoom around the galaxy!

ANIMAL SAFARI

Create a menagerie of adorable animals! Build a majestic gorilla, a koala in a eucalyptus tree, an adorable panda bear and more. It's amazing how much detail you can achieve with just a few bricks! Once you've built your animals, construct tiny habitats for them with trees, rocks or water. You might even want to build a whole safari with animal scenes and a jeep for your minifigures to ride in!

KOALA (STEP-BY-STEP)

PARTS LIST

LIGHT GRAY BRICKS

1—2 x 3 brick

2—1 x 3 bricks

1—1 x 1 brick with a stud on the side

2—1 x 1 bricks with a stud on the side (headlight)

1—2 x 3 plate

2—1 x 3 plates

3—1 x 2 plates

2—2 x 1 x 1⅓ curved slopes with recessed stud

3—1 x 1 slopes, 30 degree

2—1 x 2 plates with a socket on the end

1—1 x 2 curved slope, inverted

1—2 x 2 curved slope, inverted

ASSORTED BRICKS

2—1 x 2 dark gray plates with a ball on the side

1—1 x 2 black tile

2—eyes

2—2 x 1 x 1⅓ white curved slopes with recessed stud

1—1 x 3 white brick

1—1 x 2 white plate

1—1 x 3 white plate

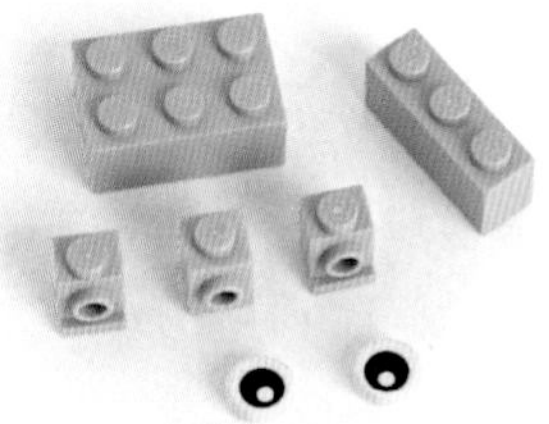

STEP 1: Gather the bricks shown for building the koala's head.

STEP 2: Place a 1 x 3 light gray brick on top of a 2 x 3 light gray brick. Then add a 1 x 1 brick with a stud on the side and two bricks with a stud on the side (headlight). Add the eyes.

STEP 3: Place a 2 x 3 light gray plate on top of the head. Then find the bricks shown.

STEP 4: Add a 1 x 2 black tile for the nose. Then add two 2 x 1 x 1⅓ white curved slopes with a recessed stud and a 1 x 1 light gray slope (30 degree) on the top of the head.

STEP 5: Gather the bricks shown for building the koala's body.

STEP 6: Place a 1 x 3 light gray plate on top of a 1 x 3 light gray brick. Place a 1 x 3 white plate on top of a 1 x 3 white brick. Then connect them with a 1 x 2 white plate as shown.

STEP 7: Add two 1 x 2 dark gray plates with a ball on the side. These will hold the arms.

STEP 8: Place a 1 x 3 light gray plate and a 1 x 2 light gray plate on the underside of the koala's body.

STEP 9: Add a 1 x 2 inverted curved slope and a 2 x 2 inverted curved slope. Then add two 1 x 1 light gray slopes (30 degree), one on each side.

STEP 10: Build the legs by attaching a 2 x 1 x 1⅓ light gray curved slope with a recessed stud on each side of the body.

STEP 11: Add the arms. Each arm is a 1 x 2 light gray plate with a socket on the side and a 1 x 2 light gray plate. Your cute koala is complete! Your koala will not balance on his own, but he can easily attach to a branch.

Build a eucalyptus tree for your koala to sit in! Eucalyptus leaves make up the majority of the koala's diet. This native Australian animal eats lots of leaves and sleeps up to 20 hours a day!

GORILLA (STEP-BY-STEP)

PARTS LIST

BLACK BRICKS

1—2 x 4 plate
1—2 x 3 plate
3—2 x 2 plates
4—1 x 4 plates
2—1 x 2 plates
4—1 x 1 plates
1—2 x 2 brick
1—1 x 2 brick
2—2 x 2 slopes
4—1 x 1 bricks with a stud on the side
2—1 x 1 bricks with a stud on the side (headlight)
2—2 x 1 x 1⅓ curved slopes with a recessed stud
1—1 x 2—1 x 2 bracket
1—1 x 2—1 x 2 bracket, inverted
2—1 x 1 slopes, 30 degree
1—1 x 2 slopes, 30 degree
1—1 x 2 tile
2—1 x 1 round plates with open stud

ASSORTED BRICKS

2—eyes
1—1 x 2 dark gray slope, 30 degree

STEP 1: Attach a 2 x 2 plate and a 1 x 4 plate to a 2 x 4 plate as shown.

STEP 2: Add another 2 x 2 plate and another 1 x 4 plate.

STEP 3: Find a 2 x 2 plate and two 2 x 1 x 1⅓ curved slopes with a recessed stud.

STEP 4: Place two 2 x 1 x 1⅓ curved slopes with a recessed stud on the back of the gorilla's body. Then add the 2 x 2 plate in front of that. Grab a 2 x 3 plate and a 1 x 2 slope (30 degree).

STEP 5: Attach the 1 x 2 slope at the back of the body, and then add the 2 x 3 plate so that it hangs off by one row of studs in the front.

STEP 6: Place a 1 x 2—1 x 2 bracket on the 2 x 3 plate from step 5. Then find a 1 x 2 plate and a 1 x 2—1 x 2 inverted bracket.

STEP 7: Place the 1 x 2—1 x 2 inverted bracket on top of the bracket added in the previous step. Then add a 1 x 2 plate on top of it.

STEP 8: Grab two 2 x 2 slopes, a 2 x 2 brick, two 1 x 1 bricks with a stud on the side (headlight), two eyes, and a 1 x 2 tile.

STEP 9: Fill in the gorilla's body by adding a 2 x 2 brick on its back and a 2 x 2 slope on top of that.

STEP 10: Add the two 1 x 1 bricks with a stud on the side (headlight) and attach the eyes to those. Then place a 2 x 2 slope and a 1 x 2 tile on top of the gorilla's head.

STEP 11: Turn the gorilla around and build the back legs by adding a 1 x 2 brick and a 1 x 2 plate.

STEP 12: Gather four 1 x 1 bricks with a stud on the side, four 1 x 1 plates and two 1 x 1 slopes (30 degree) for building the front legs.

STEP 13: Attach a 1 x 1 brick with a stud on the side and two 1 x 1 plates for each leg.

STEP 14: Build the gorilla's shoulders by adding another 1 x 1 brick with a stud on the side and a 1 x 1 slope (30 degree) on each side.

STEP 15: Attach a 1 x 4 plate to the front of each front leg. Then complete the gorilla's face by adding a 1 x 2 dark gray slope (30 degree) and two 1 x 1 round plates. These round plates have an open stud, which makes them look more like nostrils. Your gorilla is complete!

Try building a jungle scene for your gorilla with plenty of trees and plants. Gorillas eat termites and ants, but most of their diet is made up of plant stems, shoots and fruit.

GIRAFFE (STEP-BY-STEP)

PARTS LIST

YELLOW BRICKS

2—4 x 6 plates
1—2 x 4 plate
4—2 x 2 plates
5—1 x 2 plates
1—2 x 4 brick
1—2 x 2 brick
1—1 x 4 brick
5—1 x 2 bricks
1—1 x 1 brick
1—1 x 2 Technic brick
2—1 x 1 plates
1—1 x 2 slope, 30 degree
4—1 x 1 bricks with a stud on the side
2—1 x 1 bricks with a stud on the side (headlight)
8—2 x 2 round bricks

BROWN BRICKS

3—1 x 2 bricks
3—1 x 1 bricks
4—2 x 2 round bricks
4—1 x 2 plates
1—2 x 2 corner plate
1—1 x 1 plate
1—1 x 2 slope, 30 degree
2—1 x 1 cones

ASSORTED BRICKS

2—eyes
1—1 x 2 black plate
1—blue Technic pin, half length

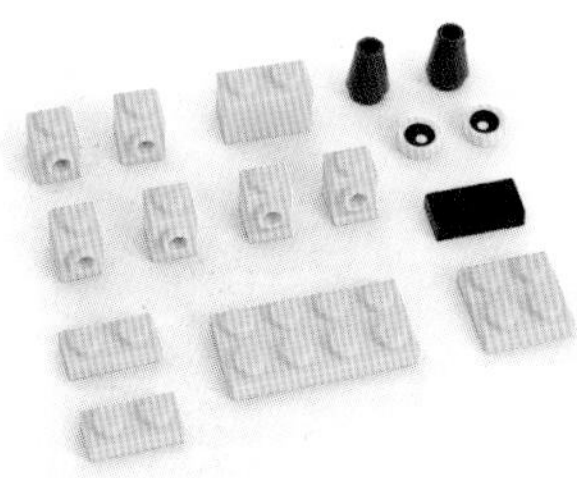

STEP 1: Gather the bricks shown for building the giraffe's head.

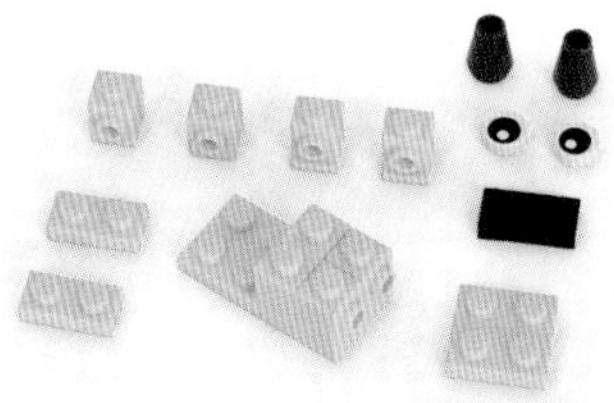

STEP 2: Place two 1 x 1 yellow bricks with a stud on the side and a 1 x 2 yellow brick on top of a 2 x 4 yellow plate.

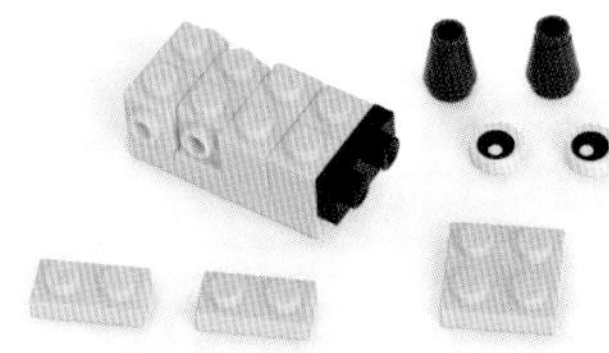

STEP 3: Add two 1 x 1 yellow bricks with a stud on the side (headlight) and then two more 1 x 1 bricks with a stud on the side. Create the nose by placing a 1 x 2 black plate on the front of the head.

STEP 4: Attach the eyes to the bricks with a stud on the side (headlight). Place a 2 x 2 yellow plate on top of the head. Add two 1 x 1 brown cones.

STEP 5: Give the giraffe ears by adding a 1 x 2 yellow plate on each side of the head.

STEP 6: Gather the bricks shown for building the giraffe's neck.

STEP 7: Place a 2 x 2 yellow plate on top of a 2 x 2 brown corner plate and a 1 x 1 yellow plate. Then add a 1 x 2 yellow brick, a 1 x 1 yellow brick and a 1 x 1 brown brick.

STEP 8: Continue building the neck by adding another 2 x 2 yellow plate, a 1 x 2 yellow plate, a 1 x 2 yellow brick and a 1 x 2 brown brick. Then add a 1 x 2 brown plate. Finish up the neck by adding a 2 x 2 yellow brick, and then attach the head.

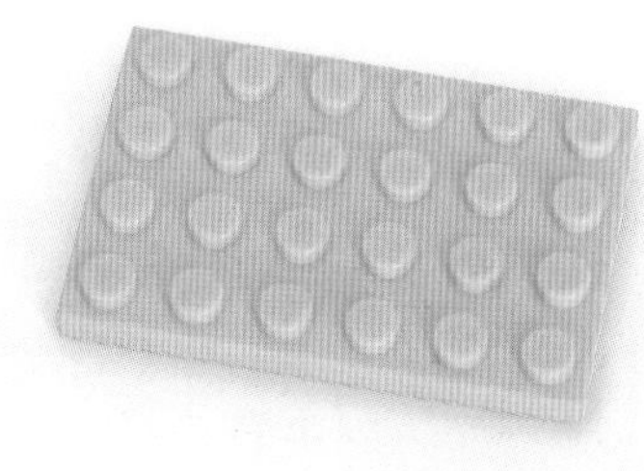

STEP 9: Build the giraffe's body. Start with a 4 x 6 yellow plate.

STEP 10: Add a layer of yellow and brown bricks to the giraffe's body, including a 1 x 2 yellow Technic brick that will hold the giraffe's tail.

STEP 11: Turn the body around so that the Technic brick is on the left. Place a 4 x 6 yellow plate on top of the giraffe's body. Then find the plates and slopes shown.

STEP 12: Give the giraffe spots on its body by adding yellow and brown plates. Place one 1 x 2 slope (30 degree) on each side of the space where the neck will sit.

STEP 13: Attach the giraffe's head and neck to the body. Then build the legs. Each leg has two 2 x 2 yellow round bricks and one 2 x 2 brown round brick. Use regular bricks if you don't have the round ones.

STEP 14: Give the giraffe a tail! Find a blue pin (half length), a 1 x 2 yellow plate and a 1 x 2 brown plate.

STEP 15: Insert the blue pin into the Technic brick on the giraffe's body. Place the 1 x 2 brown plate onto one stud of the 1 x 2 yellow plate.

STEP 16: Attach the tail to the blue pin, and the giraffe is complete!

Now build your giraffe a tree with some leaves to munch on! Be sure to make the branches the right height for the giraffe to reach with her long neck.

PARROT (STEP-BY-STEP)

PARTS LIST

1—2 x 2 red corner plate
1—1 x 1 yellow brick with a stud on the side
1—1 x 1 light gray brick with studs on opposite sides
1—1 x 1 light gray tile with a clip
1—1 x 1 black brick with studs on opposite sides
1—1 x 2 green curved slope
1—1 x 1 yellow plate with a vertical tooth
1—1 x 1 yellow plate
1—1 x 2 dark green plate with a handle on the end
1—2 x 3 orange wedge plate, right
1—2 x 3 orange wedge plate, left
2—eyes

STEP 1: The parrot's body is very simple. Start with a 2 x 2 red corner plate. Add a 1 x 1 yellow brick with a stud on the side. Then add a 1 x 1 light gray brick with studs on opposite sides and a 1 x 1 black brick with studs on opposite sides. Place a 1 x 2 green curved slope on top.

STEP 2: Add a beak by placing a 1 x 1 yellow plate with a vertical tooth under the 1 x 2 green curved slope. Then add a 1 x 1 yellow plate. Attach eyes to the black brick. Then find the bricks shown.

STEP 3: Make the parrot's tail by attaching a 1 x 1 light gray tile with a clip to the 1 x 1 yellow brick on the body. Then add a 1 x 2 dark green plate with a handle on the end. Find two 2 x 3 orange wedge plates, one right orientation and one left.

STEP 4: Attach the wings, and the parrot is complete!

Now build a tree and make your parrot perch on the branches! Look for tropical-style leaves, and you may want to add some fruit. Your parrot will be looking for something to eat!

ELEPHANT (STEP-BY-STEP)

PARTS LIST

DARK GRAY BRICKS

1—4 x 4 plate
1—2 x 4 plate
2—2 x 2 plates
1—1 x 6 plate
4—1 x 4 plates
4—1 x 2 plates
6—1 x 1 plates
2—2 x 4 bricks
2—1 x 2 bricks
10—1 x 1 bricks
2—1 x 1 bricks with a stud on the side
1—2 x 4 slope, double inverted
2—1 x 1 round bricks
1—1 x 2 plate with one finger on the side
1—1 x 2 plate with one stud on top (jumper)
2—1 x 1 slopes, 30 degree
4—1 x 2 slopes, 30 degree
3—2 x 1 x 1⅓ curved slopes with a recessed stud
1—1 x 4 curved slope, double

ASSORTED BRICKS

4—1 x 1 light gray plates
2—eyes

STEP 1: Grab a 4 x 4 plate, a 2 x 4 plate and a 1 x 2 plate with one finger on the side.

STEP 2: Place the 2 x 4 plate and the 1 x 2 plate with one finger on top of the 4 x 4 plate.

STEP 3: Add a 2 x 4 brick. Then find four 1 x 4 plates and four 1 x 2 slopes (30 degree).

STEP 4: Place two 1 x 4 plates on each side of the elephant's body.

STEP 5: Fill in the body by adding two 1 x 2 slopes (30 degree) on each side.

STEP 6: Flip over the body and add a 2 x 4 brick and two 1 x 2 bricks on the underside.

STEP 7: Find a 2 x 4 double inverted slope and two 2 x 2 plates for building the elephant's face.

STEP 8: Place both 2 x 2 plates inside the double inverted slope. Then find a 1 x 2 plate with one stud on top (jumper plate), two 1 x 1 slopes (30 degree), a 2 x 1 x 1⅓ curved slope with recessed stud, and two 1 x 1 round bricks.

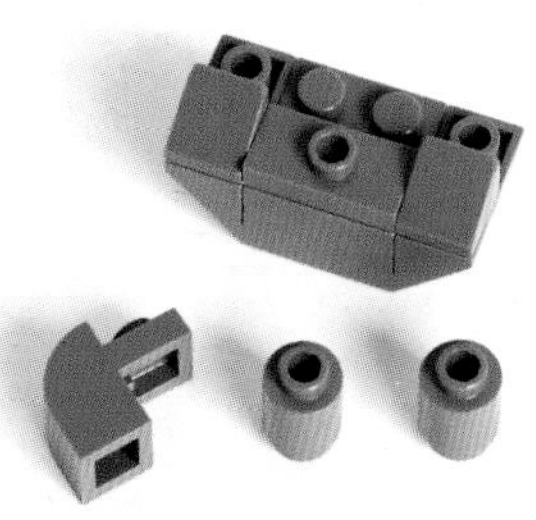

STEP 9: Place the jumper plate and the two 1 x 1 slopes (30 degree) on the elephant's face.

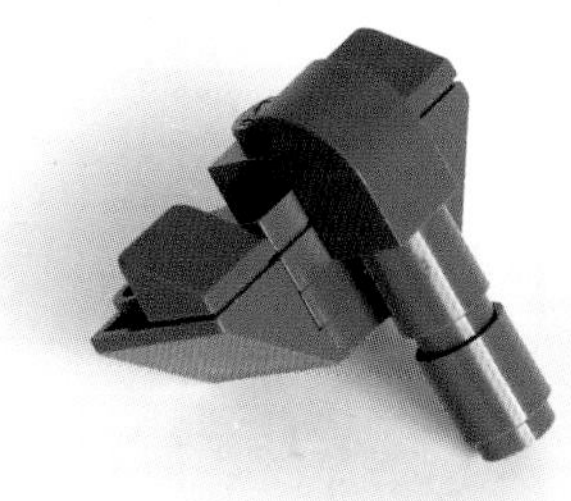

STEP 10: Build the trunk by adding a 2 x 1 x 1⅓ curved slope with recessed stud and two 1 x 1 round bricks.

STEP 11: Build the legs and add them to the body. Each leg has two 1 x 1 bricks, a 1 x 1 plate and a 1 x 1 light gray plate.

STEP 12: Attach the trunk to the elephant's body.

STEP 13: Now build the rest of the head. Grab a 1 x 6 plate and place a 1 x 2 plate on the underside on each end.

STEP 14: Add two 1 x 1 bricks with a stud on the side and two 1 x 1 bricks. Then find two 2 x 1 x 1⅓ curved slopes with a recessed stud and two 1 x 1 plates.

STEP 15: Place one of the curved slopes on each side of the head with a 1 x 1 plate under it. Then find a 1 x 4 double curved slope, two eyes and two 1 x 2 plates.

STEP 16: Attach the eyes and place the two 1 x 2 plates right above them. Then finish up the head by adding a 1 x 4 double curved slope.

STEP 17: Attach the head to the elephant, and your elephant is complete!

Build a little pool for your elephant to wade in. She likes the shade of the tree on a hot day!

Make it look like your elephant is wading in the water by removing part of each leg. Now she can get a drink!

PUFFIN (STEP-BY-STEP)

PARTS LIST

BLACK BRICKS

1—1 x 1 brick with studs on opposite sides

1—1 x 2 plate with one stud on top (jumper plate)

2—1 x 1 plates with a horizontal tooth

1—1 x 1 slope, 30 degree

2—1 x 1 plates

2—1 x 3 plates

WHITE BRICKS

1—1 x 3 plate

1—1 x 1 brick

1—1 x 1 brick with studs on four sides

ASSORTED BRICKS

2—eyes

1—1 x 1 orange slope, 30 degree

1—1 x 2 orange plate

1—1 x 1 orange round plate

1—1 x 1 light gray plate

STEP 1: Gather the bricks shown for building the puffin's body.

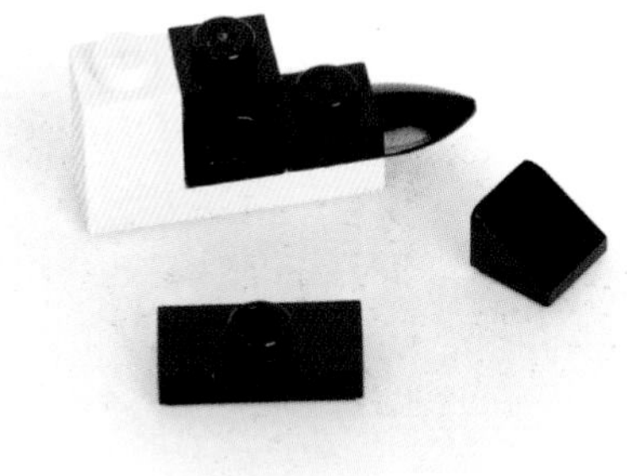

STEP 2: Place a 1 x 1 white brick, a 1 x 1 black brick with studs on opposite sides, and a 1 x 1 black plate with a horizontal tooth on a 1 x 3 white plate.

STEP 3: Add a 1 x 1 black slope on the tail and a 1 x 2 black plate with one stud on top (jumper plate) on top of the body.

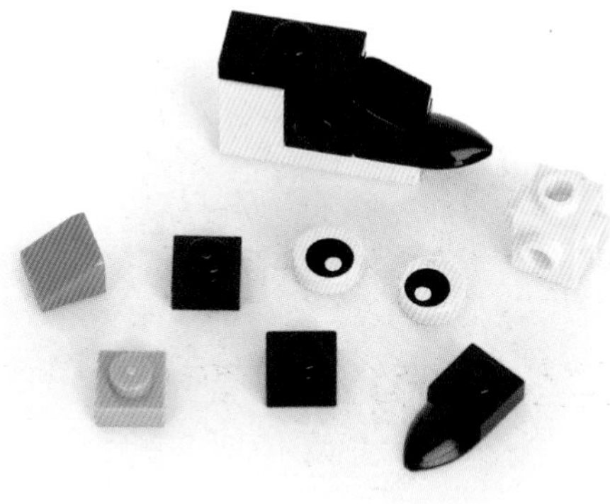

STEP 4: Gather the bricks shown for building the puffin's head.

STEP 5: Add a 1 x 1 black plate with a horizontal tooth on top of the puffin's body. Then add a 1 x 1 white brick with four studs.

STEP 6: Place an eye on each side of the puffin's head. Then add two 1 x 1 black plates, a 1 x 1 light gray plate and a 1 x 1 orange slope (30 degree).

STEP 7: Give the puffin feet by adding a 1 x 2 orange plate and a 1 x 1 orange round plate.

STEP 8: Finish up the puffin by adding two 1 x 3 black plates for wings. Your little puffin is complete!

The Atlantic puffin nests on the chilly coasts of the North Atlantic Ocean. Build a rocky seashore for your puffin to stand on. She can dive into the water to grab some fish!

PANDA (STEP-BY-STEP)

PARTS LIST

WHITE BRICKS

1—2 x 6 plate
1—2 x 4 plate
2—1 x 4 plates
1—2 x 2 plate
2—1 x 2 plates
2—1 x 2 bricks
1—2 x 2 brick
2—1 x 1 bricks with a stud on the side
1—1 x 2 slope, 30 degree
1—1 x 2 plate with one stud on top (jumper plate)
2—2 x 1 slopes, 45 degree with ⅔ cutout

BLACK BRICKS

2—1 x 1 bricks with a stud on the side
3—1 x 1 round plates
1—1 x 4 plate
1—1 x 2 brick
1—1 x 2 slope, 30 degree
2—1 x 1 slopes, 30 degree
4—1 x 1 bricks
4—1 x 2 plates

ASSORTED BRICKS

2—eyes

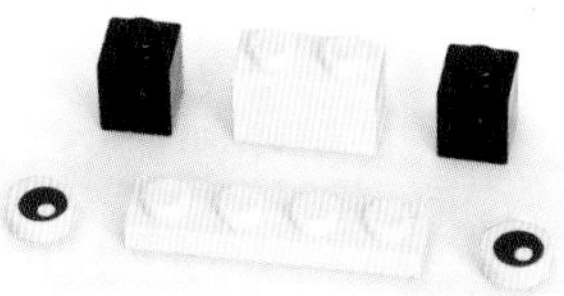

STEP 1: Find two 1 x 1 black bricks with a stud on the side, a 1 x 2 white brick, a 1 x 4 white plate and two eyes.

STEP 2: Attach the black 1 x 1 bricks with a stud on the side and the 1 x 2 white brick to the 1 x 4 white plate. Then attach the eyes to the black bricks with a stud on the side.

STEP 3: Place a 2 x 2 white plate under the head. Then add a 1 x 2 white plate on top of the head and add two 1 x 1 black round plates to be ears.

STEP 4: Place two 1 x 1 white bricks with a stud on the side on the front of the face. Attach a 1 x 2 slope (30 degree) on top of them. Then find a 1 x 2 white plate with one stud on top (jumper plate) and a 1 x 1 black round plate.

STEP 5: Make the panda's nose by attaching a 1 x 2 white jumper plate to the studs on the front of the face. Then add a 1 x 1 black round plate.

STEP 6: Find a 1 x 4 white plate, a 1 x 2 white brick, a 2 x 2 white brick, a 2 x 6 white plate and a 1 x 4 black plate.

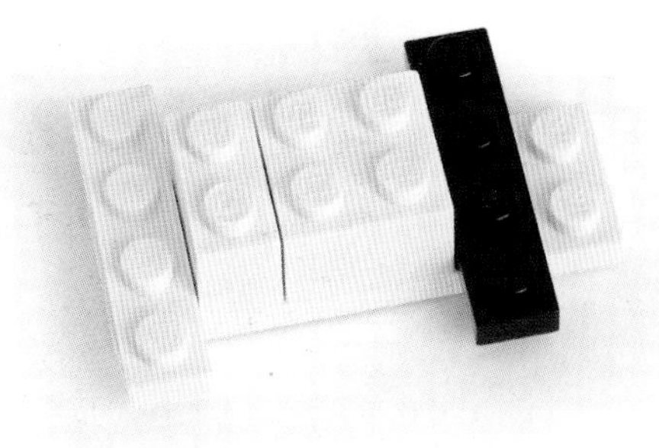

STEP 7: Place the bricks and plates on the 2 x 6 white plate as shown.

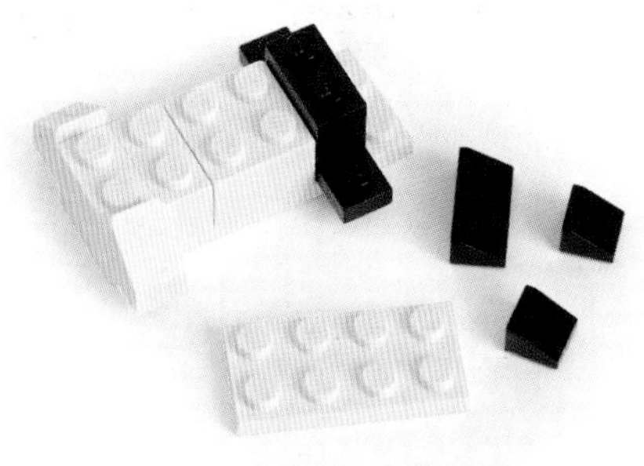

STEP 8: Add two 1 x 2 white slopes (45 degree with a cutout) and a 1 x 2 white plate on the back end of the panda. Place a 1 x 2 black brick on the 1 x 4 black plate. Then find a 2 x 4 white plate, two 1 x 1 black slopes (30 degree) and a 1 x 2 black slope (30 degree).

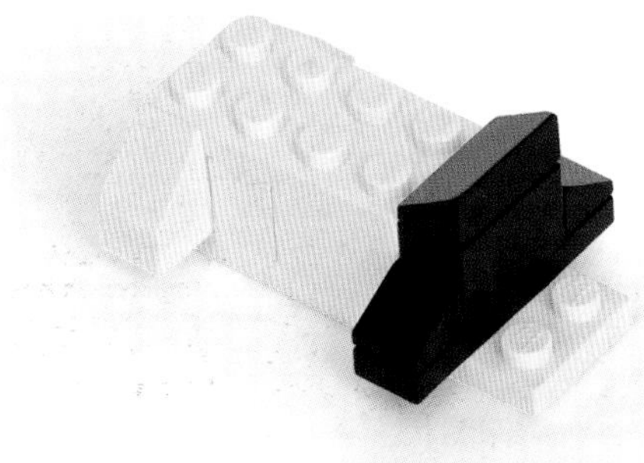

STEP 9: Place the 2 x 4 white plate on the panda's back. Add the black slopes to the front of the panda's body as shown.

STEP 10: Attach the head to the front of the panda's body.

STEP 11: Build the panda's legs and attach them to the body. Each leg is one 1 x 1 black brick and one 1 x 2 black plate. Your panda is complete!

Now build some bamboo for your panda by stacking 1 x 1 round bricks with leaves. Giant pandas live in China and eat mainly bamboo shoots and leaves. They are beautiful creatures!

ROBIN (STEP-BY-STEP)

PARTS LIST

BROWN BRICKS

1—1 x 2 plate with two fingers

2—1 x 2 plates

1—1 x 1 slope, 30 degree

1—1 x 1 brick

2—1 x 4 curved slopes, double

2—1 x 2 plates with door rail

RED BRICKS

1—1 x 4 plate

1—1 x 2 plate

1—1 x 2 slope, inverted

ASSORTED BRICKS

1—1 x 1 dark gray bricks with studs on opposite sides

1—1 x 1 dark gray slope, 30 degree

1—1 x 1 black brick with studs on four sides

1—1 x 2 black plate

1—1 x 1 black round plate

STEP 1: Gather the brick's shown for building the robin's body.

STEP 2: Place a 1 x 2 red plate under one end of a 1 x 4 red plate. Then add a 1 x 2 brown plate with two fingers, a 1 x 2 brown plate, a 1 x 1 brown slope (30 degree), a 1 x 1 dark gray brick with studs on opposite sides, and a 1 x 2 red inverted slope.

STEP 3: Add a 1 x 1 black brick with studs on four sides for the robin's head. Add eyes and a 1 x 1 dark gray slope (30 degree) for the beak. Grab a 1 x 2 brown plate and a 1 x 1 brown brick.

STEP 4: Attach the bottom of the 1 x 1 brown brick to the back of the robin's head. Then add a 1 x 2 brown plate on top. Build two wings. Each wing is a 1 x 4 brown double curved slope and a 1 x 2 brown plate with door rail.

STEP 5: Place the wings on the studs on the sides of the robin's body. Then build the feet with a 1 x 2 black plate and a 1 x 1 black round plate. Your robin is complete!

Now build a little garden for your robin to hop around in as he hunts for worms!

MINIATURE LIFE

Build tiny versions of things you use in everyday life! Construct a tiny candy machine with little round plates as colorful candy. Make a classic camera out of just a few bricks and build an intricate tiny house. Then build an adorable miniature microscope. After you've built these projects, you'll probably notice other things in real life that you can't wait to try building out of LEGO bricks!

CANDY MACHINE (STEP-BY-STEP)

PARTS LIST

Note: This parts list includes bricks needed to make a red candy machine, but you can substitute any color you like for the red bricks.

RED BRICKS

3—4 x 4 plates
1—2 x 4 plate
2—1 x 4 bricks
1—1 x 2 brick
2—1 x 2 plates
1—1 x 2 Technic brick

ASSORTED BRICKS

1—4 x 4 light gray dish
2—2 x 2 light gray round bricks
1—1 x 1 light gray round plate
6—1 x 2 x 2 clear panels
1—blue Technic pin, ½ length
About 15—1 x 1 round plates in assorted colors

STEP 1: Find a 4 x 4 red plate, a 2 x 4 red plate and two 1 x 2 red plates.

STEP 2: Place the smaller plates on top of the 4 x 4 plate as shown.

STEP 3: Add a 1 x 4 red brick on each side of the machine and a 1 x 2 brick in the back. Then find the bricks shown.

STEP 4: Insert a blue pin (half length) into the hole on a 1 x 2 Technic brick.

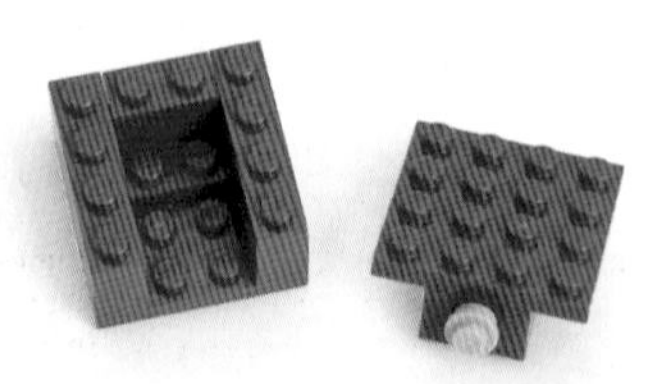

STEP 5: Attach a 1 x 1 light gray round plate to the blue pin. Then attach the 1 x 2 Technic brick to the underside of the 4 x 4 plate.

STEP 6: Attach the 4 x 4 plate with the Technic brick attached to the candy machine. Then build the sides of the candy chamber by attaching six 1 x 2 x 2 clear panels.

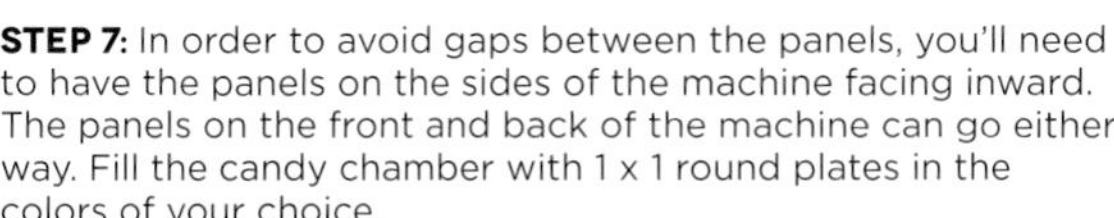

STEP 7: In order to avoid gaps between the panels, you'll need to have the panels on the sides of the machine facing inward. The panels on the front and back of the machine can go either way. Fill the candy chamber with 1 x 1 round plates in the colors of your choice.

STEP 8: Place a 4 x 4 red plate on top of the candy chamber. Then grab a 4 x 4 light gray dish. Stack two 2 x 2 light gray round bricks.

STEP 9: Build a stand for the machine by attaching the two 2 x 2 light gray round bricks to the light gray dish. Then attach the machine. Your candy machine is complete!

Build a second machine and fill it with candy. You can make it look like a different type of candy by using a different color of 1 x 1 round plates. Use brown plates for chocolate candy or fill it with pink to make gumballs!

CAMERA (CREATIVE CHALLENGE)

PARTS LIST

LIGHT GRAY BRICKS

3—2 x 6 light gray plates
1—1 x 2 light gray plate
1—1 x 2 light gray brick with two studs on the side
1—1 x 1 light gray round plate
1—1 x 1 light gray round tile
1—2 x 2 light gray round brick

BLACK BRICKS

2—2 x 6 black plates
2—2 x 2 black bricks
1—1 x 2 black brick
1—1 x 1 black round tile

ASSORTED BRICKS

2—1 x 1 clear slopes, 30 degree

Build a classic camera! Start with a 2 x 6 light gray plate. Add two 2 x 6 black plates. Then add a 2 x 2 black brick on each end and a 1 x 2 light gray brick with two studs on the side and a 1 x 2 black brick in the middle.

Finish up the camera body by adding two 2 x 6 light gray plates. Then build a flash with a 1 x 2 light gray plate and two 1 x 1 clear slopes (30 degree). Add a 1 x 1 black round tile to make a dial and a 1 x 1 light gray round plate with a 1 x 1 light gray round tile on top to make the shutter button. Then attach a 2 x 2 light gray round brick to the front of the camera to make the lens.

This project would make a great gift for a photographer! It would also look great displayed on a desk or shelf.

MICROSCOPE (STEP-BY-STEP)

PARTS LIST

DARK GRAY BRICKS

1—2 x 3 plate
1—1 x 2 slope, 30 degree
1—1 x 2 plate with one stud on top (jumper plate)
1—1 x 2 plate with bar arm up
1—1 x 1 brick with a stud on the side
1—1 x 1 plate
1—1 x 2 curved slope
1—2 x 1 x 1⅓ curved slope with recessed stud

ASSORTED BRICKS

1—1 x 2 white plate with one stud on top
1—1 x 1 translucent light blue plate
1—1 x 2 dark red plate
1—1 x 1 black round plate
1—light gray Technic pin, half length
1—1 x 1 clear round tile

STEP 1: Find a 2 x 3 dark gray plate, a 1 x 2 dark gray slope (30 degree), a 1 x 2 white plate with one stud on top (jumper plate), and a 1 x 1 translucent light blue plate.

STEP 2: Attach the 1 x 2 slope (30 degree) and the white jumper plate to the 2 x 3 dark gray plate. Then place the 1 x 1 translucent light blue plate on top of the white jumper plate. This is the microscope slide. You can substitute a 1 x 1 plate in another color if you want to or leave it off.

STEP 3: Add a 1 x 2 dark red plate and a 1 x 2 dark gray plate modified with a bar arm up.

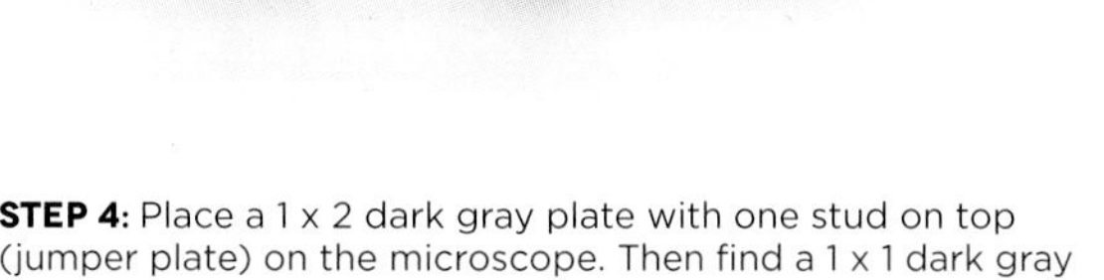

STEP 4: Place a 1 x 2 dark gray plate with one stud on top (jumper plate) on the microscope. Then find a 1 x 1 dark gray plate, a 1 x 1 black round plate and a 1 x 1 dark gray brick with a stud on the side.

STEP 5: Place a 1 x 1 plate on top of the dark gray jumper plate. Then add a 1 x 1 brick with a stud on the side and attach a 1 x 1 black round plate to the brick.

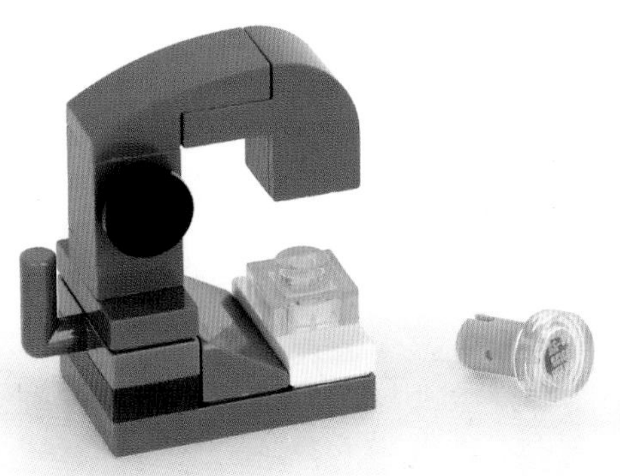

STEP 6: Add a 1 x 2 curved slope. Then add a 2 x 1 x 1⅓ dark gray curved slope with a recessed stud. Build the lens of the microscope by attaching a 1 x 1 clear round tile to a light gray pin (half length).

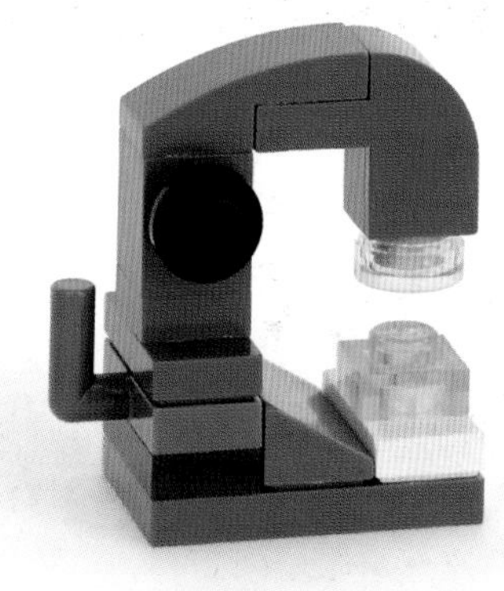

STEP 7: Insert the light gray pin into the dark gray curved slope, and your microscope is complete!

MINIATURE HOUSE (STEP-BY-STEP)

PARTS LIST

TAN BRICKS

2—4 x 4 plates
1—2 x 8 plate
5—1 x 4 plates
1—1 x 3 plate
1—1 x 1 plate
1—1 x 8 brick
1—1 x 6 brick
5—1 x 4 bricks
2—1 x 3 bricks
6—1 x 2 bricks
2—1 x 1 bricks
1—1 x 1 brick with a stud on the side

LIME GREEN BRICKS

4—2 x 4 lime green plates
2—1 x 4 lime green plates
1—1 x 6 lime green plate
1—1 x 2 lime green plate
1—1 x 1 lime green plate

ASSORTED BRICKS

2—6 x 10 light gray plates
5—1 x 4 light gray tiles
1—1 x 3 light gray tile
1—1 x 2 brown tile
5—1 x 1 clear bricks
10—2 x 4 dark blue slopes
4—2 x 2 dark blue slopes
1—plant stem with three leaves
1—1 x 1 red round plate with hole
2—flowers

STEP 1: Build an adorable family home on a tiny scale! Use two 6 x 10 light gray plates for the base.

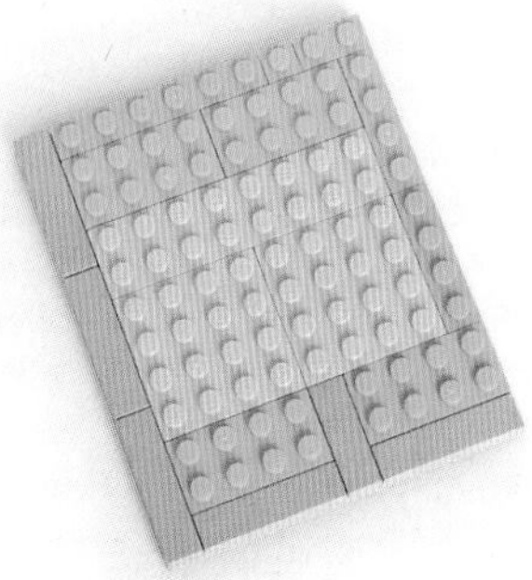

STEP 2: Join the two 6 x 10 plates together to make a 10 x 12 rectangle. Add two 4 x 4 tan plates and a 2 x 8 tan plate to make the bottom of the house. Add lime green plates for the yard area and light gray tiles for the sidewalk. Use plates instead of tiles for the sidewalk if needed.

STEP 3: Add a border of tan plates around the house and a 1 x 1 tan brick with a stud on the side.

STEP 4: Add bricks around the perimeter of the house. Use 1 x 1 clear bricks for the windows. If you don't have clear bricks, white bricks also work well for windows. Find a 1 x 1 tan plate and a 1 x 2 brown tile for the front door.

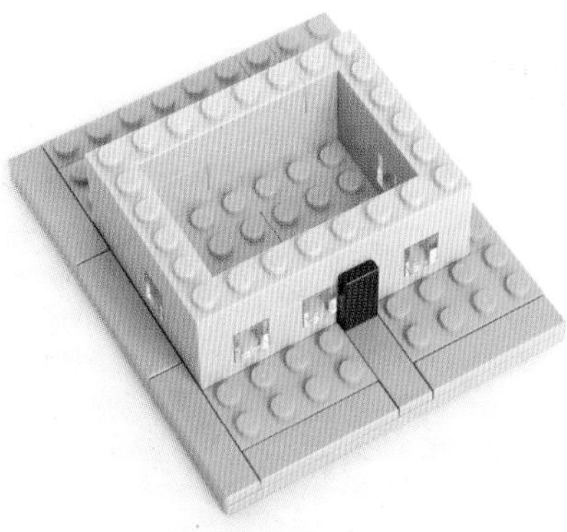

STEP 5: Place the 1 x 1 tan plate on top of the 1 x 1 brick with a stud on the side. Attach the door. Then add another row of tan bricks.

STEP 6: Build a roof! Place two 2 x 4 dark blue slopes on the front of the house and two on the back. Add a 1 x 4 tan brick on each side.

STEP 7: Add another row of dark blue slope bricks, and place a 1 x 2 tan brick on each side of the house.

STEP 8: Finish up the roof with a final row of 2 x 4 dark blue slopes. Then find some tiny plants to landscape your house!

STEP 9: Slide a plant with three leaves into a 1 x 1 round plate with a hole. It's the perfect size for a tiny tree! Add flowers to make bushes. Your tiny house is complete!

AMAZING IDEA

Build a tiny neighborhood! Make more houses or try building a taller apartment building. Create a tiny store or a tiny library. What other ideas can you think of?

MICRO ROBOT CREW

Build some fun micro robots that are detailed, posable and super cool! Robots are a great project to tackle with all the odds and ends at the bottom of your tub of bricks because you can use almost any pieces you find. And robots can be built in many different ways! Give them wheels, feet or tracks. Use eyes for eyes, or use round plates, tiles or even wheels. Find a friend and build robots together. It will be fun to see what you come up with!

RETRO BOT (STEP-BY-STEP)

PARTS LIST

RED BRICKS

2—2 x 3 plates
2—1 x 2 plates
1—1 x 3 brick
1—1 x 1 brick
1—1 x 1 brick with a stud on the side
2—1 x 1 bricks with a stud on the side (headlight)
2—1 x 2 grills
4—1 x 1 round bricks

LIGHT GRAY BRICKS

2—2 x 3 plates
2—1 x 2 plates with a clip on the end
2—1 x 2 plates with a socket on the end
1—1 x 2 plate
1—antenna

DARK GRAY BRICKS

2—1 x 2 plates
2—1 x 2 plates with a ball on the side
1—1 x 1 brick with a stud on the side
1—1 x 2 grill
2—1 x 1 round plates

ASSORTED BRICKS

2—2 x 3 black plates
2—1 x 1 white round bricks
2—1 x 1 silver round plates

STEP 1: Gather the bricks shown for building the robot's head.

STEP 2: Attach a 1 x 3 red brick, a 1 x 1 red brick and two 1 x 1 red bricks with a stud on the side (headlight) to a 2 x 3 black plate. Then add two 1 x 1 silver round plates as the eyes.

STEP 3: Place a second 2 x 3 black plate on the top of the head.

STEP 4: Gather the bricks shown for building the body of the robot.

STEP 5: Attach two 2 x 3 red plates to a 2 x 3 light gray plate. Then add two 1 x 2 red plates.

STEP 6: Place a 1 x 1 dark gray brick with a stud on the side and a 1 x 1 red brick with a stud on the side in the center of the body. Then add a 1 x 2 dark gray plate with a ball on the side and a 1 x 2 red grill on each side.

STEP 7: Finish up the body by adding a 2 x 3 light gray plate and two 1 x 1 white round bricks to make the neck.

STEP 8: Attach the head to the white round bricks. Then build the legs and feet with red round bricks and 1 x 2 dark gray plates. Add arms. Each arm is a 1 x 2 light gray plate with a socket on the end and a 1 x 2 light gray plate with a clip on the end.

STEP 9: Add an antenna to the robot's head and place a 1 x 2 light gray plate on his back. Add two 1 x 1 dark gray round plates to the light gray plate. Your robot is complete!

The clips on the robot's hands make it easy for him to hold all kinds of tools!

SPECIALIZED ASSISTANCE MODULE (SAM) BOT (STEP-BY-STEP)

PARTS LIST

DARK GRAY BRICKS

1—4 x 4 round plate

1—2 x 4 plate

2—1 x 2 Technic bricks

1—1 x 2 slope, 30 degree, printed with dials

2—1 x 2 plates with a clip on the end

2—1 x 2 plates with a pin hole on top

LIGHT GRAY BRICKS

2—1 x 4 hinge plates with swivel top

2—1 x 2 plates with a pin hole on the bottom

1—1 x 3 Technic liftarm

2—Technic axle and pin connectors, perpendicular, 3 studs long with a center pin hole

ASSORTED BRICKS

2—1 x 5 blue Technic liftarms

1—2 x 2 blue turntable

1—blue axle pin

6—black Technic pins with friction ridges

1—1 x 2 yellow Technic brick

1—2 x 2 yellow plate

1—lime green Technic axle and pin connector, perpendicular

1—1 x 1 lime green plate

1—1 x 2 lime green curved slope

2—dark tan axles, 3 studs long with stud

2—1 x 1 translucent blue round plates

2—1 x 1 medium azure slopes, 30 degree

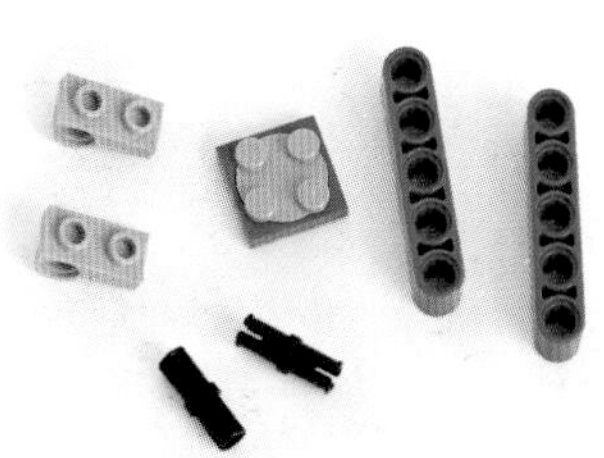

STEP 1: Gather the bricks shown to build the base of the Specialized Assistance Module Bot (SAM Bot).

STEP 2: Place a 2 x 2 blue turntable on top of two 1 x 2 light gray plates with a pin hole on the bottom. Insert black pins into the second hole from the end on two 1 x 5 blue liftarms.

STEP 3: Insert the black pins into the holes in the light gray plates.

STEP 4: Gather the dark gray bricks shown.

STEP 5: Attach a 2 x 4 dark gray plate to the top of a 4 x 4 round plate. Then add a 1 x 2 Technic brick on each end of the 2 x 4 plate. Add a 1 x 2 dark gray slope (30 degree) printed with dials.

STEP 6: Insert a blue axle pin and a black pin into a 1 x 3 light gray liftarm.

STEP 7: Insert the black pin into the hole on a 1 x 2 yellow Technic brick. Then attach the yellow Technic brick to the robot's body.

STEP 8: Slide a lime green axle and pin connector (perpendicular) onto the blue axle pin. Substitute with any other color if needed. Insert a black pin. Then find the bricks shown.

STEP 9: Place the 2 x 2 yellow plate on the right side of the robot and the 1 x 1 lime green plate and 1 x 1 lime green curved slope on the left.

STEP 10: Find two light gray axle and pin connectors (perpendicular, 3 studs long with a center pin hole), two dark tan axles (3 studs long with a stud) and two 1 x 1 translucent blue round plates.

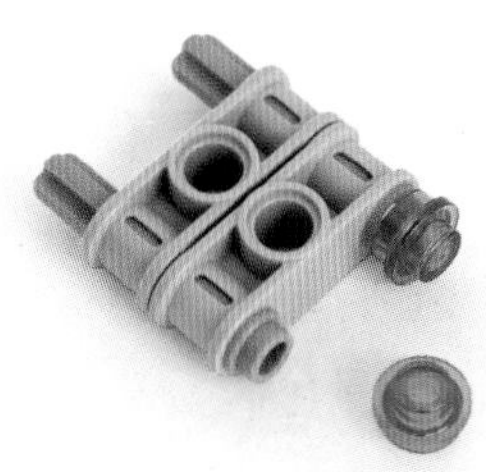

STEP 11: Slide the two dark tan axles through both axle and pin connectors. Attach the translucent blue round plates to the axles to make eyes.

STEP 12: Attach the robot's head to the black pin.

STEP 13: Gather the bricks shown for building the robot's arm. You'll need two sets of these pieces.

STEP 14: Place a 1 x 2 dark gray plate with a pin hole on top and a 1 x 2 dark gray plate with a clip on the end on a 1 x 4 light gray hinge plate. Then insert a black pin and add a 1 x 1 medium azure slope (30 degree).

STEP 15: Build a second arm for the robot.

BUILDING TIP

The friction ridges on the blue pin allow you to tilt the robot's head upward, and it will stay in place.

STEP 16: Attach the pins on the arms to the Technic bricks on the robot's body, and your SAM Bot is complete!

The SAM Bot's posable joints allow it to assist with a multitude of tasks. You can turn his head from side to side and tilt it up and down. His arms move up and down and bend at the elbows, and you can also swivel his entire body.

ZIP THE WHEELED BOT (CREATIVE CHALLENGE)

PARTS LIST

LIGHT GRAY BRICKS

1—2 x 4 brick

2—1 x 2 plates

2—1 x 1 bricks with a bar handle

2—2 x 2 light gray plates with wheel holders

2—antennas

ASSORTED BRICKS

1—1 x 4 tan brick with four studs on the side

2—black droid arms

2—2 x 1 dark gray slopes with cutout

1—1 x 2 dark gray brick with ridges

1—1 x 2 white grill

2—1 x 1 translucent green round tiles

4—wheels with a hole for a wheel holder

Use the pictures to build this adorable robot on wheels. The antennas on Zip's head and his widely spaced eyes give him a cute and quirky look. Use droid arms to give him arms that can hold tools or other accessories.

The body of the robot is a simple 2 x 4 light gray brick that sits on top of two 2 x 2 light gray plates with holders and four small wheels. Add two 1 x 2 light gray plates and then two 2 x 1 dark gray slopes with a cutout to build the back of the body.

ARTIFICIAL INTELLIGENCE BOT (CREATIVE CHALLENGE)

PARTS LIST

LIGHT GRAY BRICKS

1—2 x 4 plate
2—2 x 2 plate
1—1 x 2 plate
2—1 x 2 bricks
2—1 x 2 plates with a socket on the end
1—1 x 2 plate with one stud on top (jumper plate)
2—2 x 2 plates with wheel holders
1—1 x 2 slope, 30 degree
1—1 x 1 tile with clip
1—1 x 2 tile, printed with gauges

DARK GRAY BRICKS

1—2 x 4 plate
2—1 x 2 curved slopes
2—1 x 2 plates with a ball on the side
2—1 x 2 plates with a ball and a socket
1—1 x 1 plate with a horizontal clip
1—1 x 2 grill
1—phone handset

ASSORTED BRICKS

1—2 x 2 white turntable
2—1 x 2 tan bricks with two studs on the side
4—wheels
1—1 x 2 red slope, 30 degree
2—1 x 2 red plates with one stud on top (jumper plate)
2—1 x 1 medium azure round plates
2—1 x 1 translucent red round plates

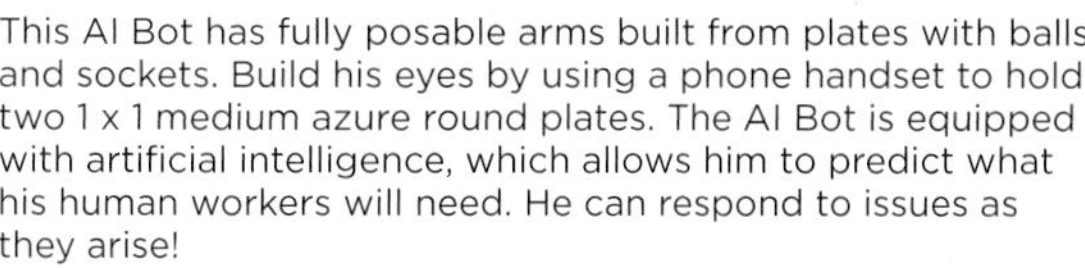

This AI Bot has fully posable arms built from plates with balls and sockets. Build his eyes by using a phone handset to hold two 1 x 1 medium azure round plates. The AI Bot is equipped with artificial intelligence, which allows him to predict what his human workers will need. He can respond to issues as they arise!

Build the base of the robot's body from a 2 x 4 dark gray plate and plates with wheel holders. Place two 1 x 2 dark gray plates with a ball on the side at the top of the body. These will hold the arms. Use a 2 x 2 turntable to make the robot's head turn.

This robot's mouth is built from two 1 x 1 translucent red round plates. Another great option is to use a 1 x 2 plate in any color. Finish up your robot with details like a tile that has dials and gauges printed on it, colorful buttons or grills.

PLAY AND DISPLAY

You may have never thought of LEGO bricks as an art material, but they can be used to create fabulous works of art. Just as you would use colored pencils or paint to draw a design on paper, you can also "draw" a design with bricks. Use your bricks to build all kinds of awesome mosaic pictures. Design an artistic city skyline with buildings in a variety of shapes and colors. Then use your bricks to build yourself in a self-portrait! Construct colorful treasure boxes, build a display stand for your minifigures and then see what other ideas you come up with for using your LEGO bricks in amazing displays!

CITY SKYLINE

CREATIVE CHALLENGE

Design your own city skyline in miniature form. This is such a fun project because you'll be able to use your creativity to make your city look just like you want. Choose a variety of colors for the buildings, and experiment with different building shapes to make an awesome skyline. If you don't have enough windows or translucent bricks for the windows, you can use white or light gray bricks.

KEY ELEMENTS

2—8 x 16 light gray plates

Basic bricks in assorted colors

14—1 x 2 x 2 clear panels for windows

25—1 x 2 clear translucent bricks for windows

White or light gray bricks to use as windows

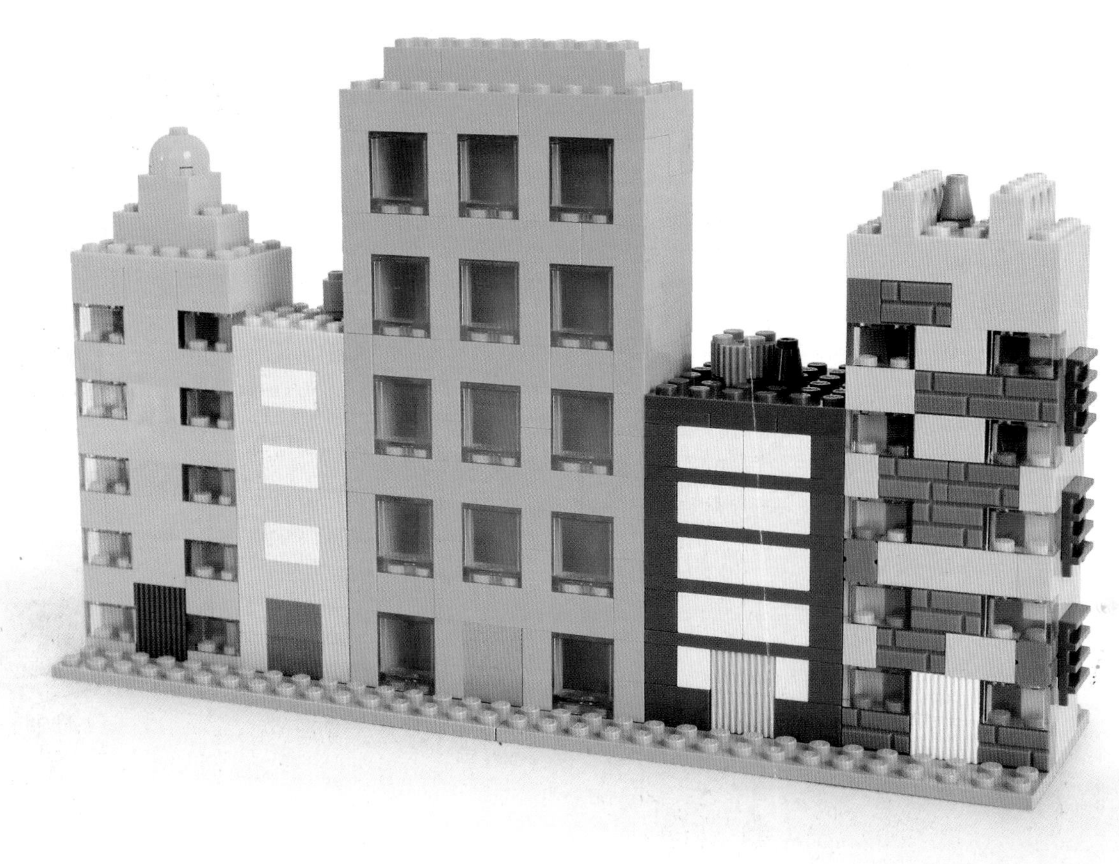

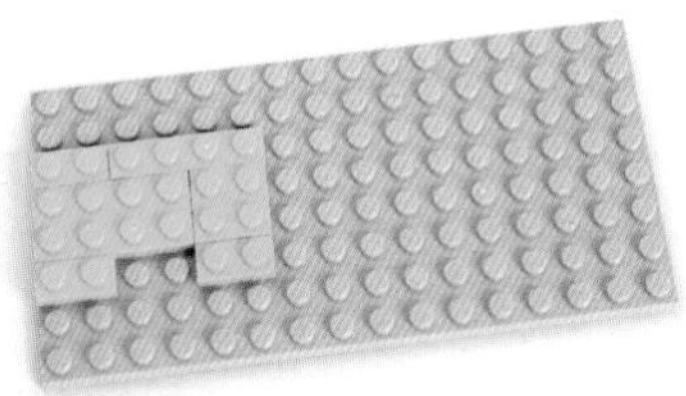

Construct your city on top of two 8 x 16 plates, or use any size plates you'd like. Start by building the outline of your first building. Use plates at the bottom of the building if you want a little color showing under the first-floor windows.

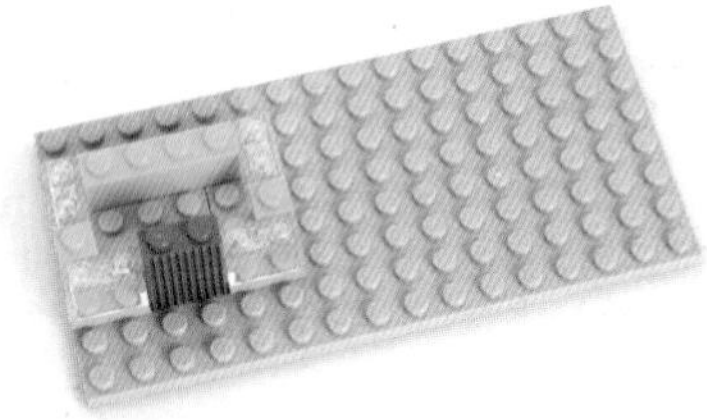

Add bricks and 1 x 2 translucent bricks to make the windows. Bricks that have ridges make a great door. The ridges add some texture to the design and make it more interesting.

Keep building more layers of bricks and windows until the building reaches the height you'd like.

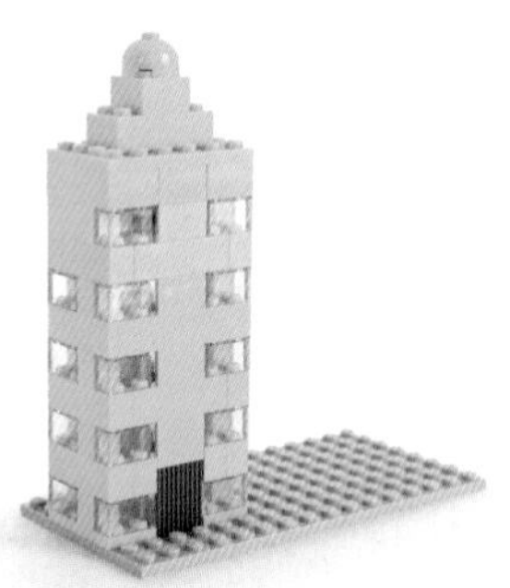

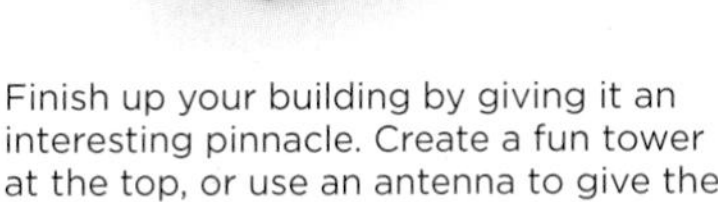

Finish up your building by giving it an interesting pinnacle. Create a fun tower at the top, or use an antenna to give the building a thin spire.

Once you've got one building complete, start adding more! The bricks from the buildings will hold a second 8 x 16 plate in place. Try using different colors for the buildings, and use white or light gray bricks for windows if you don't have enough translucent bricks. Your skyline will look its best if you vary the heights of the buildings rather than making them all the same size.

This building has fire escape ladders built into the side. Each time you add a ladder, place two 1 x 2 plates on top of it to make it equal to the level of the bricks around it. It's also fun to try combining plain bricks with bricks that are modified with a masonry design.

Your completed city skyline will look awesome displayed on your desk or on a shelf! It would also be fun to make this project as a gift to someone.

AMAZING IDEA

Try designing some of the buildings to look like buildings that are in your own city or town!

MINIATURE GOLF

CREATIVE CHALLENGE

Use your LEGO bricks to design your own miniature golf course! This is a fun project to do with friends. Each person can build their own golf hole, and then you can take turns trying them out. Add obstacles to your golf course such as ramps, hills and even a moving propeller! Can you get a hole in one?

KEY ELEMENTS

2—16 x 16 plates per hole or one 32 x 32 baseplate

Various bricks and plates

2 x 3 slopes for building ramps

1 x 4 x 3 window frames to use as holes

1—1 x 12 brick or Technic brick for the golf club

1—1 x 2 brick for the golf club

1—black propeller, 9-stud diameter

1—blue axle pin

1—light gray Technic axle, 3 studs long

1—1 x 2 Technic brick

1—1 x 3 black liftarm with two axle holes and a pin

1—light gray Technic axle connector

2 x 4 tiles—optional

A few marbles

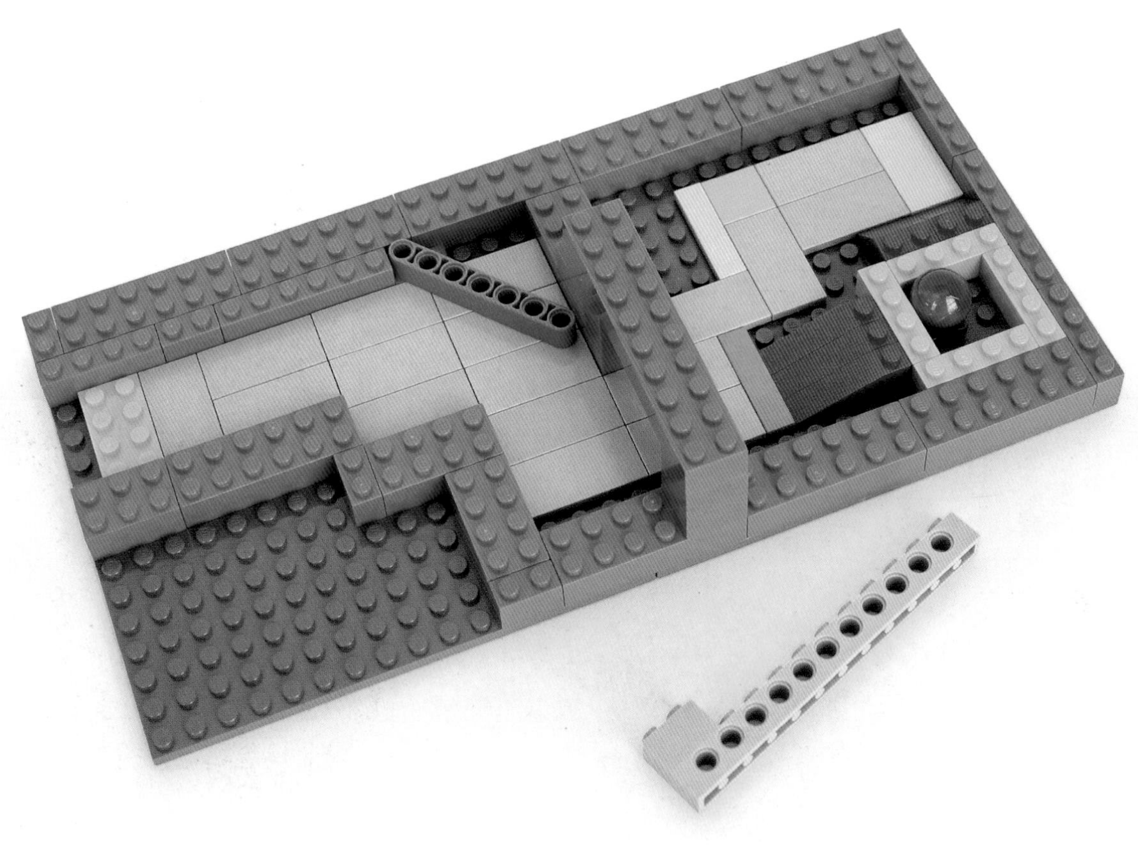

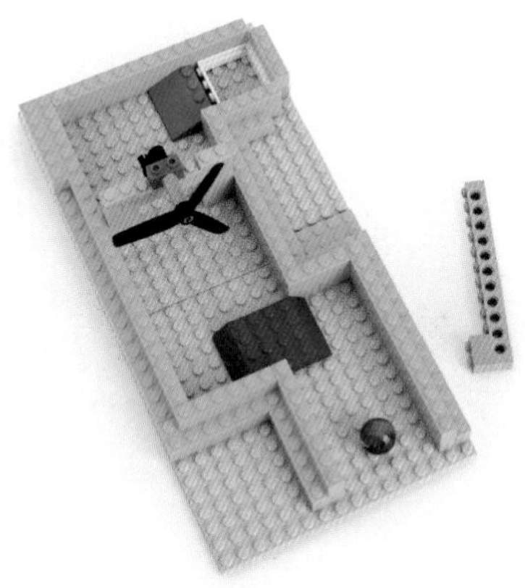

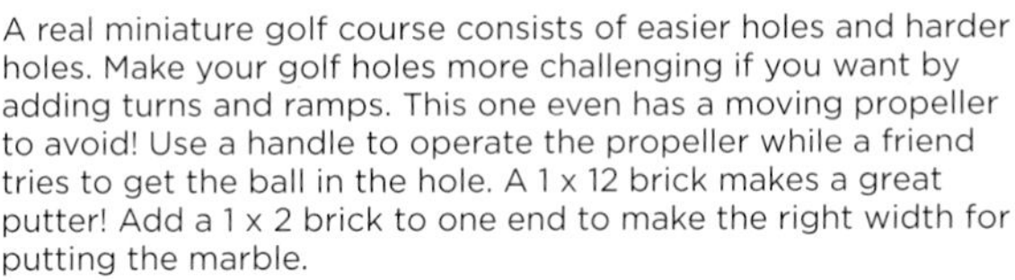

A real miniature golf course consists of easier holes and harder holes. Make your golf holes more challenging if you want by adding turns and ramps. This one even has a moving propeller to avoid! Use a handle to operate the propeller while a friend tries to get the ball in the hole. A 1 x 12 brick makes a great putter! Add a 1 x 2 brick to one end to make the right width for putting the marble.

Insert the blue pin into the propeller. Then attach the axle connector to the axle end of the pin.

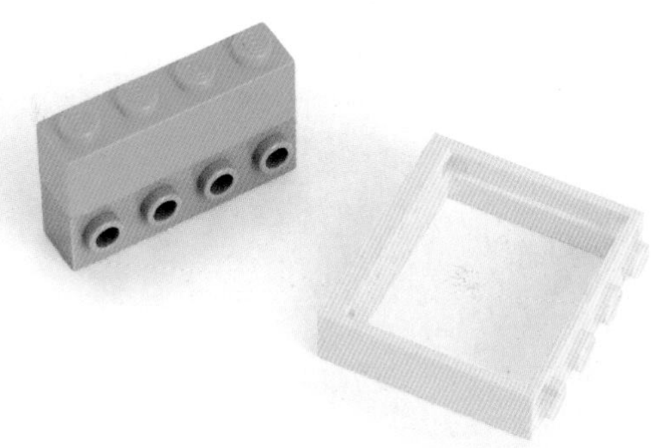

A window frame makes a great hole for the marble golf ball! Grab a 1 x 4 brick that has four studs on the side.

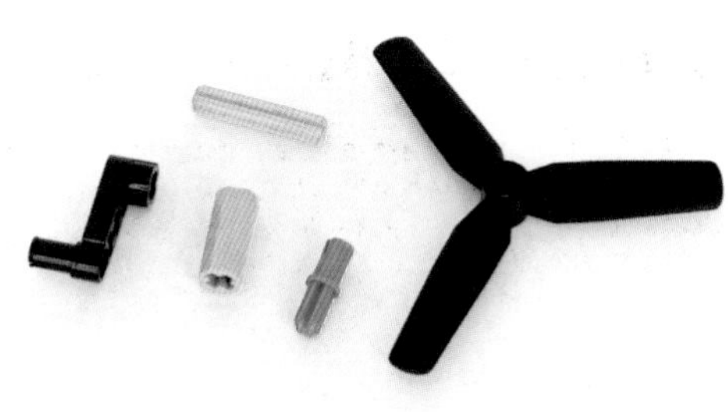

To build a moving propeller for your golf course, grab a light gray axle (3 studs long), a blue axle pin, a light gray axle connector, a 1 x 3 liftarm with two axle holes and a pin, and a black propeller (9-stud diameter).

Slide an axle (3 studs long) into the connector. Slide a 1 x 2 Technic brick onto the axle, and then add a 1 x 3 black liftarm with two axle holes and a pin. The pin on this piece makes a great handle. Build a support structure under your propeller.

Attach the window to the brick with studs on the side. Then you can build this into the layout of your golf course.

Use slopes to build a hill for the marble to travel over. You'll also want to use slope bricks to make a ramp leading up to the hole.

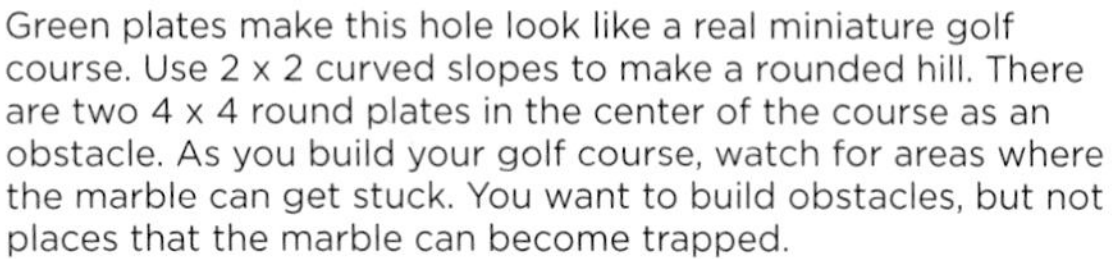

Green plates make this hole look like a real miniature golf course. Use 2 x 2 curved slopes to make a rounded hill. There are two 4 x 4 round plates in the center of the course as an obstacle. As you build your golf course, watch for areas where the marble can get stuck. You want to build obstacles, but not places that the marble can become trapped.

If you have enough of them, you may want to cover your golf course with a layer of tiles. The smooth surface will make it much easier to navigate the marble through the course. Technic liftarms are great for creating an angled wall in your course. The holes in the liftarm can be attached to a stud on a brick or plate. Attach one end of the liftarm to a plate, and then swivel it to the right angle. See if you can bank a shot off the angled wall!

SELF-PORTRAITS

CREATIVE CHALLENGE

Have you ever thought of designing a LEGO version of yourself? You can put together a minifigure that looks like you, or you can build yourself with bricks! Try creating a brick picture of your face. Choose bricks that match your skin tone, hair color and eye color. Do you wear glasses? Then build those into your picture! You can also build yourself wearing your favorite shirt, hat or hairstyle.

KEY ELEMENTS

1—32 x 32 baseplate
Various bricks in the colors of your choice

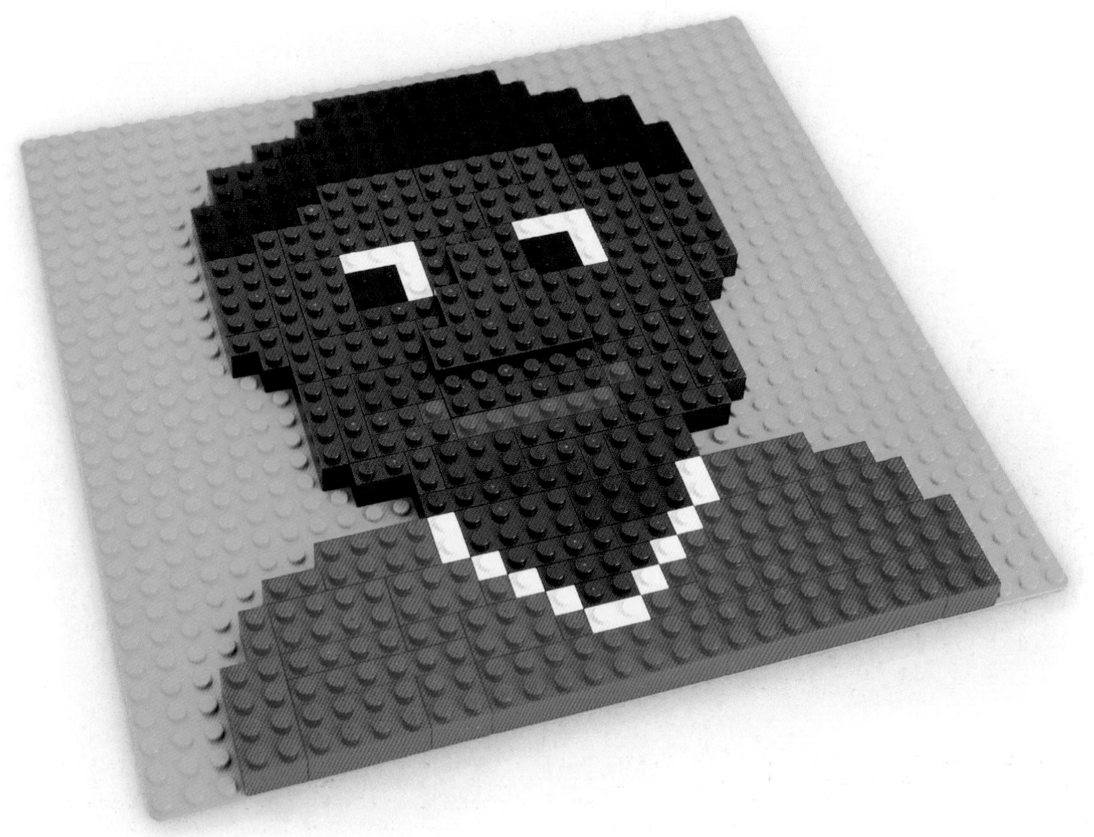

AMAZING IDEA

You might want to display your self-portrait! Lean the baseplate against a shelf, or try putting your baseplate inside a shadowbox frame.

You might want to look in a mirror as you build so that you can determine the right proportions for your face. For example, your eyes should be about halfway down your head. The tops of your ears are likely just above your eyes. As you start building your self-portrait, you'll want to center it on the baseplate. Count the studs to make sure that the first row you build has an equal number of open studs on either side of it.

Noses can be tricky to build. It works well to build your nose with plates. If you feel like you can't tell the difference between your chin and your neck, you might also want to add some plates at the bottom of your face to create a visual difference between the two.

When choosing the size of your eyes, 2 x 2 or 3 x 3 eyes both work well. Use black bricks for pupils or add some color to your eyes. Decide how you want to build your mouth. Do you want to be smiling? Or laughing with your mouth open? You might want to build yourself with a V-neck shirt like the picture.

You can use your bricks to build all kinds of hairstyles! Add a small row of bricks to look like ribbons in your hair. Build short hair, long hair or hair in ponytails. Once you have built your own self-portrait, you might want to build the rest of your family! Or try building a brick portrait of a friend!

PEG SOLITAIRE GAME

CREATIVE CHALLENGE

Here's a fun game that you can play by yourself! The goal of this game is to remove as many pegs as possible from the game board. Pegs are removed by jumping over them with another peg. The peg that is "jumped over" can be removed. With practice, you'll figure out which moves are the best to make!

KEY ELEMENTS

1—8 x 16 tan plate
15—1 x 2 plates with one stud on top (all the same color, or a mix of colors)
14—1 x 1 cones in the colors of your choice

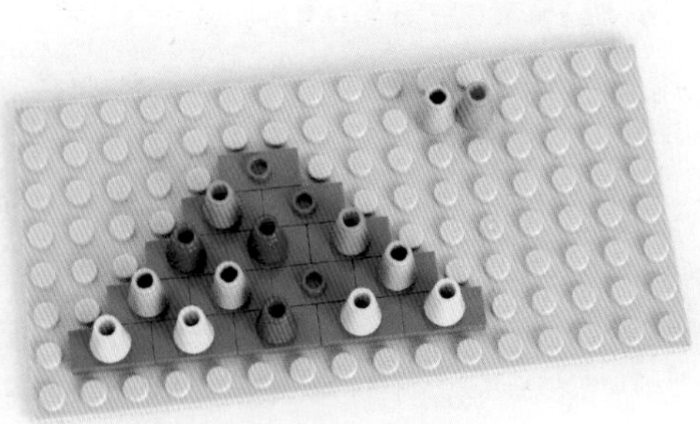

Set up your game board by attaching fifteen 1 x 2 plates with one stud on top. Arrange them with one plate in the first row, two in the second, three in the third and so on. Then add 1 x 1 cones. There should be one fewer cone than plates so that one plate is open.

Now make your first move. The red peg jumped over the light gray peg, and so the light gray peg was removed.

Then the orange peg at the top of the game jumped over another orange peg to land in the open space. The orange peg that was jumped over is removed. There is space on the plate to hold the pegs that have been removed, which makes it much easier to keep track of them.

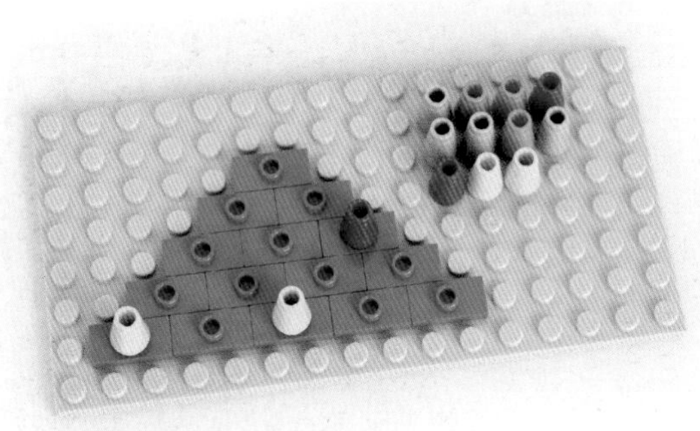

Pegs must be directly next to each other or diagonal to each other in order to jump over them. Once you can't jump over any more pegs, the game is over! How many pegs are left? See if you can choose your moves so that you only have three or fewer pegs remaining. Can you make it to only one left?

Play with a friend! Build a second game board so that you can share the fun with someone else.

TREASURE BOXES

CREATIVE CHALLENGE

Build a box to hold your favorite treasures! These brick boxes can be used to store minifigures, coins, jewelry, marbles, a rock collection and so much more. Decide what you want your box to hold, and then build the size of your box to match. Or make a treasure box as a gift for a sibling or friend!

KEY ELEMENTS

2—8 x 16 plates per box, or choose a different size

Various bricks in the colors of your choice

Tiles to decorate the box lid

Slope bricks for the box lid

Various tiles for the top edge of the box

Plates, 1 stud wide, for securing the lid

10—2 x 4 light gray tiles

1—2 x 2 light gray tile

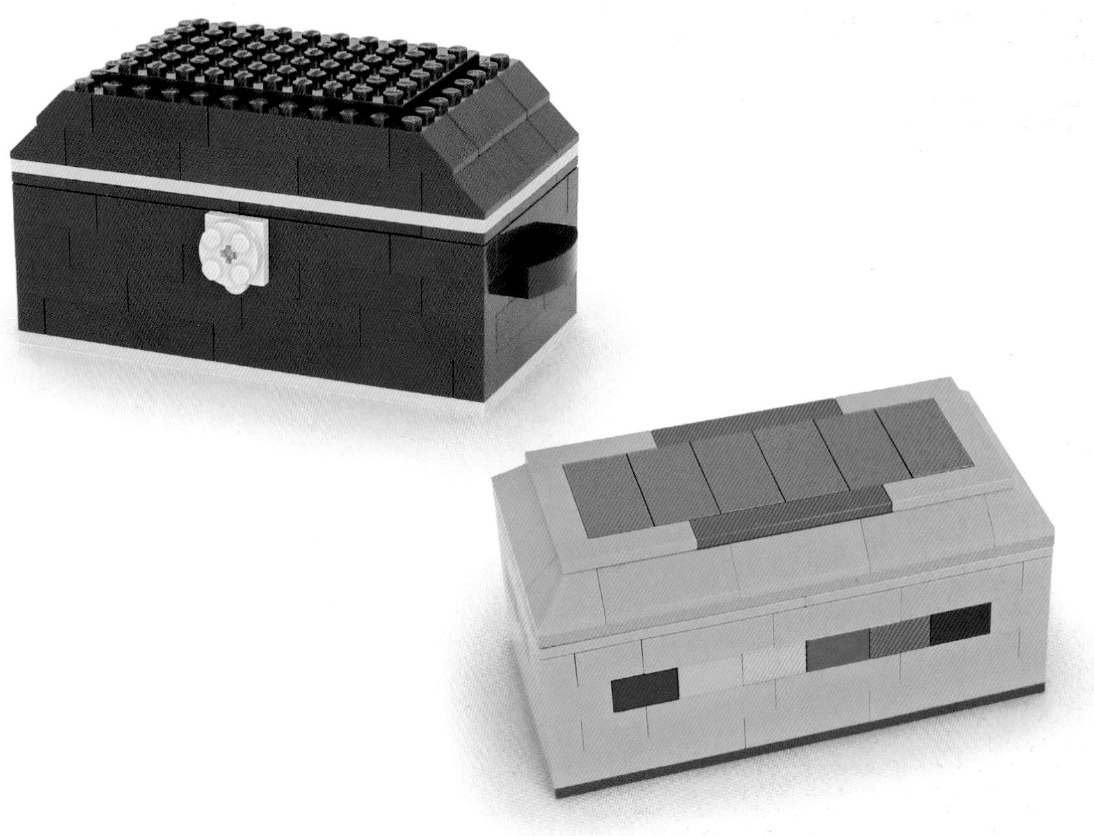

Start building your box by grabbing an 8 x 16 plate. Build a row of bricks around the perimeter and add a colorful design. Cover the bottom of the box with tiles if you have them.

Make your treasure box four bricks high or keep going if you want a deeper box. Then place tiles around the top edge of the box.

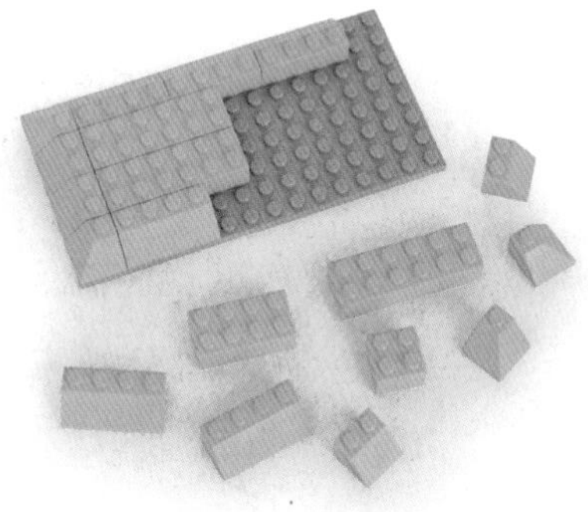

Now it's time to build the lid. Grab another 8 x 16 plate. You can make the lid flat or add slope bricks to give it a fun shape.

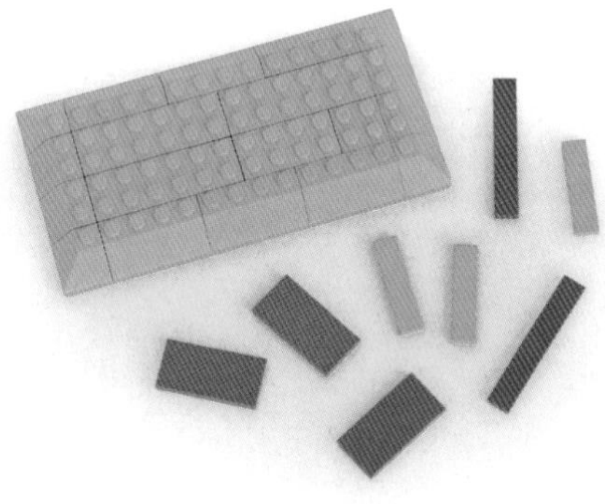

Fill in the center of the lid with bricks. Then find some tiles in your favorite colors for decorating the lid.

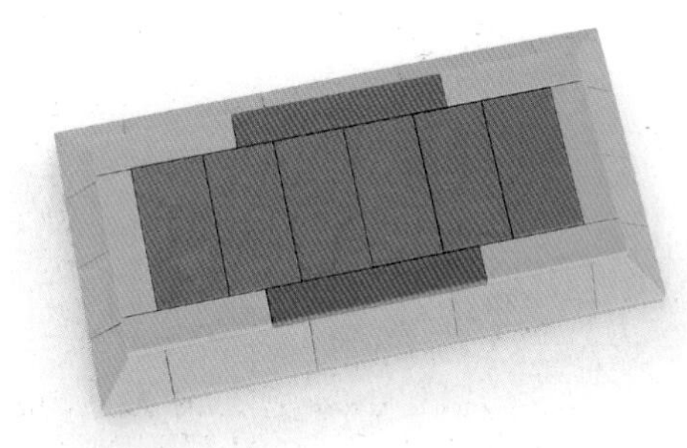

Build a pattern with tiles on the lid. Make it a solid color or create a design with multiple colors. You can even spell a word with tiles or plates or build a shape like a heart. It's totally up to you!

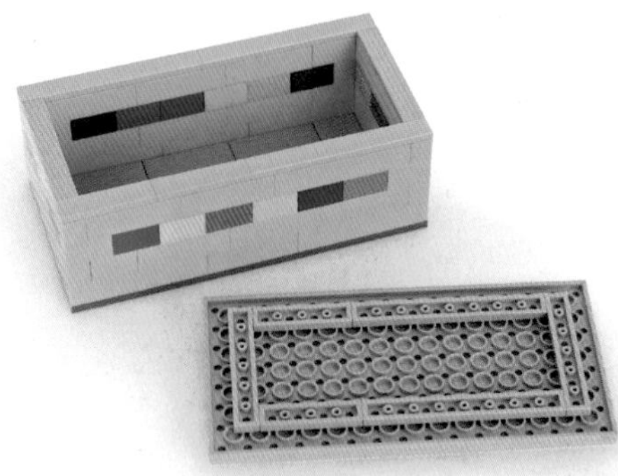

If you set the lid on your treasure box, it will slide off. To keep it from sliding, add a row of plates around the underside of the lid. The plates should be one stud away from the edge. When you place the lid on the box, this row of plates will fit inside the top of the box and make it secure.

Try making a treasure box that looks like a treasure chest! Use brown bricks and add two rows of slopes to the lid of the box to give it that treasure chest shape.

Build handles on your treasure chest by building two 1 x 1 brown bricks with a stud on the side into each side of the box. Attach a 1 x 1 brown plate to each stud. Then add a 1 x 4 double curved slope.

Build two 1 x 1 brown bricks with a stud on the side into the front of your treasure box so they can hold the lock. Find a 1 x 2—1 x 2 tan hinge and a 2 x 2 tan round plate to build a decorative padlock on the front of your treasure box.

Attach the 1 x 2—1 x 2 hinge to the studs on the front of the box. Then add a 2 x 2 tan round plate. Your treasure box is complete! What will you store in your treasure box? Maybe it will be a great place to save up your cash! Or use it to store a collection of tiny toys.

BRICK ART MOSAICS

CREATIVE CHALLENGE

Create beautiful works of art out of bricks! Grab a baseplate and gather up your basic bricks, because there are so many amazing things to build. It's like drawing pictures, except with bricks! And with this type of picture, there are no mistakes. If you don't like how your picture is turning out, just remove the bricks and try again until your mosaic looks just right.

KEY ELEMENTS

1—32 x 32 baseplate per picture
Basic bricks in all colors

HOUSE

Build a house! Make a mosaic that looks like your own house, or design your dream house. There are a couple of different ways to approach building mosaics. You can fill in every stud on the baseplate, or you can just build the objects and leave the space around them open. This house mosaic is an example of one where every stud has a brick on it.

There's another choice you can make with mosaics as well. You can use only basic bricks, or you can add three-dimensional elements to your picture. For example, the flowers and door handle in this mosaic stand out from the rest of the picture.

STEAM TRAIN

Build a classic steam train engine with a coal tender car. This mosaic combines basic bricks with three-dimensional elements, such as the 4 x 4 dark gray dishes used for the wheels.

Use 1 x 2 brown plates with one stud on top (jumper plate) as railroad ties. Then add long gray bricks to make the track. The 4 x 4 dish wheels are attached to two 2 x 2 dark gray round tiles with a hole. Insert the stud on the dish into the hole.

RAINBOW

Here's a fun project that will cheer up a rainy day! Build a colorful rainbow and puffy white clouds. If you use a blue baseplate, you won't need to fill in the sky with blue bricks.

DINOSAUR

Build a mighty Tyrannosaurus rex! Choose a color for your T-rex and a lighter color for its belly. Then start building the shape of its body. Then build more dinosaurs! A stegosaurus or a brachiosaurus would work well. You might want to add a scene around your dinosaur with a river, volcano or trees.

MINIFIGURE DISPLAY STAND

CREATIVE CHALLENGE

Put your favorite minifigures on display! Use your bricks to create a simple and effective display stand that can hold plenty of your best figures. The great part about this minifigure display stand is that it's easy to rearrange your minifigures or change out which ones you have on display. Choose your favorite colors to build your display stand. It will look great in your bedroom or playroom!

KEY ELEMENTS

1—8 x 16 plate
Various bricks in the colors of your choice

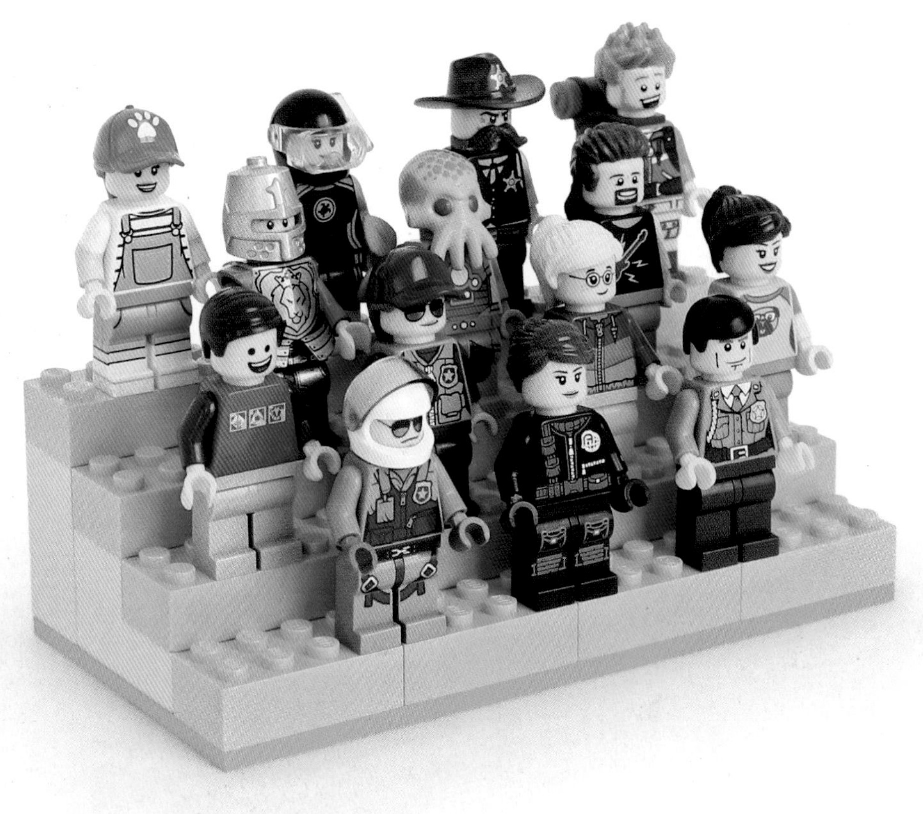

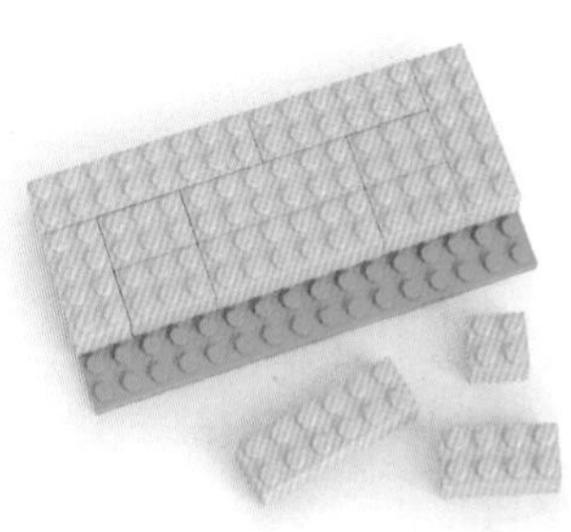

Grab an 8 x 16 plate and some bricks. Cover the plate with bricks, but leave two rows of studs open.

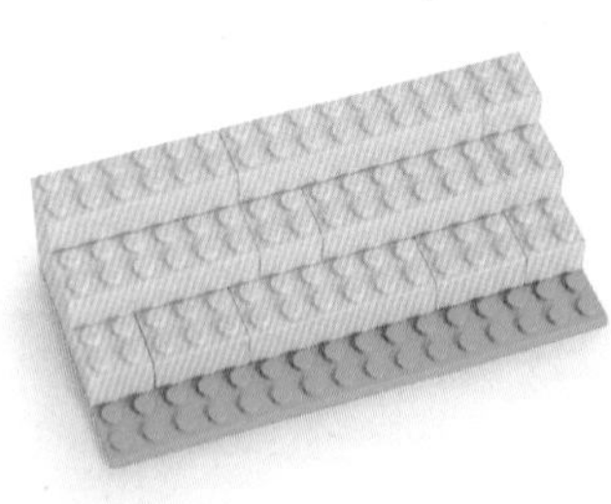

Keep adding bricks until you have three rows that look like a staircase.

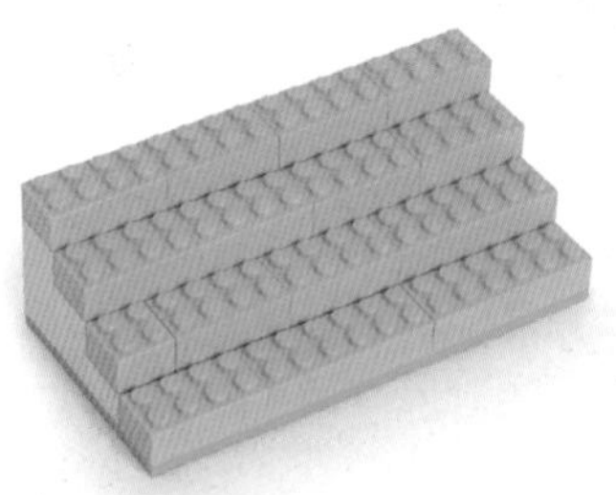

Then add another row of bricks on each step. It looks good if all of these bricks are the same color, but it doesn't really matter. The color of the bricks pictured is medium azure. Other great color choices are blue, gray, red, lime green, black or white. Really ANY color would be great!

Your completed display stand will hold fourteen minifigures. Stagger the minifigures when you place them on the steps so that you can see more of each one.

If you have enough bricks, you can make a larger version of the minifigure display stand that can hold 33 minifigures! The base for this display stand is a 16 x 16 plate and an 8 x 16 plate. Build five rows of brick steps, and then add a sixth row in the front by attaching plates.

That's a lot of room for displaying minifigures! This is a great way to showcase a large collection. It might be worth ordering bricks in the color you want to build this awesome display.

AMAZING IDEA

Your display stand does not have to be made of solid bricks. You can leave open spaces in the bottom layers to save on brick usage. Just make sure that your design is sturdy!

ACKNOWLEDGMENTS

I am so extremely grateful for all those who contributed time and skill to this project.

Thank you to Page Street Publishing, and especially to my editor, Sarah. As always, you have worked hard to make this book the best it could be. Thank you for your help and encouragement!

Thank you to Jens Ohrndorf for allowing us to use your gorilla design. It's an awesome gorilla!

Thank you to the Spangler family for your helpful feedback on the projects and your enthusiasm and encouragement!

Thank you to my son Owen for working enthusiastically on this book. Owen built several projects including the 1960s race car, police car, Humvee, ATV, tiny car, pirate ship, surf shop, parrot and elephant.

Thank you to my son Aidan for building the train mosaic.

Thank you to my son Gresham for designing Edmund the dragon, the baby dragons, baby troll, wizard, witches' lair, one of the agent speeders, the drone launch station, crab, koala, puffin and robin.

Thank you to my son Jonathan for designing the sports coupe, green race car, piano for the band and the bedroom desk with lamp.

Thank you to my daughter Janie for creating the rainbow mosaic.

Most of all, I am so thankful for my husband Jordan and his unending support for all my creative pursuits! Thank you for putting up with LEGO bricks everywhere and constant discussions of what we should build next. Our life is such a fun adventure!

ABOUT THE AUTHOR

Sarah Dees is the creative mind behind the popular website Frugal Fun for Boys and Girls. She's the author of the bestselling LEGO project book series. Her other books are:

Incredible LEGO® Creations from Space with Bricks You Already Have

Awesome LEGO® Creations with Bricks You Already Have

Epic LEGO® Adventures with Bricks You Already Have

Genius LEGO® Inventions with Bricks You Already Have

She is an educator; wife to her wonderful husband, Jordan; and a busy mom of five LEGO-loving kids. She enjoys learning and exploring the outdoors with her kids, as well as creating all kinds of neat LEGO projects. It's not unusual for her playroom floor to be covered with LEGO bricks—with the entire family building! Her website is a fantastic resource for crafts, activities, STEM projects and games that kids will love. Check out her latest projects, including LEGO ideas, at frugalfun4boys.com.

INDEX

T

U

V

W